The Peninsular War

Aspects of the Struggle for the Iberian Peninsula

THE PENINSULAR WAR

Aspects of the Struggle for the Iberian Peninsula

General Editor: Ian Fletcher

Foreword by
His Grace The Duke of Wellington
KG LVO OBE MC

SPELLMOUNT
Staplehurst

British Library Cataloguing in Publication Data:
A catalogue record for this book is available
from the British Library

Copyright © Spellmount Limited 1998

Foreword © The Duke of Wellington 1998

ISBN 1–873376–82–0

First published in the UK in 1998 by
Spellmount Limited
The Old Rectory
Staplehurst
Kent TN12 0AZ

1 3 5 7 9 8 6 4 2

The right of the contributors to be identified
as the authors of this work has been asserted by them
in accordance with the Copyright, Designs
and Patents Act 1988

Typeset in Palatino by Palimpsest Book Production Limited,
Polmont, Stirlingshire
Printed in Great Britain by
TJ International Ltd, Padstow, Cornwall

Contents

List of Plates

1. Carlos IV (1748–1819), King of Spain. Dominated by his wife, the 'toothless and incontestably ugly' Maria-Luisa, and her lover, Manuel Godoy, it was Carlos' feud with his son, Ferdinand VII that led to Napoleon's intervention and, ultimately, the outbreak of the war in Spain.
2. Ferdinand VII (1784–1833), Prince of the Asturias. Napoleon, whose support Ferdinand had sought, tired of the bickering between Carlos and his weak and hapless son, had the latter sent under guard to the Château of Valençay, where he was to remain until 1814.
3. Joseph Bonaparte (1768–1844), King of Spain. Never happy in his appointment, Joseph nevertheless proved a benevolent if reluctant ruler of Spain. He was no great military commander and was recalled to France after his crushing defeat at Vittoria on 21 June 1813.
4. Sir Arthur Wellesley (1769–1852), 1st Duke of Wellington. The dominant figure of the Peninsular War, Wellington commanded the Anglo-Portuguese army throughout the war, save for a brief spell when he returned to England for the inquiry into the Convention of Cintra.
5. Sir John Moore (1761–1809). Commanded the British army in the Peninsula during its ill-fated Corunna campaign in the winter of 1808–9. He was mortally wounded at the battle of Corunna on 16 January 1809, the British victory which enabled the army to escape the clutches of the pursuing French and return to England.
6. André Massena, Prince of Essling (1758–1817). Commanded the Army of Portugal and was Wellington's most dogged opponent. His failure before the Lines of Torres Vedras, his subsequent costly retreat and his defeat at Fuentes de Oñoro led to his recall by Napoleon in 1811.
7. Marshal Nicolas Soult, Duke of Dalmatia (1769–1851). Generally recognised as a good organiser of troops rather than a brilliant battlefield commander, Soult led the pursuit of Moore during the Corunna campaign. Expelled from Portugal by Wellesley in 1809, he was recalled and subsequently served in Germany. He returned to the Peninsula in 1812 and, following the French disaster at Vittoria in 1813, was made Commander-in-Chief in Spain, a post he held until the end of the war in April 1814.
8. The role of the Spanish guerrillas in the Peninsula was later acknowledged by Wellington to have been one of the main factors in the Allied victory over the French. Here, General Franceschi-Delonne is ambushed and taken by 'El Capuchino' and his men near Toro in May 1809. He died of fever whilst in captivity in 1810.
9. 'Assassination'. The French laboured under a great disadvantage with every hill and rock seemingly concealing a guerrilla. It was fatal to wander too far from camp, straggle on the march or fall asleep on picquet duty, whilst

despatches sent to France travelled under strong cavalry escorts in order to ensure their safe delivery.

10. Berg Infantry Officer, probably 2nd Regiment. A good illustration of a standard infantry officer in field dress during the Peninsular War. This junior officer has adapted to the exigencies of campaigning in Spain by acquiring brown trousers, a haversack and a walking stick. In addition, German officers in Spain seem to have favoured pistols carried in large holsters slung over the shoulder. *From the collection of Col. John Elting, USA, retd.*

11. Nassau Infantryman, 1810. Nassau's soldiers regularly earned praise for their appearance and good discipline as well as their tactical competence. *From the collection of Col. John Elting, USA, retd.*

12. Berg Infantryman, 1809. This illustration shows one of Baden's infantry soldiers early in the campaign. He still wears the large, heavy 'Raupenhelm' (crested helmet), but has procured trousers of Spanish brown cloth. Although the helmet was later replaced by a shako this uniform remained essentially unchanged for the duration of the war. *From the collection of Col. John Elting, USA, retd.*

13. Baden Artillery Officer and Gunner, 1810–13. These figures provide a good contrast to the infantrymen, showing the gunner with covered shako and haversack and the officer's bicorne. Note also the officer's pistol holster. *From the collection of Col. John Elting, USA, retd.*

14. 'Campagne en Espagne, 1809.' French infantry in action in a smoke-filled house in Spain.

15. A lancer and infantryman of the Polish Vistula Legion which served in the Peninsula from 1808 until 1814. Their greatest exploits were the charge at Somosierra in November 1808 and the destruction of Colborne's brigade at the battle of Albuera in May 1811.

16. The Fusilier Brigade advances in line at the battle of Albuera, 16 May 1811. One of the great episodes of the war, the Fusiliers' charge turned the tide of battle in favour of the Allies.

17. The 5th (Northumberland) Fusiliers demonstrating that infantry, even in line, were capable of attacking cavalry. This painting by Simkin shows the 5th engaging in such an attack at El Bodon on 25 September 1811. The 5th won the distinction of wearing white plumes in their caps following an action against the French at St Lucia in 1778.

18. 'A British Soldier taking two French officers at the Battle of the Pyrenees.'

19. The Tower of Belem, Lisbon. French prisoners were housed here prior to being transferred to England. *Paul Chamberlain.*

20. Portchester Castle. Many French prisoners, captured in the Peninsula and elsewhere, were kept here. The castle and its prisoners are the subject of a set of paintings by Captain Durrant, a British officer who served at Portchester during the Napoleonic Wars. *Paul Chamberlain.*

21. Fraternisation in the Peninsula. British light dragoons exchange news and views with French cavalry at the outposts. Such exchanges were commonplace in the Peninsula.

22. French infantry under fire from British Royal Horse Artillery. Note the baggy, striped trousers worn by the man on the right and by the man falling back in the centre.

Unless indicated otherwise all illustrations were supplied by Ian Fletcher.

Foreword

by His Grace The Duke of Wellington KG LVO OBE MC

The Peninsular War has always been for me a subject of absorbing interest and I suppose this stems from both family links and the fact that I was myself a regular soldier for nearly thirty years. As such I have always been very conscious of the debt of gratitude that the British Army owes to the Great Duke. After five years of hard campaigning in the Iberian Peninsula the Duke's soldiers in 1814 constituted probably the finest Field Army this country has ever produced. It was fit, professional and well administered, and it laid the foundations of excellence which have maintained the British Regular Army as the finest in the world for close on two centuries.

The reasons for this pre-eminence are not hard to find. Wellington was not only a great commander he was also a superb trainer of men. The list of books he took with him on his long and tedious journey to India in 1796 gives one the clue to his determination to succeed in his chosen profession, somewhat unusual one has to admit in someone of his background. Furthermore, as still quite a young officer and in an age not noted for its sobriety, the standing orders he laid down for the fitness and training of the men under his command in the 33rd of Foot are an object lesson even by today's standards.

But Wellington was not only a great trainer of men, he was an innovator. In the Peninsula, the Divisional system, a properly organised intelligence network and a chain of supply in the form of the Royal Wagon Train (the forebears of the RASC, now the RLC), bears witness to his contribution to the creation of the Regular Army we know today. All these innovations resulted from the lessons he had learnt in his years of campaigning as a young officer, particularly in India. He was still only in his early forties in Spain and Portugal, and his physical fitness and his ability to ride prodigious distances on a marvellous string of horses enabled him invariably to be in the right place at the right time. As one of his soldiers said, 'his presence on the battlefield was worth ten thousand men'.

Over the last forty years or so, I have been lucky enough to spend a good deal of time in Spain, and I have made it my business to visit nearly all the battlefields of the campaign. Many of them remain much as they were in the Great Duke's time. Such is the wealth of contemporary accounts of these long-ago battles that one can still visualise, when visiting them, the sequence of events as they unfolded.

This book will, I am sure, add much to our knowledge and appreciation of a fascinating campaign.

1998

Introduction

One of the main problems when writing about the Peninsular War is that it is often difficult to fathom just when the conflict began. Was it 1807, when Junot marched across Spain in order to invade Portugal? Or was it 1808, following the risings in the Asturias in March of that year and the infamous 'Dos de Mayo' in Madrid some two months later?

Certainly 1808, which saw the first military clashes of the war as well as Britain's entry into the conflict, has a strong case. But if that isn't bad enough, what do we actually call the war? In Britain, of course, we call it the Peninsular War. In Spain it is called the War of Independence, although a Spanish friend of mine was at pains to ask me, 'independence for whom?' Well, such is Anglocentrism that I am plumping for both 1808 and the Peninsular War as both the beginning and the title of the war. Anniversaries are, by and large, no big thing but they do, from time to time, provide us with nice pegs upon which we can hang the results of much research, organise visits or conferences, put on re-enactments and generally reflect upon the events which have helped shape our world. The battle of Waterloo, for example, is commemorated by way of a large scale re-enactment every five years whilst each year the small village of Albuera, in southern Spain, marks the anniversary of the great and bloody battle fought just outside it on 16 May 1811. I have attended the celebrations in Albuera on two occasions and am sure that the men who fought themselves to a bloody standstill on that fateful day would feel very proud, if a little bemused, to know that their efforts were still being remembered each year, not only by the Spanish people, but by the descendants of some of the famous regiments that took part – the 'Buffs', 'Die Hards' and Royal Fusiliers – as well as representatives from the governments of Spain, Portugal, France, Britain, Poland and Germany.

There are other events throughout Europe each year marking the anniversaries of other famous battles. By way of marking the 190th anniversary of the start of the Peninsular War, I have had the privilege of assembling a team of distinguished historians, each of whom has written about a different aspect of the struggle. Histories abound on the war in the

Peninsula, as can be gauged by a look at the bibliography in this book, and so the aim was not to produce just a straightforward account of the war, but to focus on different topics, to look at the contributions made by the various combatant nations and also to study one or two subjects which usually fall outside the scope of general histories.

Philip Haythornthwaite looks at the relationship between the combatant soldiers and demonstrates that, although there was little love lost on the field of battle, enemies could live in relative harmony elsewhere. He also takes a look at the French experience in the Peninsula. The role of the Spanish guerrillas has always been seen as a somewhat heroic one, which Charles Esdaile shows was not always the case. Indeed, Charles has been largely responsible for much revisionist work on the guerrillas. Napoleonic drill has long been the stuff of many a book, but few can explore the subject with the same grasp as Paddy Griffith. The contribution made by German troops in the Peninsula – on both sides – has often gone overlooked, something which Jack Gill puts to right in his chapter on the Rheinbund.

The eminent historian, David Chandler, explores some of the complexities of siege warfare in his contribution whilst John Grehan puts the case for the Portuguese army, Wellington's 'fighting cocks'. The end result for many a French soldier was – if not a shallow and unmarked grave – a place of confinement in one of His Majesty's prisons, be it on land or on one of the dreaded 'hulks', the terrible prison ships, so hated by them. Paul Chamberlain, an expert, deals with the subject in his chapter. My own contributions include an outline of the war, a look at Wellington's part in the Allied victory, and a bibliographical essay on Wellington's army.

Of course, there are many aspects of the war which do not feature in this book – it is often forgotten that over 50,000 Italians fought in the Peninsula, for example – but a book of this kind can only be so long. It is, however, hoped that the areas studied here will serve to shed more light on what Napoleon called 'the Spanish Ulcer', the war that gnawed away at his resources and helped bring about his abdication in 1814.

May I take this opportunity most sincerely to thank the contributors for their efforts and last, but by no means least, His Grace the Duke of Wellington for honouring this book with his Foreword.

Ian Fletcher
Rochester 1998

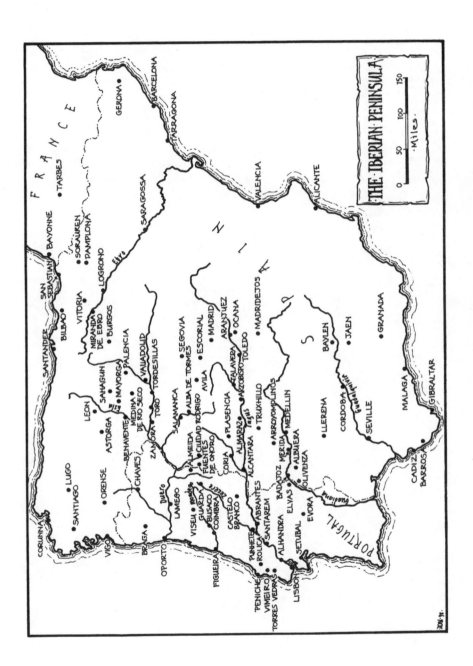

CHAPTER I

The Peninsular War

Ian Fletcher

It can be argued that the Peninsular War exploded into life on 2 May 1808, when the Madrid mob turned upon those French troops who were attempting to carry off to France Don Francisco, the youngest son of King Carlos IV and Queen Maria Luisa of Spain. It can also be argued that it began on 9 May, in Oviedo, the capital of the province of the Asturias, when the people came out in open revolt, declaring war on Napoleon Bonaparte some two weeks later. In truth, the events which led to the war began on 18 October 1807, when General Andoche Junot, at the head of 25,000 troops of the Army of the Gironde, crossed the Bidassoa river and set foot on Spanish soil in order to begin his long march to the Portuguese capital of Lisbon. By a strange irony, it was to be that very same month, six years on, that Arthur Wellesley, then Marquess of Wellington, crossed the very same river to invade France and begin his final drive to victory in the Peninsula, a victory which would help bring about the first downfall of Napoleon in April 1814.

Portugal had long been due for Napoleon's attention, for when he stepped from his boat onto the banks of the river Niemen after concluding the Treaty of Tilsit with the Russian czar and Frederick William III of Prussia in July 1807, he did so having decreed that both Sweden and Portugal, the only European powers still to implement his Continental System, would be forced to do so. This system effectively banned all European countries from trading with Britain, France's last remaining enemy, in the vain hope that he would be able to starve her into submission. The Portuguese regent, John, somewhat timidly bowed to pressure from both France and her ally, Spain, and declared her ports closed to British shipping. He was not, however, prepared to order the incarceration of all British citizens resident in his country and the seizure of their property. Unfortunately for the regent, this was not good enough to satisfy Napoleon's demands, and the response was Junot's advance into Spain, through which he would have to march in order to reach Lisbon.

Junot's march to Lisbon is one of the great dramatic episodes of the war. At the head of his 25,000 troops he set off at a rather leisurely pace on 18 October 1807, and just over three weeks later had reached Salamanca, a distance of 300 miles. The normal route would take him on through Ciudad Rodrigo and into Portugal, past Almeida, down to Coimbra and south to Lisbon. It was the usual invasion route for armies entering Portugal and, indeed, it was the route by which Massena pursued Wellington in the late summer of 1810. However, anxious that Junot should reach Lisbon before Portuguese resistance could be organised, Napoleon ordered him to change his route and, when he reached Ciudad Rodrigo, redirected him south to Alcantara and the Tagus valley. From here he was to march to Abrantes and then south-west to Lisbon. As anyone who has ever travelled the route between Ciudad Rodrigo and Alcantara will know, it is a bleak, barren wilderness of rugged but often spectacular scenery. In his efforts to get to Lisbon, Junot's men became strung out, there were little or no supplies forthcoming, and when he reached Lisbon on 30 November he did so at the head of just 1,500 exhausted, tattered and rain-soaked soldiers. To add insult to injury, Junot discovered that the Portuguese royal family had sailed for Brazil the day before. It was fortunate that the Portuguese offered no resistance at all, otherwise Junot would have found himself on a decidedly sticky wicket. However, Portugal was taken, or at least Lisbon was, and Junot quickly set about disbanding the Portuguese army whilst trying to stamp his own authority on the city. The British ambassador, meanwhile, took ship aboard the *Hibernia*, the flagship of Sir Sydney Smith, whose squadron arrived to begin blockading the mouth of the Tagus.

There is little need to go into the politics which were brewing up behind the scenes whilst Junot's men marched south across Spain. Suffice to say that events in Spain had been simmering away for some time before they finally came to the boil in that late autumn of 1807. Spain was, in theory, ruled by the inane King Carlos IV and his shameless, immoral wife, Queen Maria Luisa, of whom Sir Charles Oman, the great historian of the Peninsular War, wrote that she 'was about the most unfit person in Europe to be placed upon the throne at the side of such an imbecile husband'. In reality this hapless pair were dominated by the corrupt Manuel Godoy, the so-called 'Prince of the Peace'. He had long since been their favourite, and had risen to power as much by his manipulations in the corridors of power as by his many amorous nights in the Queen's bedchamber. Some acrimonious squabbling between the king and queen and Godoy, on one side, and the king's son, Ferdinand, Prince of the Asturias, on the other led eventually, in April 1808, to all of them being summoned by Napoleon to Bayonne where he proposed to discuss the matter of the Spanish throne. After all, both parties had sought his backing during their recent arguments which had seen, amongst other things, Ferdinand's imprisonment for treachery and Carlos' abdication in favour of his pardoned son. The shadow of the French emperor, in fact, had long been cast over affairs at the Escurial, and he watched delighted as the internal strife within the royal family opened the way for his invasion of the country which had undoubtedly been his objective all along. Indeed, as early as January 1808, French troops began to cross the Pyrenees and the Spanish court watched and waited with a sense of unease as column after long column of French troops snaked over the Pyrenees into northern Spain ostensibly to march in support of Junot. By the beginning of March the important fortresses of Pamplona, San Sebastian, Barcelona and Figueras were in French hands after what Oman called 'cynical effrontery and mean cunning'.

These despicable events were followed by a further act of treachery by Napoleon at Bayonne, when he declared his intention to dissolve the Bourbon family and install a French prince on the Spanish throne. By 10 May 1808, both Carlos and Ferdinand had duly signed away their rights to the Spanish throne in favour of Napoleon, and Ferdinand was to spend the next six years in the Château of Valençay under the watchful eye of his keeper, Talleyrand.

With the political antics over, it became a simple fight for survival for the Spanish people and, as we have seen, there were outbreaks of violence against the French in Madrid on 2 May, the famous 'Dos de Mayo', which was ruthlessly suppressed by Murat, commanding the French troops in Madrid. There followed the rising already mentioned in the Asturias as well as a series of brutal sackings of Spanish towns by the invading French armies. Saragossa held on bravely in the north whilst Andalucia felt the force of Dupont's troops as they pushed south.

The initial clashes between the French and Spanish armies went much the way of the French, including their crushing victory at Medina del Rio Seco on 14 July 1808. But the really significant event took place some five days later, when some 20,000 French troops, under Dupont, hemmed in along the Guadalquivir between Andujar and Baylen, surrendered to the Spaniards under Castanos. It was the first time one of Bonaparte's armies had surrendered, and was the catalyst which was to bring Britain into the war on the side of the Iberian nations.

Spanish emissaries from the Asturias had arrived in London on 7 June and had sought assistance from Canning, the Foreign Secretary, who promised them arms, ammunition and money. Before the end of the month, other representatives from other insurgent juntas arrived on similar missions. But it was Dupont's surrender at Baylen that convinced the British government that the time had finally come for a strike against

Napoleon on mainland Europe, and preparations were made for an army to be despatched to the Peninsula.

The British force selected for the task consisted of some 9,000 troops who were originally destined to sail to South America in an attempt to resurrect British designs on that continent, designs which disappeared into oblivion following Whitelocke's disastrous attack on Buenos Aires in July 1807. The projected plan was abandoned, fortunately, and the force ordered to proceed to the Peninsula under the command of Sir Arthur Wellesley, the Chief Secretary of State for Ireland. Wellesley, destined to become the dominant figure of the war, sailed to Spain and then to Portugal, where he landed on 1 August, to be joined four days later by 5,000 men under Sir Brent Spencer. But even as Wellesley's men were tossed ashore by the rolling Atlantic breakers Sir Arthur received a despatch from Castlereagh informing him that he was to be superseded by Sir Hew Dalrymple and Sir Harry Burrard, whilst another gifted soldier was likewise on his way to the Peninsula to supersede him there. This was Sir John Moore.

Wellesley took this somewhat depressing news philosophically and decided that, as the other generals would not arrive for a few days yet, he might as well make the most of his opportunity and try to achieve as much as he could whilst he still commanded the army. His march south took him to Brilos and it was here, on 15 August 1808, that a rifleman of the 95th Rifles fired the first shot of the British campaign in the Peninsula. It was also during this skirmish that Lieutenant Bunbury, of the same regiment, achieved the somewhat unwanted distinction of becoming the first British officer to be killed in the war. Two days later, at Roliça, the British army fought its first battle of the war, a skirmish by later standards, when Wellesley drove Delaborde from his position north of the village and then from the heights to the south of the village of Columbeira.

On 21 August Wellesley achieved an even greater victory, at Vimeiro. Here, on the slopes in front of the village, the French columns first experienced the power of the British infantry line which sent them reeling back in defeat. It also saw the first of a series of unhappy British cavalry charges, on this occasion the culprits being the 20th Light Dragoons, the regiment's commanding officer being killed into the bargain. The victory made more than a few people sit up in the halls of the mighty throughout Europe and, indeed, was the beginning a series of great victories which would take Wellesley from Lisbon to Toulouse. However, his satisfaction was tempered by the arrival, first of Burrard and then Dalrymple, both of whom seemed unable to act in consolidation of Wellesley's victory. The two elderly generals appeared to be paralysed and Wellesley could do nothing but kick his heels in frustration as the beaten French army was allowed to extricate itself unmolested.

However, Junot, commanding the French, was no fool and he realised the perilous position in which he now found himself, trapped as he was on the Lisbon peninsula. There was little choice but to ask for an armistice. Otherwise he faced a retreat back into Spain and a long and dangerous march to Burgos, where the nearest French troops were to be found, across territory infested with guerrillas who would, no doubt, reduce his army to a mere skeleton should he decide to risk this course of action. No, it was too dire to contemplate, and General Kellerman was duly despatched to solicit terms from the British. The result was the infamous Convention of Cintra, whereby the French army was allowed to sail away in British ships, with its arms and much of its accumulated plunder, back to the safety of France. Portugal was cleared of the hated invaders at the stroke of a pen and without the loss of a single life or the need for prolonged sieges. After all, the fortresses of Elvas, Almeida and Peniche all had strong garrisons, protected by strong walls. The pen, on this occasion, certainly did prove mightier than the sword, but the stunned British public did not see it the same way. An enemy army was there to be crushed and defeated, not to be tamely shipped home in British ships. Public outrage was so widespread, in fact, that an inquiry was set up and both Burrard and Dalrymple were recalled to explain themselves, a disillusioned Wellesley already having returned home on leave. The court found no fault with Wellesley, who was acquitted of any wrong doing. Burrard and Dalrymple, on the other hand, whilst avoiding any severe censure, never returned to the Peninsula and, indeed, faded into the backwaters of British military history.

With the trio of British generals back in England, command of the army in Portugal devolved upon Sir John Moore, a great and experienced soldier whose methods of training light infantry remain perhaps his greatest legacy. Moore had arrived in Portugal shortly after Dalrymple but had declined to become involved with the business at Cintra. Reinforcements had increased the size of his army to 30,000 infantry with a further 15,000 expected to arrive in northern Spain in October 1808 under Sir David Baird. Moore planned to leave 10,000 troops in Lisbon whilst he himself, with the main body of the army, marched north into Spain to join up with Baird. From here, he would march upon Burgos and form a junction with the Spanish generals, but he had no idea of just who he was to co-operate with.

Moore began his advance from Lisbon on 26 October 1808, his force being split into four columns, the most southerly of which saw artillery and cavalry travelling via Badajoz and Talavera to Salamanca, the chosen place of concentration. The army began to concentrate towards mid-November, but while Moore waited at Salamanca, he received information that the Spaniards had been scattered to the winds by Napoleon – who had ventured south of the Pyrenees in person with the intention of sweeping the British into the sea – and that there was little prospect of co-operating with them. Consequently, Moore issued orders for a retreat towards Corunna and Vigo, while the British reinforcements under Baird, which had finally landed during the first week of November, were ordered to turn about and march back the way they had come. However, on 4 December, Sir John Hope's column finally staggered into Salamanca to find that Moore had changed his mind and had decided to advance instead. This decision was based upon assurances given to him by the Spaniards who claimed they were about to begin a defence of Madrid. Moore decided that he would march north to Burgos after all and threaten Napoleon's communications with France. By doing so he hoped to draw the French away from Madrid and afford the defenders some time to organise themselves. Little did he know, however, that by the time his advance began, on 11 December, Madrid had been in the hands of the French invaders for a whole week, having fallen on 4 December, the very day that Hope's column arrived at Salamanca.

One of the characteristics of the Corunna campaign was the way in which both sides groped around in almost complete ignorance of the whereabouts of each other. This lack of reliable intelligence was highlighted on 23 December when Moore received an intercepted despatch that told him the bad news that Madrid had fallen. This, however, was accompanied by information that Soult was isolated with a fairly weak force in his front, upon which Moore decided to attack him. The optimism with which Moore's army began its march was cruelly shattered by the news that Napoleon was leading his imperial legions over the snows of the Guadarrama Pass in order to drive 'the hideous leopard' into the sea. British hopes were dashed, as were hundreds of British muskets, as Moore's men threw them to the ground in utter frustration. The retreat to Corunna had begun.

Events in Galicia were, therefore, turning sour for the British. And, even as they contemplated the thought of a gruelling retreat, their Spanish Allies were reeling from one defeat after another as the French began to push out into Spain. The Spanish armies had already been defeated at Medina, as we have seen, and by the end of the year they would experience further disasters at Gamonal, Espinosa, Cardadeu and at Molins de Rey. And yet the Spaniards themselves were to make a major contribution to the war in Spain merely by their presence, and would prevent the French from turning their full attention to the relatively small British – and later Anglo-Portuguese – army. When the war was over Wellington paid a great tribute to the Spanish guerrillas, suggesting that without their contribution he could not have driven the French from the Peninsula. But we must never overlook the role of the Spanish armies themselves, who doggedly and bravely maintained a threatening presence in the field in spite of a succession of defeats. In fact, the Spaniards themselves would come to regard the role of the British army as being a fairly minor one, given the fact that until 1813 all that the Spanish people ever seemed to see of their allies was during a retreat – 1809, 1810, 1811 and even 1812 saw the British conducting retreats to Portugal. Indeed, it is interesting to note the amount of fighting done between 1808 and 1814 by both the Spanish and Anglo-Portuguese armies. A relatively crude but nevertheless useful exercise is to compare the number of trophies captured during the war by the two Allied armies. The Spanish armies captured some 11 eagles and 31 flags from their French opponents compared to just 6 eagles and 16 flags captured by the Anglo-Portuguese. This, admittedly, is a simple exercise but it does give some indication of the amount of fighting done by the Spanish armies, something which is very often overlooked by historians today who tend to focus on the role of the guerrillas.

On 16 January 1809, Sir John Moore and his savage, tattered and exhausted army, turned in anger on their French tormentors who had hustled and harried them through the snow-covered mountains of Galicia. They demonstrated that, in spite of the terrible conditions endured by them during the horrors of the retreat, they were still capable of fighting and, indeed, delivered a loud message to the French, that a British soldier is never more at his dangerous and magnificent best than when his back is firmly against the wall. At the battle of Corunna, the British army turned and fought off successive French attacks to enable itself to embark aboard the ships of the Royal Navy, waiting anxiously in the harbour. Sadly, Sir John Moore was not amongst them, for as his men shuffled onto the ships, he lay dying in a house in the Canton Grande of a terrible wound to the chest and shoulder. As the first ships began to sail away towards England, Moore was lowered into his grave and there, on the ramparts of the Old Town, he was left alone with his glory.

While Moore had been busy in Spain Wellesley was in England, defending himself against charges which had arisen following the Convention of Cintra. Fortunately, he was acquitted and by April 1809 he was back in command of the British army in Portugal. The task facing him was not an enviable one, and his arrival in Portugal came on the back of another succession of Spanish defeats at Valls, Ciudad Real and the Medellin. The city of Zaragosa had also fallen after a heroic defence by the population and their commander, Palafox. Indeed, some 54,000 inhabitants perished in the two month siege during which the French fought their way into the city, house by house, in savage and bitter fighting.

Within three weeks of landing, Wellesley had formulated his plan for the forthcoming campaign, to drive Soult from Portugal before marching south into Spain to link up with the Spaniards against Victor. The crossing of the Douro at Oporto was one of Wellesley's most daring operations, involving small groups of British infantry who crossed the river in wine barges while the French defenders peered aimlessly out to the west and to the sea, from which direction they expected the British attack to come. By the time Soult realised just what was going on, Wellesley's men had fortified the Bishop's Seminary, a large building to the east of the town, whilst Sherbrooke's brigade crossed the river from the suburb of Villa Nova. The operation was a complete success, and so ended the second French invasion of Portugal. Wellesley was back and he was not to leave the Peninsula until the war was finally over in 1814.

Wellesley's return had been a great success and, for a general who has long since been regarded as a defensive-minded soldier, his victory at Oporto is all the more significant. However, it did not herald the beginning of a period of British success in the Peninsula. When Wellesley marched into Spain to meet his Spanish allies, he must have done so with some degree of trepidation, given the absence of co-operation shown towards Moore during the latter's ill-fated Corunna campaign. He was not to be disappointed. He met the ageing General Cuesta in a small village close to Almaraz and, even by the dim light of the burning torches by which he inspected Cuesta's men, he could see that he was going to have his work cut out if he was to forge a working relationship with them. The Spaniards regarded the British as heretics whilst they themselves were loath to do today what they could put off until tomorrow. They were also very proud men and could not bring themselves to accept orders from their British Allies. As it turned out, their first major battle together, at Talavera on 27–28 July 1809, ended in victory for them, although the brunt of the fighting fell fairly and squarely on the red-jacketed soldiers whose firepower and steady lines proved too much for Victor's French columns. It was a costly victory for Wellesley – some 5,365 British soldiers were killed or wounded – but it was one which earned for him the title 'Wellington'.

The battle of Talavera ushered in a period of fourteen months of great anxiety for Wellington as his army watched and waited on the Portuguese-Spanish border for Massena to begin the third French invasion of Portugal. Elsewhere, however, the war went on, with the Spaniards winning at Tamames on 18 October 1809, their first victory since Alcaniz on 23 May that year. This victory, however, was more scant reward for a year of hard endeavour which had seen their armies beaten yet again at Almonacid, Ocana and Alba de Tormes, and the city of Gerona fall after another violent siege. It was this fourteen month period that saw the emergence of the so-called 'croakers', British officers even of high rank, who advocated an abandonment of the campaign in the Peninsula and who conspired ineffectively but irritatingly against Wellington. The commander-in-chief was not to be put off by the croakers, but their coffee-house whisperings and whinges were a constant source of annoyance to him. The views of the croakers found voice amongst politicians at home who saw little point in remaining in the Peninsula and, indeed, when Ciudad Rodrigo and Almeida fell to Massena in the summer of 1810, Wellington's position looked more than a little precarious. However, unbeknown to all but a few of his closest confidants, Wellington had been planning ahead for such an eventuality. Indeed, on 26 October 1809, Wellington had ordered the construction of a series of defensive lines to be laid out across the Lisbon peninsula from the Atlantic to the Tagus. These were the famous Lines of Torres Vedras, since dubbed 'the cheapest investment in military history' and certainly one of the best kept secrets in history. Wellington, with unerring accuracy, predicted that the French invasion would be too strong to hold back on the border itself and that his army would have to retreat to the relative security of the lines, by which time the Portuguese population north of Lisbon would have been driven inside the lines along with their livestock and crops, leaving the land to be laid waste behind them. He even predicted that he would turn and make a stand along the way, which he did at Busaco. It all fell out as he expected.

Throughout the spring and summer of 1810 Wellington's army watched and waited on the Portuguese border as Massena's preparations for the third French invasion prospered. There were numerous skirmishes on both the Coa and Agueda rivers as the newly formed Light Division, under the command of its controversial leader, Robert 'Black Bob' Craufurd, strove mightily to prevent the ever-probing French from piercing Wellington's outpost line in order to gain information on Allied troop dispositions. Much of the reputation of the Light Division as being Wellington's elite division was gained during this period, and not once did it let its commander down. The chain of outposts along the Coa and Agueda was such that, as Sir Charles Oman later wrote, 'the whole web of communication quivered at the slightest touch'. Indeed, the seeds sown by Sir John Moore during his famous period of training of light infantry at Shorncliffe can be said to have come to fruition on the rocky chasms of the Coa. But if the Light Division enjoyed a period of prolonged and active service at the outposts, the rest of the army wallowed in frustration and idleness which gave more weight to the arguments of the 'croakers' who now, more than ever, saw little point in remaining in the Peninsula, particularly with the prospect of a French invasion in strength looming on the horizon. Many officers grew jealous of the Light Division and its escapades and, as one of its officers later recalled, the mere mention of the words 'outposts' or 'Light Division' was enough to turn many officers' wine ration into vinegar! That the Light Division performed sterling work on the border there can be little doubt, but there was more than the occasional episode which sent Wellington into the depths of frustration, none more so than at Barquilla, on 11 July 1810, and, more particularly, at the infamous combat of the Coa, on 24 July. During this latter action Ney's VI Corps attacked Craufurd as he prepared to bring his division back over to the left bank of the Coa. Attacked in strength, Craufurd was driven back pell-mell on the Coa, across which there lay just a single bridge which quickly became the scene of much confusion and chaos as the British and Portuguese infantry came tumbling down the hillsides to cross it. That the Light Division managed to escape at all was down purely to the skill of the division's battalion commanders, for all control at higher level was lost almost immediately. A tally of 392 casualties was the price for Craufurd's folly in delaying far longer than he ought to have done whilst the French also suffered heavily, mainly in their attempts to pass the bridge after Craufurd's men had crossed it. Craufurd's reputation was dented, even if Wellington wrote that his mistake was one of judgement rather than intention. It could have been far worse, however, for the loss of the Light Division might have given the croakers more ammunition than even Wellington could have resisted. It is just as well that elsewhere in the Peninsula French efforts were concentrated mainly in Catalonia, Valencia and Andalucia as they sought to consolidate their stranglehold on the country.

By the end of August 1810, both Ciudad Rodrigo and Almeida were in Massena's hands, the latter most fortuitously after one of the first shots fired by his guns ignited a leaky powder keg, the train of which led back to the main magazine. Some 500 Portuguese were killed by the ensuing explosion. The extra time, which a prolonged defence of Almeida Wellington hoped would buy, was now spent and his army was forced to withdraw into Portugal a little more hurriedly than was originally planned. While the army trudged west the construction of the Lines of Torres Vedras, or Lines of Lisbon as they were originally called, gathered pace. Engineer officers were despatched to Lisbon to report on their progress, some of whom suggested that the lines would not hold back the French for five minutes and that the Portuguese would run at the first shots. However, things were to turn out quite differently.

For the moment there was still the matter of a delaying action, which Wellington had predicted, and it came on 27 September 1810 with the battle of Busaco.

The morning of the 27th dawned grey and misty, and found the Allied army settled in atop a ridge which towered some 1,810 feet above sea level and extended for over eleven miles north from the Mondego. That the French even considered a frontal attack on this position is testament to both their confidence and ability, but these qualities alone would not be enough to dislodge the Allied defenders and a series of attacks by Massena's columns were driven back after some hard fighting, leaving Wellington in possession of the ridge. However, some miles to the north Massena's troops discovered a route by which they were able to outflank Wellington's left flank and once again the Allied army was chivvied along towards Lisbon.

On 10 October 1810, Wellington's army finally entered the lines with Massena close behind. It was a bewildered Massena, too, for he gazed up in astonishment at the defences, the existence of which he was completely unaware. In fact, the concept of the lines had been known only to a very few select officers close to Wellington. True, many people knew of the construction of various forts and redoubts but few appear to have appreciated the way in which they linked together to form what was to prove an impenetrable barrier to Massena who only once, at Sobral on 14 October, tested them in any strength and with little success. Massena lingered before the lines for three weeks before deciding to pull back to Santarem, a few miles to the north, where provisions could be obtained, the land occupied by his troops in front of the lines having been stripped bare. Once more the French settled down to wait and watch but for what? There was no help forthcoming from far-off Paris, whilst Wellington himself showed little inclination to move out from the safety of the lines, fed and supplied as he was by the ships of the Royal Navy. The situation dragged on until 5 March 1811, when British picquets moved forward to discover that the very stiff French sentries in front of them were, in fact, dummies stuffed with straw. Massena was on the retreat.

The French retreat through Portugal was marked by outbursts of savagery as village after village was laid waste and put to the torch. Indeed, the roads taken by Massena's army were strewn with the corpses of murdered men, women and children, many of whom had been tortured first. Wellington's men were horrified by what they saw. The French themselves did not escape punishment and any stragglers who strayed too far from the main French columns were bound to fall prey to the watching, waiting Portuguese guerrillas who were capable of evening the score in the most terrible manner.

As Massena's starving army marched north it was followed all the way by Wellington who ensured that the pressure was kept on all the way back to Spain. There were fights at Redinha, Pombal, Cazal Nova, Foz d'Arouce – where the French lost one of their prized Imperial 'eagles' – and finally at Sabugal, before Massena was finally thrown back over the border and into Spain. The third and final French invasion had come to a disastrous end. So decisive did the Lines of Torres Vedras prove, that the present Duke of Wellington was moved to write that, 'if in the course of the history of war a battle had taken place in which one side lost 30,000 men and the other a matter of a few hundreds, it would have echoed down the pages of history as the greatest victory ever won. But that, in fact, is the decisive nature of Massena's defeat at the Lines of Torres Vedras . . . it was possibly the most decisive victory that Wellington won during the entire Peninsular Campaign.'

Portugal was clear of Massena's army but there still remained in the fortress of Almeida a French garrison under General Brennier, and it was the operation to relieve them that led to the final confrontation in the Peninsula between Wellington and his most dogged and able adversary, Massena. The battle of Fuentes de Oñoro was fought over three days, between 3 and 5 May 1811, and saw a great deal of bloodshed in the maze of small streets and alleyways of which the village consisted. Wave after wave of French infantry crossed the Dos Casas stream to do battle with Wellington's men in the streets only to be thrust back again after severe and savage hand-to-hand fighting. The battle continued with a series of assaults on the village while away to the south French pressure forced Wellington to withdraw his right flank, the squares of the Light Division covering the operation in what was later described as 'a series of rhythmical evolutions which suddenly transformed the deadly orthodoxy of Hyde Park reviews into a dance of life'. Massena's attempt to relieve the garrison of Almeida ended in failure, and a few days later a messenger was on his way from Paris bearing a despatch from the Emperor recalling him to France and informing him that Marshal Auguste Marmont was to assume command in his place. Ironically, Brennier blew up the fortifications of Almeida shortly before midnight on 10 May and bravely led his garrison through the Allied blockade to safety with the loss of 360 men, an operation which an exasperated Wellington claimed had turned the victory at Fuentes de Oñoro into a defeat.

With Massena gone, the biggest threat to Wellington's progress was removed. However, in the south Marshal Soult, who had already driven Moore from Spain, but who had in turn been driven from Portugal by Wellington in 1809, returned to the Peninsula to begin the conquest of Estremadura and Andalucia. His operations got off to an optimistic start with the capture of both Olivenza and Badajoz, coupled with the French victory at Gebora. Like other French commanders he was to find his task in Spain to be a far cry from operations in central Europe and ultimately was to fail. Soult and Marmont were just two of a series of French commanders sent to the Peninsula to deal with both the Spanish and Anglo-Portuguese armies. In the event none of them was successful, thanks in part to interference from Paris by Napoleon himself who never really appreciated the difficulties facing his commanders, he himself paying only a brief visit south of the Pyrenees in the winter of 1808–9. He also underestimated the dangers posed to his southern border by an increasingly successful Allied army. Of course, he was more often than not tied down by affairs in central Europe, in particular the ill-fated Russian campaign of 1812. But one wonders whether Napoleon made a significant error in not taking the war in the Peninsula more seriously. It appears to have been to him merely a drain on French resources – a 'running sore' or 'ulcer' he was to call it later – but in reality it was much more than this. Indeed, not only did it provide an inroad into France from the south, taking the pressure off the often beleaguered Allied powers in the north, but it gave the British army the opportunity of honing a fine blade of what began as a blunt instrument; after all, the army went into the Peninsula campaign on the back of a very patchy war record. The victories in Egypt and India were as distant a memory as they were far off in terms of distance, whilst the disasters of El Hamet in Egypt in 1807 and Buenos Aires in the same year were fresh in the memory. Only the small but significant victory of Sir John Stuart's army at Maida could be held up with any satisfaction at the outset of the war. Therefore, the long years of war in the green valleys of Portugal, on the dusty plains of Leon, and atop the rugged mountains of the Pyrenees gave Wellington's men the opportunity to graduate from a small and delicate army into what Wellington described in November 1813 as 'the most complete machine for its numbers now existing in Europe'. It was a chance grabbed eagerly by Wellington's men and they were not to let their commander down.

Of course, in 1811 the British army had a long way to go before it was in a position to earn such high praise from Wellington as that which he accorded it in 1813. But it had seen off Massena and for that Wellington could be thankful, as he had proved his most dogged enemy. Marmont was a different case altogether and his term of office would last barely fourteen months. Meanwhile, the main theatre of operations shifted to the south, to Estremadura and Andalucia. In May and June 1811, the Allied army laid siege to the fortress of Badajoz, but with little success. Indeed, the siege operations only served to demonstrate that Wellington's engineers were simply not up to the job and that it would take a very real effort to snatch the place from the grasp of the French. How true this was to prove in April 1812. The siege operations at Badajoz were interrupted by the battle of Albuera, fought on 16 May 1811, between Beresford and Soult. It was the bloodiest battle of the war in terms of sheer pummelling. The Allied victory was purchased at a terrible cost to the British infantry, however, who stood there pouring out volley after volley into the packed ranks of Frenchmen who gave as good as they got until they could take no more. 'Survivors who took part did so as in a dream,' the great historian of the British army, Sir John Fortescue, later wrote, 'with a little inclining to the centre but above all a desire not to run.' And he was right. But one wonders whether the dream was really a nightmare, for it surely must have been for those brave men on both sides who stood opposite each other, firing blindly through the smoke into the dark ranks opposite them. Albuera was the most controversial battle of the war, owing to the bad position adopted by Beresford and to his efforts to redeem the position which he should have taken up in the first place. Only the steadfastness of the stoical British infantrymen saved him that day. Indeed, Soult later said that the day was his but that the British did not know it and would not run.

But it was not all bad news in 1811. Indeed, at Barrosa, on 5 March, Sir Thomas Graham led his men up the hill there to defeat Victor's Frenchmen in a fierce battle, during which Sergeant Patrick Masterman took the Imperial 'eagle' of the French 8th Line Regiment. It was the first of six such trophies to be taken during the war. Meanwhile, Marmont's tenure of office began with a series of long, drawn-out manoeuvres and counter-manoeuvres on the Spanish-Portuguese border, culminating in a stand-off as the year came to a close. Winter arrived and the campaigning season duly came to an end. Or so Marmont thought. For while his men settled down for the winter, Wellington's men busied themselves in making preparations for their assault on Ciudad Rodrigo, the first of the great fortresses to fall to them.

The strategic importance of Ciudad Rodrigo lay in the fact that it commanded the northern corridor between Spain and Portugal, whilst Badajoz commanded the southern. Before Wellington could even consider advancing into Spain, he would have to prise these guardians of the frontier from the French; they were not called 'the keys of Spain' for nothing. Wellington's thrust was aided by further interference from Napoleon who ordered the withdrawal of 12,000 French troops under Montbrun from the border in order to assist Suchet in the east, a move which gave the Allied commander greater freedom of movement. The siege of Ciudad Rodrigo began on 8 January 1812 amidst snow and biting cold winds. The frozen ground made digging almost impossible to begin with, but through sheer hard work the infantry – Wellington possessed no such luxury as a corps of sappers and miners – managed to dig trenches or 'parallels' in which the guns were placed in batteries. They sapped forward from the Greater Teson, the hill overlooking the town, and down to the Lesser Teson, a lower height just a few hundred yards from the walls of the fortress itself. By the evening of 19 January all was ready. Wellington's gunners had laid low the walls in two places, creating two practicable breaches. Craufurd's Light Division was to storm the Lesser Breach whilst the 3rd Division would assault the Greater Breach. Two diversionary attacks were also to be made, one across the bridge over the Agueda against the defences below the castle and another from the convent of Santa Cruz against the left of the main breach. The attack was duly delivered by the storming columns which moved forward in the darkness, feeling their way towards the breaches under fire from the French defenders. Craufurd's Light Division was first up, scrambling their way up and into the Lesser Breach meeting relatively light resistance. In fact, so quick was their passage into the town that, after turning to their right in order to clear the ramparts as far as the Great Breach, many of them were killed when the French exploded a huge mine beneath it. Scores of British troops from the 3rd Division were sent flying into the air along with several men of the Light Division who had been too quick for their own good.

The town was taken, but at a cost. Both commanders of the respective storming columns were lost during the assault, Mackinnon being killed by the great mine and Craufurd being mortally wounded by a French musket ball as he stood upon the glacis, urging his beloved Light Division forward. A further 562 officers and men also became casualties during the storming. The first of the two great fortresses was now in Wellington's hands, but there was a darker and more significant aspect to the successful storming, for, in the event of such a success, nobody appears to have considered what they should do afterwards. No British army had ever taken a town by storm in the Peninsula – indeed, the British army had not taken a regularly fortified town in Europe since Drogheda in 1649. When Wellington's men broke into Ciudad Rodrigo officers lost control of their men and there was a period of disorder during which they broke open houses and shops in search of drink and plunder. Some buildings were also set on fire. The disorder was relatively short lived and order was restored after a few hours. The most significant aspect of these disturbances was that it gave Wellington's men a taste of what they could expect to enjoy at Badajoz, their next objective, for if affairs were bad at Rodrigo they would be much worse there in the maze of small, dark streets where order would be virtually impossible for British officers to maintain over any troops determined to break free from the rigours of army discipline. Furthermore, Badajoz had a long history amongst the British troops of being a distinctly hostile town and had shown itself thus during the aftermath of Talavera in 1809 when British troops – particularly the wounded – were afforded a less than friendly welcome from their supposed Spanish allies. Also, Wellington's men had besieged the town twice before, in May and June 1811, without any success, and this served only to increase their determination to settle the score when they revisited the town in April 1812. The situation cannot be summed up any better than by a passage from William Grattan, an officer of the 88th (Connaught Rangers), who wrote, 'the capture of Badajoz had long been their idol; many causes led to this wish on their part; the two previous unsuccessful sieges, and the failure of the attack against San Christobal in the latter; but above all, the well known hostility of its inhabitants to the British army, and perhaps might be added, a desire for plunder which the sacking of Rodrigo had given them a taste for. Badajoz was, therefore, denounced as a place to be made an example of; and most unquestionably no city, Jerusalem exempted, was ever more strictly visited to the letter than was this ill-fated town.'

First of all, of course, Wellington had to move his army south, which he began to do in February 1812. A series of ruses were employed to lead the French into believing that there would be no further offensive moves for the time being. The number of sick and wounded in hospitals was exaggerated, some senior officers were allowed to go home on leave, whilst Wellington himself remained at Freneida until 5 March. Then, quickly, and without fuss, he slipped away to join his army which had appeared to the west of Badajoz. The great siege was about to begin.

The siege of Badajoz was, from the outset, a race against time with relieving French armies marching to the town's assistance. Wellington was again hampered by a lack of decent siege tools whilst the digging devolved once again on the ordinary line regiments. The weather conspired against him also, with the rain pouring down in torrents during the first days of the siege which began on 16 March. However, by sheer hard work and through the skill of Wellington's gunners, two breaches were made in the strong walls of the town – in the bastions of the Santa Maria and La Trinidad – with another being blasted on 5 April through the curtain wall which connected them. With time running out, Wellington – probably with a heavy heart, for he almost certainly would have liked more time to batter the walls – issued his orders for the assault. The main storming columns were to be provided by the 4th and Light Divisions, who were to attack the breaches, whilst Picton's 3rd Division was to make a diversionary attack by escalading the walls of the Moorish castle in the north-eastern quarter of the town. Leith's 5th Division was to make a second diversionary attack, on the Pardaleras fort and against the San Vincente bastion.

When the cathedral bells in Badajoz tolled the hour of ten o'clock on the night of 6 April 1812, they heralded the beginning of the most momentous, dramatic and terrible night of the whole Peninsular War. The 4th and Light Divisions were hurled against the walls of Badajoz no less than forty times, but in vain. Each time they were thrown back by the tenacious defenders who were commanded by Governor Armand Phillipon, as staunch an opponent as Wellington would come up against in the Peninsula. But while the French defenders taunted and jeered their increasingly desperate attackers at the breaches, other British troops were pouring over the ramparts at the castle and at the San Vincente to render their efforts useless. Soon, British bugles could be heard faintly above the roar at the breaches and, as the defenders realised the enemy was approaching from behind them, resistance ceased and Badajoz was won. It was won at a tremendous cost, however, for no fewer than 3,752 British and Portuguese troops became casualties, including over 800 killed, and most of these were confined to a relatively small area at the breaches. Little wonder that Wellington broke down and wept when he saw the horrifying carnage there on the morning of 7 April.

Inside the town, meanwhile, those who had survived the assault unleashed their full power against the town and its unfortunate population. Shops and houses were sacked, their contents looted, women and young girls were raped and murdered, convents were sacked and pillaged and all manner of atrocities committed that defy description. Seventy two hours later – an astonishing length of time for an army to be out of control – the debauchery died down. Wellington's efforts to restore order, including the erection of a gallows that, incidentally, was not used, came to nothing and, as Napier later wrote, 'the disorder subsided rather than was quelled'.

Many may claim, with some justification, that Wellington's men were entitled to embark upon their course. After all, by fighting on after practicable breaches had been made in the walls of the town – the convention current at the time dictating that garrisons should surrender in such an event – the French waived all rights to mercy. Wellington himself later wrote that if he had slaughtered the garrison at Ciudad Rodrigo he would have saved the flower of his army at Badajoz. But he did not, the garrison at Badajoz fought on, and the consequences were left for all to see. Curiously, it was not the French garrison which suffered, but the population, leading one to suspect that the British troops were bent on such a design from the outset. As Grattan says, Badajoz was a town to be made an example of.

Wellington's army staggered away from Badajoz and returned north to avert a renewed threat to Ciudad Rodrigo by Marmont, who quickly withdrew. The subsequent operations saw Wellington march east to Salamanca, which was entered on 17 June 1812. There followed a period of marching and counter-marching by both French and Allied armies before Marmont pushed his luck too far on 22 July at the small village of Los Arapiles, a few miles south of Salamanca. Here, the French extended their left too far in an attempt to cut Wellington's retreat to Portugal and, as a horrified Marmont watched the disastrous manoeuvre unfold before him, Wellington's divisions struck south against his columns, destroying one after another. So much, therefore, for the defensive-minded and over-cautious reputation of the British commander. The battle did not go completely in Wellington's favour, however, for after Pack and Cole had seen their attacks thwarted by some stout French resistance, the French commander, Clausel – both Marmont and his successor, Bonnet, had been struck down and carried from the field – launched a counter-attack which almost succeeded. Fortunately, Wellington displayed his powers of foresight again, and while Cole's men rallied, Clinton's 6th Division was thrust by him into the gap to prevent the French from snatching a drawn battle, if not victory itself, from what had earlier appeared to be a disaster. As night fell, Marmont's defeated army was driven from the field in disorder and it was only the darkness, and an extensive wood to the south of the battlefield, that saved the French from a greater disaster. Wellington did not pursue the French. Why should he? Had he not despatched Carlos D'España's Spanish troops to Alba de Tormes to hold the only bridge over the Tormes river? There was no other way for the retreating French to cross the Tormes and it would be a simple matter for his army to advance the following morning and scoop them all up. Unfortunately, D'España had withdrawn his men without orders and had not the courage to inform Wellington of this unauthorised move. The commander-in-chief's reaction – he was never one to tolerate the slightest deviation from his orders – can be easily imagined. Despite this disappointing conclusion, the battle of Salamanca was a crushing defeat for the French and was one which, in the opinion of one of the defeated French generals, raised Wellington's reputation throughout Europe to that of Marlborough.

The victory at Salamanca opened the way to Madrid which was entered by Wellington on 12 August. It was a time of great optimism for the Allies in Spain, for not only had the first eight months of the year yielded some of the great triumphs of the war, but Napoleon had begun to withdraw large numbers of French troops from the Peninsula in preparation for his ill-fated attack on Russia. Unfortunately, the optimism was to be sadly misplaced. In September Wellington made his way north-east to undertake the siege of the castle of Burgos, perched high on a hill overlooking the town. Burgos was not the sort of fortified town found at Ciudad Rodrigo or Badajoz and, indeed, the castle was relatively small and apparently easy game for the Allies. However, Wellington left behind him the 3rd, 4th, 5th and Light Divisions, his veteran storming divisions, and chose to attack the castle with troops from the 1st Division who had pleaded with him to be allowed to show what they could do. Sadly, his decision went against him and the combination of inexperienced troops, the usual lack of siege tools and, more significantly, a woeful lack of heavy guns – he undertook the siege with just three heavy guns – resulted in his only major failure of the war.

From start to finish the siege was little short of a fiasco and, apart from the successful storming of the hornwork of San Miguel, prior to the siege proper beginning, there was little to cheer during the month-long siege. The various assaults went in piecemeal and were all thrust back by the French defenders – during an assault on 4 October, the French even obtained a copy of Wellington's plans for the assault from a dead British officer – and, on 8 October, Edward Cocks, a favourite of Wellington's and an officer of great promise, was killed helping repulse a French sortie. Wellington wept at Cocks's funeral and with his death it is said that Wellington's heart went out of the siege. Finally, on 21 October, the Allied army packed up and departed for Madrid, ironically, three days after Napoleon got himself out of his own particular mess at Moscow. The ensuing retreat by Wellington and his army did not end until they had reached Ciudad Rodrigo and the Portuguese border after what Wellington himself called 'the worst scrape I ever was in'. Indeed, many of those who had experienced both the retreats to Corunna and Burgos said afterwards that the latter was by far the worse. Therefore, 1812, a year begun with such a burst of energy, ended as a damp squib.

It must be remembered, however, that the two key fortresses of Ciudad Rodrigo and Badajoz were still in Allied hands, and throughout the winter of 1812–13 and the following spring, Wellington's men recovered, reinforcements arrived from England and by May the army was ready to begin its great advance from Portugal into Spain, and the campaign which would see the decisive battle of the Peninsular War and end with Wellington poised for the invasion of France.

Throughout the six years of Britain's involvement in the Peninsula they had received vital support from the Spanish guerrillas whose part in the war Wellington later freely acknowledged. They were a real thorn in the flesh for successive French commanders whose resources were drained by having to keep a continual watch over their shoulders for guerrilla activity. By the time of the Vittoria campaign, King Joseph was forced to send escorts of up to 1,500 men in order to ensure that his despatches reached Paris, manpower that he could ill afford. Indeed, such was the omnipresent threat from these covert killers that the various French armies could never concentrate against Wellington, for had they been able to do so his position in the Peninsula would have become untenable. Instead, he was able to deal with the French armies separately, and by the time they did manage to concentrate, as at Vittoria – where the armies of the South, of Portugal and of the North combined – his own army had grown both in numbers and in stature to deal with them. One must also remember that the French armies in Spain were armies of occupation and as such had a duty to go hunting these guerrillas, and not just sit back and become penned in like sheep in their respective headquarters. Their resources were stretched to the limit by having to leave occupying forces in major towns and cities, otherwise as soon as they moved on they would find a guerrilla force in their rear. It was a most difficult situation for them. The reputation of these unlikely but most valuable allies has for years been as patriotic heroes, but recent research has shown that this is partly myth, and that although some guerrilla units and their leaders were indeed invaluable to Wellington's war effort – Julian Sanchez's cavalry were converted to regular cavalry at the end of the war, for example – many guerrillas used the war as an excuse to rob and take whatever they pleased under the guise of patriotism. The real losers at the end of the day were the Iberian people who had to endure both the Allied and French armies, as well as the guerrillas. All parties took what the villagers had to offer, the only difference being that Wellington's men paid for their supplies (usually), whereas both the French and the guerrillas took theirs by force. The end result for the villages was the same; they were left with very little. The Vittoria campaign of 1813 began with General Foy's troops, away in the north of Spain, engaged in such a hunt for guerrillas, something which was to prevent him from joining Joseph at Vittoria, and as the war entered the Pyrenees and Navarre, Spanish guerrillas, who had been quite active there throughout the war, stepped up their operations. Their efforts were, as Wellington said, an important factor in his eventual triumph.

The Vittoria campaign began with a touch of theatre from Wellington who, on crossing the Portuguese border, turned in his saddle and said, 'Farewell Portugal, I shall never see you again.' He never did. The campaign involved an Allied advance in four columns, not along the great high road to France, but north of it, outflanking each successive French position as they went. In this way, strong French positions on the Douro and Esla rivers were turned without having to fight. It was a tremendous achievement, and was one conducted in great secrecy for the French never really knew where the main Allied army was until it had passed them. Even Burgos, the great stumbling-block in 1812, was avoided, the French abandoning the castle after blowing it up on 14 June. Eventually, the Allied columns converged to the west and north-west of Vittoria on 19 June, ready to do battle. King Joseph's armies had converged on Vittoria some days before, a huge convoy of accumulated treasure, paintings, gold and silver accompanying them, as did an astonishing array of non-fighting personnel, of camp followers, French civilians and ministerial staff, wives and *afrancesados*, the pro-French Spaniards who had thrown in their lot with the enemy.

On 21 June Wellington's troops burst from the hills surrounding the valley of the Zadorra, the river which winds its way along the horse-shoe-shaped valley floor, over which the deciding battle of the war was to be fought. Wellington was trusting much to his subordinates, Hill, Graham and Dalhousie, particularly the latter two whose instructions were to feel their way into the action depending on events unfolding on their respective right flanks. For a commander rarely used to delegating, Wellington was placing a huge responsibility on their shoulders and, indeed, things did not quite come off as planned. They did work well enough, however, for Wellington to achieve one of his greatest victories, a victory which looked likely from the moment Hill's 2nd Division began driving the French along the summit of the heights of Puebla on the French left, to open the battle. By 10am Graham's column had cut the main road to Bayonne, thus preventing the possibility of any direct escape to France, and when Picton's 3rd Division stormed the bridge of Mendoza during the early afternoon, Joseph's prospects became decidedly bleak. The French were driven from successive positions after severe fighting, but when Gazan abandoned his position on the French left, Joseph's army gave way and there followed unprecedented scenes as it streamed away to the east along the road to Salvatierra and Pamplona, abandoning in its haste over 150 guns. The French lost over 8,000 men, but this could have been immeasurably worse had it not been for the old curse of the British army – plunder. For what really saved the French from complete destruction was the convoy of treasure which the British troops caught up with to the south and east of Vittoria. When the wagons were ripped open the British troops could not believe their eyes – or their luck, for they had taken possession of a vast treasure trove, the like of which had never been seen before in the history of warfare. Soldiers filled their pockets with coins and jewels, French officers' baggage, loaded down with accumulated plunder, was pillaged and distributed amongst the men, whilst scores of unfortunate women were taken after being abandoned in the rout. Madame Gazan, the wife of the French general, was captured but returned to her husband shortly afterwards and indeed, King Joseph himself narrowly avoided capture when, after finding his carriage caught in the jam outside Vittoria, he hastily took to his horse, scrambling out of one side of his carriage as Colonel Wyndham, of the 10th Hussars, fired his pistol through the other door. Marshal Jourdan's baton was captured by a corporal of the 18th Hussars and sent by Wellington to the Prince Regent who in turn made him Britain's first Field Marshal.

Wellington, however, was in no mood for such niceties on the evening of 21 June and the morning of 22 June for, as at Salamanca, he had seen the French army escape his clutches once again, this time due to the plundering of the French baggage train. It was this episode which moved him to refer to his men as 'the scum of the earth' in a despatch to Lord Bathurst. This was slightly unfair to a large part of the army, however, for whole regiments of infantry and cavalry saw none of the treasure, forming up and pitching camp to the north of the town following the battle itself and as such taking no part in the disgraceful aftermath. But few could blame the men. Arrears of pay were commonplace in the British army and the prospects were none too cheerful for the private soldier. So, why not fill your pockets with gold and silver? Of course, whether they managed to hold on to their ill-gotten gains is doubtful, for the majority of the windfall would probably have been spent on the usual army pleasures before the campaign was over.

There must have been a great sense of both disappointment and *déja vu* in Wellington's headquarters during the days immediately following the battle. Like Salamanca, he had achieved a great victory, but once again the French had been allowed to get away, whereas if all had gone to plan both of the French armies at these two battles ought to have been totally destroyed. In the case of Vittoria it was particularly unfortunate, for the consequence was that Marshal Soult, who assumed command in the Peninsula shortly afterwards, was able to launch a counter-attack in the Pyrenees the following month, as well as ensuring that Wellington would have a fight on his hands when he invaded France towards the end of the year.

The victory on 21 June had far-reaching consequences for, even as the battle was being fought, Napoleon had negotiated a treaty with the Austrians and Prussians. The consequences of the outcome of the battle of Vittoria were not lost on Napoleon who tried his best to suppress the news from both the Austrians and Prussians. He was unsuccessful, however, and on 21 August the treaty was repudiated and hostilities broke out once again. Vittoria, therefore, can be said to be one of the most decisive and important battles of the Napoleonic period.

Junot, Victor, Massena, Marmont and Joseph. To this list of Wellington's main adversaries in the Peninsula must now be added Marshal Soult for, following the disaster at Vittoria, he was chosen by Napoleon as the next French commander to attempt what all the previous incumbents had failed to do, namely, to stop Wellington. As we have already seen, he enjoyed success in 1809 against Moore but was on the receiving end at Oporto in May the same year. He had also been frustrated by the Allies at Albuera in 1811. His first task now was to restore the shattered morale of the French troops. This proved easier than expected, for it was the generals who appear to have suffered the greatest loss of confidence and, indeed, the ordinary French soldier had fought well at Vittoria; unfortunately he did not fight well enough and his cause was not helped by the ineptitude of Gazan. This, coupled with the fact that the French army was now fighting not as an army of occupation but as an army about to defend its homeland, made Soult's job far easier than it might otherwise have been and as he fell back, his position, ironically, became stronger as he was retreating upon his base, namely Bayonne.

Soult's first counter-attack came on 25 July, the first day of what was known as the battle of the Pyrenees, a series of actions which lasted until 2 August. Why Soult gave up the passes at Maya and Roncesvalles, and then attacked them is slightly puzzling but that was his course of action, and when he attacked these two passes on Sunday 25 July, ostensibly in an attempt to relieve the garrison of Pamplona, he was partially successful, particularly at Maya where troops from Hill's 2nd Division were driven along the ridge which runs east of the pass and down into the valley of the Baztan. D'Erlon, commanding the French, chose not to press down in pursuit, however, and save for the capture of the pass itself, little was gained strategically by the French. A different and far more serious situation occurred at Roncesvalles, however, where Cole was attacked on the same day by Clausel and Reille. His men held the French in check for most of the day until dense fog brought the curtain down on the day's fighting. Unnerved by this, and fearing the French might get around his flank, he pulled back and withdrew his men south. When Wellington, who was away to the west at Lesaca during the day, heard about this he was not too perturbed as there was a good defensive position at Zubiri, a few miles to the south. Unfortunately, Cole, who had been joined by Picton, had completely lost his nerve and fell back far beyond there, to Sorauren, almost at the gates of Pamplona, much to Wellington's great dismay and in direct disobedience of his orders. Cole and Picton may have been great fighters and the latter one of the army's real firebrands, but, as Wellington said, 'when I am obliged to quit them they are children'.

Wellington rejoined Cole at Sorauren on 27 July and, after narrowly avoiding capture by French cavalry as he coolly dictated an order to Fitzroy Somerset, he rode up alone in front of his men to assume command. The first troops he came upon were Portuguese who, since May 1809, had called him 'Douro' and it was this shout that now went up. It must have been one of the memorable moments of the war as the chant, 'Douro! Douro!' rang out, a cry taken up in turn by each British regiment as it rolled along the mountainside from left to right. The effect of this chanting must have been as inspiring to the Allies as it was disheartening to the French. Indeed, observing the effect it had upon his men, Wellington, who usually disliked such worshipping – 'if they cheer you one day, they may turn against you the next', he claimed – indulged it, and when he peered through his telescope across the valley at Soult he saw a man whose heart must surely have just sunk. Wellington spent the wet and stormy night of 27 July wrapped in his cloak upon the hillside along with his men. By the end of the Napoleonic Wars such storms would become the omen of victory for Wellington's men, preceding as they did the victories at Salamanca, Sorauren and Waterloo.

Soult's attack was duly delivered on 28 July in the usual style, dense blue columns ascending the steep hills on which the Allies were positioned. All credit must be given to the French during the Pyrenees campaign for the stamina they showed in even attempting to force the Allied line, for as at Roncesvalles and, to a lesser extent, Maya, they had to negotiate long and difficult marches before they could engage Wellington's men. At Sorauren the fighting was hard and on the Allied left inroads were made in their line. But French successes were short-lived, and they were thrown back at bayonet point by determined Allied counter-attacks. The battle subsided into stalemate and both armies remained where they were throughout 29 July, during which further British reinforcements arrived, and when Soult moved on the 30th he was attacked with vigour by Wellington and driven back over the mountains into France. His attempt to relieve Pamplona had failed.

While the fighting in the Pyrenees had been going on, Sir Thomas Graham had been supervising the siege of San Sebastian, the third of Wellington's great sieges in the Peninsula. Once again, the operation was unsatisfactory and the first assault on the place, on 25 July, failed. On 31 August another assault was made, in broad daylight, and in full view of hundreds of spectators who came from the surrounding towns and villages to watch. The Allied troops ran the gauntlet of fire across the shallow waters of the Urumea river to attack the breaches made in the sea wall but the attack stalled, held up by determined French resistance, until Graham gave orders for his guns to open fire over the heads of the attacking troops and on to the French defenders. This innovation worked to perfection, to which the line of headless French bodies testified. British and Portuguese troops pressed their faces into the rocks whilst a stream of shells smashed into the defenders above them, driving them back and allowing the Allies to enter the town. General Rey, commanding the garrison, pulled his men back to the safety of the castle at the top of Monte Urgull, where they surrendered on 7 September. Once again, there followed the usual scenes of disorder as the town was sacked, the rioting made all the worse by a fire which all but destroyed the old town. Many considered the aftermath at San Sebastian to have been worse than Badajoz, which may be true. Perhaps the many diarists of the day had exhausted themselves during that particular episode and, to prevent repetition, said merely that San Sebastian was as bad, and made worse than Badajoz by the fire. The Spaniards themselves added to the controversy by claiming that Wellington himself had ordered the town to be put to the torch as a penalty for its continued trading with France, a notion scoffed at with indignation by him. Indeed, Wellington held an internal enquiry into the cause of the fire, after which he was perfectly satisfied that his men had done no wrong.

With San Sebastian taken, only the city of Pamplona remained in French hands. There was, of course, a French army under the redoubtable Marshal Suchet still operating on the east coast of Spain, and for a while Wellington considered moving east against them. However, he chose to push on to the French border, leaving Pamplona to be blockaded rather than besieged in the regular manner. Pamplona eventually capitulated on 25 October 1813. Suchet was eventually forced to relinquish his hold in Catalonia and was forced back towards the Pyrenees, crossing back over the French border in late 1813 with just 15,000 men.

On the very day that San Sebastian fell to the Allies, Soult launched what was to be the last battle fought by the French army in Spain, the ill-fated San Marcial offensive of 31 August. This was Soult's last-ditch attempt to relieve San Sebastian but, like the battle of the Pyrenees which was intended to relieve Pamplona, it failed. Soult's men crossed the Bidassoa river to attack the Spanish troops at the top of the steep heights opposite. The battle saw one of the few occasions where, having learned from their British allies, the Spanish troops waited patiently at the top instead of charging down at the enemy. The result was that, as the French neared the top of the heights, the Spaniards opened fire before rushing at the French and driving them back at bayonet point. That the French troops noticed large red columns waiting behind the Spaniards perhaps had something to do with their less than vigorous attack, but little should be taken away from the Spaniards and their commanding officer, Bernadin Freire, who at one stage of the battle appealed to Wellington for British help. Wellington, observing that the French were as good as beaten, refused, saying, 'if I send you the English troops you ask for, they will win the battle; but as the French are already in retreat you may as well win it for yourselves.' The result was a belated win for the Spanish army, which had enjoyed few successes since its great victory over the French at Baylen in 1808.

By the first week of October Wellington was poised to begin his long-awaited invasion of France. Facing him along a sixteen-mile front were just 47,000 French troops, thinly spread and concentrated around the lofty mountain, La Rhune, which dominates the whole area. There were close to 15,000 French troops in this sector with a further 14,000 away to the east. Just 10,000 troops defended the sector between the Rhune and the Atlantic as this area was considered to be impassable and the least likely target of Wellington's main thrust. Sadly for Soult, it was this very front that Wellington planned to attack. He gave orders for diversionary movements to be made away to the east while several smaller ruses were staged intended to deceive the French. Indeed, he himself rode to Roncesvalles to visit the 6th Division and made sure that the French knew he was there. It was all intended to tease, torment and badger the French into believing that the invasion would be made over the hills and tracks around La Rhune.

At about 7.30 on the morning of 7 October the red trail of a rocket sent spiralling into the grey morning sky signalled the beginning of the Allied invasion of France. The 1st and 5th Divisions stepped off from their positions on the southern bank and began crossing the Bidassoa, local shrimpers leading the way to guide the Allied troops across the shallow estuary. By 11.30 Wellington's men were firmly in possession of the northern bank having driven back the French defenders who retired to another position farther north. The fighting was fiercer above Vera, where the Light Division attacked French positions on the Bayonet Ridge, but by early afternoon they were in possession of all their objectives. More important, the French defenders on the Rhune, faced with being cut off from the main French positions, withdrew across the ravine which divides the Rhune from the Lesser Rhune and took up positions behind walls and amidst the rocky crags of the latter's razor-backed crest.

That afternoon, Wellington perhaps reflected upon his early victories at Roliça and Vimeiro, at the despair of Moore at Corunna, and at his own long list of personal triumphs from Oporto to the Pyrenees. Finally, after those long years of fighting, he had seen his army cross the Bidassoa and set foot upon the so-called 'sacred soil' of Napoleon's France, surely, one of the greatest moments of Wellington's life.

There was a lull of just under a month before Wellington struck next, driving Soult from his positions along the line of the Nivelle river. The operation was similar to the crossing of the Bidassoa, Wellington attacking a position of about twenty miles in length, defended by around 63,000 French troops, thinly spread along the whole line. During the past few weeks the French troops had been busy constructing forts and redoubts on most of the more prominent hilltops to create a strong position which would have to be attacked frontally by Wellington. His plan was a reverse of that employed during the Bidassoa operation. On this occasion, Hope's 1st and 5th Divisions, with two Spanish divisions, were to tease the enemy on his right, close to the Atlantic. The main Allied attacks, however, were to be launched in the centre against the Rhune, and between Sare and the bridge over the Nivelle at Amotz. Hill was to attack the French left at the same time.

The battle of the Nivelle was fought on 10 November 1813, and was another great success for Wellington and his army who swept all before them, driving the French from their forts after some stiff fighting in places. The great chronicler of the war, William Napier, present during the attack on the Lesser Rhune, wrote, 'The plains of France so long overlooked from the towering crags of the Pyrenees were to be the prize of the battle, and the half-famished soldiers in their fury, broke through the iron barrier erected by Soult as if it were but a screen of reeds.' By the end of the day Soult had been driven back upon Bayonne, his military base. For him, the day had been another disaster, although his position still grew stronger as he fell back upon Bayonne, with the Nive river on his left flank and the Atlantic on his right, a narrow front defended in depth by his men. For Wellington it was a different story. He had seen his army achieve yet another great victory and, even though he was never one to lavish praise upon his men, he was moved to call his army 'probably the most complete machine for its numbers now existing in Europe'. High praise indeed, but justified.

A further four weeks passed before the two armies next clashed, on 9 December, the first day of the four-day battle of the Nive. Soult was firmly pinned against Bayonne and the river Ardour, but he had the advantage of being able to operate either to the left or right of the Nive river, which ran south from Bayonne, by virtue of the bridges in the city. Wellington, on the other hand, had divided his force, Hill taking the eastern or right bank of the Nive whilst Wellington occupied the west or left bank of the river with his left flank resting upon the Atlantic. Hill crossed the Nive on 9 December, his intention being to threaten Soult's retreat to the east and the interior of France. However, on 10 December Soult counter-attacked and drove back Wellington's left flank for almost three miles, the centre of the latter's army – the Light Division – being driven back to Arcangues, where it halted the retirement. The main French attacks were thwarted, but this did not deter them for Soult persisted in his pushes on 11 and 12 December, but to little avail.

The main action came on 13 December, a battle since known as the battle of St Pierre. The pontoon bridge linking Wellington and Hill was washed away by heavy rains, thereby isolating Hill on the right bank of the Nive. Soult was able, therefore, to transfer his men to that side and attack, knowing that he had about four hours to defeat Hill before the pontoon was restored and before reinforcements arrived from Ustaritz, the next crossing point south on the Nive. The action began at 8am, when Soult's columns loomed out of the morning gloom to begin their attack. The next four hours saw some extremely hard fighting as Hill strove to maintain his position, throwing in most of his reserves in the face of determined French attacks. Fortunately, Wellington's most trusted subordinate proved more than capable of winning the game before Wellington himself arrived with reinforcements. Hill, in fact, chose to close the battle with the men under his command and, as the commander-in-chief rode up, he declared Hill the victor, declining to take command and adding, 'My dear Hill, the day's your own.'

The year of 1813 ended with Wellington firmly established in southern France and with the great French military base of Bayonne in his grip. Indeed, on 23 February 1814 the vice was further tightened when his men crossed the Adour river and began blockading the town from the north, by which time Soult had retreated east, leaving around 14,000 French troops to garrison the town. On 27 February Wellington's army fought its last major battle in open ground amidst the green, lush slopes of the main Dax-Orthes road. There was little stopping the Allied army at this stage of the war, and when its columns ascended the long, gradual slopes to attack the enemy, they were triumphant once again, the French putting up a stiff fight at the village of St Boes but not stiff enough to stop the Allied juggernaut.

The pursuit of Soult's army took Wellington to Toulouse, where he arrived during the closing week of March, his men fighting a couple of sharp actions along the way at Aire and Tarbes. It is quite ironic that such a satisfactory war – from Wellington's point of view – should come to such an unsatisfactory finale with the messy and bloody assault on Toulouse on 10 April 1814. Over 4,500 Allied troops became casualties by the end of a day which saw them clear the French from their positions along the Calvinet Ridge, against 3,200 French casualties. The result of the battle gave Wellington his final triumph – albeit a kind of pyrrhic one – in the Peninsula. Six long, hard years of fighting were finally over, although the battle need never have been fought at all. Indeed, Napoleon had already abdicated on 4 April, although Wellington was not to receive news of the event until 12 April, two days after the battle of Toulouse. Soult, in fact, did not accept defeat until 17 April. And yet even though Napoleon had abdicated and the war, in theory, was at an end, there was still time for more blood to be shed, the blood of 1,733 Allied and French casualties to be precise during the sortie from Bayonne on the night of 14 April 1814 when French troops issued from the gates of the citadel on the north bank of the Adour to drive back the British and German troops blockading from the north. The French were eventually driven back after a night of fierce, confused fighting, leaving Major-General Hay dead and Sir John Hope wounded and captured. For what? The French governor, Thouvenot, claimed not to have known about events elsewhere in France, but one cannot believe anything other than that the sortie was launched purely out of malice, and as a final, desperate act of a mischievous French soldier.

Not counting the event which ostensibly sparked off the Peninsular War – Junot's invasion of Portugal in November 1807 – the war lasted from 1808 until 1814. These six long years of warfare were Britain's greatest contribution to the first downfall of Napoleon and were a constant drain on French manpower and resources. It was no coincidence, in fact, that Napoleon called the war 'the Spanish ulcer', for that was exactly what it was, a 'running sore'. Many consider the war in the Peninsula to have been a mere sideshow when compared to the great campaigns in Russia, Austria and Germany, and perhaps they are right. Wellington was never in a position to threaten Paris strategically, which was the object of the wider game, but the Anglo-Portuguese army got a grip of affairs in Spain and Portugal and, along with the Spanish armies and the guerrillas, never really let go. They hung grimly on at times, but by the end of 1813 they were across the French border, by which time Napoleon must have suspected that his time was running out. Similarly, the great battles at Salamanca and Vittoria were never on the scale of Wagram, Borodino, Austerlitz and Leipzig, but none of the Austrian, Prussian or Russian armies could claim such a record on the field of battle as Wellington's, in spite of Napoleon sending a succession of tried and tested marshals and generals against him. Wellington defeated them all. And, of course, he defeated Napoleon himself – with a lot of help from the Prussians – when he finally came face to face with him at Waterloo. The great battle, fought there on 18 June 1815, has rightly gone down as the greatest of all European land battles, one that in effect kept the peace of Europe for a further ninety nine years. Unfortunately, Waterloo has tended to overshadow the achievements of Wellington's Anglo-Portuguese army in the Peninsula, an army which barely lost a gun, let alone a battle, and there are few armies which can boast a similar record. The Peninsular War should, therefore, be rightly considered to be much more than a sideshow, for it was an integral part of the final downfall of Napoleon, and if Waterloo was won on the playing fields of Eton, then it was the dusty battlefields of the Peninsula on which the seeds of that final victory were sown.

CHAPTER II

'That unlucky war': Some aspects of the French experience in the Peninsula

Philip J Haythornthwaite

Writing of his experiences in the Peninsula, a French officer commented on the 'anxious and disturbed life' which he and his compatriots had endured 'during these Spanish campaigns; there would be no resemblance between their history and that of others of the same kind, if it were possible to collect all the circumstances of them. By the side of heroic and sublime actions will be found others that are most atrocious and sometimes most grotesque'[1]. Among all the campaigns waged by Napoleon's troops, the Peninsular War was not only the most protracted but among the most unpleasant and demoralising; and played a significant part in Napoleon's eventual defeat.

The emperor himself made no attempt to conceal this fact, remarking that: 'That unlucky war ruined me; it divided my forces, obliged me to multiply my efforts, and caused my principles to be assailed . . . All the circumstances of my disasters are connected with that fatal knot: it destroyed my moral power in Europe, rendered my embarrassments more complicated, and opened a school for the English soldiers'[2].

Napoleon's involvement in the Peninsula occurred at a time when his fortunes were in the ascendant, following his victories at Austerlitz and Jena, and the diplomatic settlement at Tilsit. Spain was then in alliance with France, and French troops first traversed the country in order to invade Portugal. Had Napoleon limited himself to this objective, he could have avoided the entanglement which was to prove so costly; but the government of Spain inspired little confidence as an ally. The ineffectual King Carlos IV was dominated by his wife and her favourite, chief minister Manuel Godoy, 'Prince of the Peace'; the heir-apparent, Ferdinand, Prince of the Asturias, was no more talented than his father, and was the focus for opposition to Godoy, towards whom he maintained a bitter animosity. Consequently, the first French troops to enter Spain experienced a reception very different from that encountered on subsequent occasions: Louis Lejeune discovered that: 'The troops of the

Emperor had been received as friends . . . everywhere our soldiers were welcomed as liberators . . . on every road laurel branches had been cut down to form triumphal arches beneath which the Emperor of France, the redresser of the grievances of the people, was to pass . . . the loyal populace, who now received us as if we were their brothers, impatiently awaited the day when the Emperor should arrive in Madrid. They hoped that he would remove the hated minister [Godoy] and restore the royal authority of Carlos IV, or place it in the hands of his son Ferdinand . . .'[3].

Godoy's conduct in 1806 can only have confirmed Napoleon's suspicions about the untrustworthy nature of his Peninsular ally; and although Godoy's anti-French pronouncements had ceased upon Napoleon's victory over Prussia, they were not forgotten. Napoleon's hand was forced by the public uprising of March 1808 against Godoy, which culminated in the Prince of the Peace being driven from office and the king abdicating in favour of Ferdinand. Faced with the threat of a new and possibly anti-French regime, Napoleon decided that he had to depose the Bourbon monarchy and instal his own, in the person of his brother Joseph. In giving this the appearance of legitimacy by the restoration of Carlos IV as king, who then voluntarily resigned the throne in favour of Joseph, Napoleon must have hoped to prevent much unrest. His miscalculation of popular support for Ferdinand and opposition to the French was a serious error.

Although, at least in his own view, there were pressing political and military reasons for his actions, in order to secure Spanish support and her resources for the war against Britain, Napoleon maintained that he had also acted in the interests of the Spanish people. As he was being conveyed to Elba he told his British host, 'that Spain was the natural friend of France, and enemy of Great Britain, that it was the interest of Spain to unite with France in support of their commerce and foreign possessions . . . He did not invade Spain, he said, to put one of his own family on the throne, but to revolutionize her; to make her a kingdom *en règle*, to abolish the inquisition, feudal rights, and the inordinate privileges of certain classes'[4]. This he continued to maintain, but was more forthcoming when discussing the war during his exile at St Helena:

'Events have proved that I committed a great fault in the choice of my means; for the fault lies in the means much more than in the principles. It cannot be doubted that, in the crisis in which France then was, in the struggle of new ideas, in the great cause of the age against the rest of Europe, we could not leave Spain behind, at the disposal of our enemies; it was absolutely necessary to enchain her, voluntarily, or by force, in our system. The destiny of France required this: and the code of the welfare of nations is not always that of individuals. Besides, to political necessity was here superadded for me the force of right. Spain, when she saw me in danger, Spain, when she saw my hands were full at Jena, had almost declared war against me. The insult ought not to pass unpunished: I could declare war in my turn, and assuredly the success could not be doubtful. It was this very facility which misled me. The nation despised its government: it called loudly for a regeneration. From the height to which Fortune had raised me, I considered myself called, I considered it worthy of me to accomplish in peace so great an event. I was solicitous to spare blood, that not a drop should stain the Castilian emancipation, I therefore delivered the Spaniards from their abominable institutions; I gave them a liberal constitution; I deemed it necessary, perhaps too lightly, to change their destiny . . . I had done the greatest benefit that ever was conferred on a nation – so I said to myself, and so I still say. The Spaniards themselves, as I have been assured, thought so in their hearts, and never complained of any thing but the forms. I expected their blessings, but I was disappointed: disdaining interest, they thought only of the insult: they were indignant at the idea of an affront, enraged at the sight of force, and all flew to arms . . . but, if they triumphed, they have been cruelly punished for it. Perhaps they are to be pitied. They deserved better'[5].

In addition, he also admitted that 'it was impossible to leave the Peninsula a prey to the machinations of the English, the intrigues, the hopes, and the pretentions of the Bourbons'[6]. Napoleon commented upon the methods he employed: 'I ought to have given a liberal constitution to the Spanish nation, and charged Ferdinand with its execution. If he had acted with good faith, Spain must have prospered and harmonized with our new manners. The great object would have been obtained, and France would have acquired an intimate ally and an addition of power truly formidable. Had Ferdinand, on the contrary, proved faithless to his new engagements, the Spaniards themselves would not have failed to dismiss him, and would have applied to me for a ruler in his place'[7]. However, for his attempt to seize 'the singular opportunity, held out to me by fortune, for regenerating Spain, rescuing her from the yoke of England, and intimately uniting her with our system', Napoleon knew that posterity would judge him severely: 'I engaged very inconsiderately in the whole affair; its immorality must have shown itself too openly, its injustice too glaringly, and the transactions taken altogether, present a disgusting aspect, more particularly since my failure; for the outrage is no longer seen but in its hideous nakedness, stripped of all loftiness of idea, and of the numerous benefits which it was my intention to confer. Posterity, however, would have extolled it had I succeeded, and perhaps with reason, on account of its vast and happy results. Such is our lot, and such our judgment in this world! But I once more declare, that in no instance was there any breach of faith, any perfidy or falsehood, and, what is more, there was no occasion for them'[8].

Whatever the merits of his opinions, Napoleon was correct in his assessment that: 'At all events, that unfortunate war in Spain was a real affliction, and the first cause of the calamities of France'[9]. As he came to realise, he underestimated the capacity of the Spanish nation to resist his occupation of its country, although the motivations behind the Spanish reaction were much more complicated than the simplistic view of loyalty to the deposed Bourbon monarchy, even if that did provide a figurehead. Napoleon's view of how he expected them to react found an interesting echo in the opinion of William Cobbett, that opponent of British government policy, who as late as November 1811 declared that, as the Spanish troops had a reputation for not defeating the French, then the Spanish people could not be serious about wanting to expel the occupying forces; indeed, faced with discussions about whether the Inquisition should be reinstituted by the independent Spanish government, 'Can any man believe, that, with this before their eyes, the people of Spain will enter heartily into a war against the French? Is it not much more likely that they will look upon them as their real deliverers?'[10], which was what Napoleon claimed to be his original intention concerning what he termed the 'abominable institutions'.

Napoleon might also be excused for not expecting Britain to intervene so decisively, nor that they would find a general of Wellington's skill, sufficient to frustrate the best efforts of Napoleon's own subordinates. Support at home for the British presence in the Peninsula was not universal, a comment of 1809 expressing the opposing view most colourfully: 'Were the entire Spanish Peninsula engulphed in the Ocean, it could not excite less interest than it does now . . . our aid can never afford relief to a People who persist in attending to their own private squabbles, rather than to the public good'[11], but the maintenance of a British army in the Peninsula had diplomatic as well as military consequences, in providing Britain with the prestige of maintaining the struggle against Napoleon, useful when negotiating with other states which shared their opposition.

Despite failings in the French methods of campaigning, and despite the tribulations heaped upon the French forces by the Spanish irregular forces, until the end of 1811 at least Napoleon had a good chance of success. While Wellington's army remained confined to Portugal (although keeping it there occupied the efforts of large numbers of French troops), in the remainder of the Peninsula the French achieved notable successes, and given adequate resources it is likely that they could, ultimately, have crushed the opposition. The early mass insurgency was replaced by more organised guerrilla activity, but even those guerrilla forces which were organised conventionally had only a limited chance of achieving success in the open field. Had Napoleon maintained his determination to succeed despite the costs, it is likely that he could, eventually, have eliminated sufficient Spanish opposition to permit him to fall upon Portugal in overwhelming strength, with the previous supply problems alleviated by the presence of a pacified Spain in his rear. Another criticism which might be made of Napoleon's maintenance of the war is that Spanish resistance provided a beacon for insurgent movements elsewhere in French-occupied territory. Such effects can be overestimated; while Spanish resistance may have been quoted as something to be admired and emulated, there was no mass insurrection in Germany, for example, to any degree comparable with that in Spain, and those which did occur, for example the Tyrolean risings, were influenced by factors other than a knowledge of what was happening in the Peninsula.

The most crucial year of the Peninsular War was 1812, when Napoleon's campaign against Russia not only reduced the supply of troops which he was able to commit to Spain, but actually caused the withdrawal of experienced units for use elsewhere; and his reverses in the east ensured that the position in the Peninsula could not be rectified by the return of the forces necessary to prevent ultimate defeat. Napoleon could have decided earlier than he did that the Spanish war was not worth its cost, but to withdraw would have been a terrible blow to his prestige, and by the time he did decide to abandon the enterprise it was already too late.

At an operational level, there were failings in the conduct of the Peninsular War, despite the considerable French successes which must have encouraged the belief that ultimate victory was possible, at least until comparatively late in the war. Questions were raised about the quality of troops initially committed to Spain, a decision perhaps influenced by the knowledge that the Spanish military establishment had been neglected for years and was hardly as formidable as other armies already defeated by France. The troops first deployed in Spain included a considerable proportion of 'provisional' units, ad hoc assemblies lacking established regimental identity, and 'Legions of Reserve', untried conscripts; in effect, 'second line' troops rather than seasoned elements of the *Grande Armée*, with only a relatively small proportion of veteran troops. Dupont's command, perhaps the most obvious example, comprised one battalion of the Seamen of the Imperial Guard, six of Swiss, nine of Legions of Reserve, four of provisional infantry and two of the *Garde de Paris*, and all the cavalry were provisional units.

Dupont's surrender at Bailen, one of the greatest reverses suffered by French arms to that date, might have led Napoleon to reconsider his

Spanish policy; but, as Marbot observed, 'his rage was fearful. Up to then he had regarded the Spaniards as on a par in courage with the Italians, and supposed that their rising was merely a peasant revolt which would quickly be dispersed by a few French battalions. But his eagles had been humbled, and French troops had lost the prestige of unbroken victory. Deeply must he have regretted that he had allowed his army to be composed of recruits, instead of sending the veterans whom he had left in Germany'[12]. Napoleon's decision to pour into the Peninsula more troops and experienced commanders set in motion what he was to describe as his 'Spanish ulcer', a continual drain upon his resources.

The war upon which Napoleon embarked in the Peninsula differed from his successful earlier campaigns, not least in the geographical nature of the country and the lack of a single objective, the attainment of which would have ensured French victory, such as the destruction of a single field army. A further consideration was that, at least until the Russian expedition of 1812, Napoleon had been able to superintend the most important aspects of campaign in person; which was not the case in Spain.

Significant problems lay in the realm of command. The difficulties of scale were severe enough, with problems of communication exacerbated by popular hostility, but these were made infinitely worse by the lack of central direction and authority. Napoleon had concentrated power in his own hands, so that his subordinates had limited experience of independent command; this system was less disadvantageous in a campaign sufficiently small to enable Napoleon to superintend all important matters in person, but could have severe consequences when subordinates were left largely to their own devices. Even worse was what happened in the Peninsula, where there was no central authority able to insist upon co-ordination of effort, and where commanders of individual forces were beset by mutual jealousy, suspicion and reluctance to assist their fellows.

Although Joseph was nominally Napoleon's deputy, and invested with the prestige of kingship, his authority was diminished from the beginning both by Napoleon's interference in even the smallest matters, and worse in that Napoleon sent orders to the individual army commanders and required their reports to be sent to him, rather than via King Joseph. The latter complained with little result; in one especially sad letter of February 1809 he offered to resign the crown, remarking that: 'I have not your entire confidence, and yet without it my position is not tenable . . . I devote to business all my faculties from 7 in the morning till 11 at night . . . I have no real power beyond Madrid, and even at Madrid I am every day counteracted . . . if I must be insulted even in my own capital; if I am denied the right of naming the governors and the commanders who are always before me, and make me contemptible to the Spaniards and powerless to do good; if, instead of judging me by results, you put me on trial in every detail – under such circumstances, Sire, I have no alternative . . . a Spaniard has let me know that he has been ordered to give to Marshal Duroc, day by day, an exact account of all that I do . . . my misery is as much as I can bear . . . if there is on earth a man whom you esteem or love more than you do me, I ought not to be King of Spain, and my happiness requires me to cease to be so . . .'[13].

Compounding the problem of command was the way Napoleon organised French forces in Spain; from 1810 there were six separate armies, the only supreme commander being the absent Napoleon. This tended to diminish the effectiveness of the very considerable numerical strength committed to the Peninsula; in mid-1811, for example, the following were the six separate armies and their approximate overall strengths (the latter greater than the field strength): Army of Aragon (Suchet) 51,000; of Catalonia (Macdonald) 30,000; of the Centre (Joseph) 25,000; of the North (Dorsenne) 99,000; of Portugal (Marmont) 58,000; of the South (Soult) 90,000. Had it been possible to co-ordinate these large numbers towards a single objective, much might have been achieved, but a large proportion of troops had to be deployed on anti-guerrilla duties and to protect bases and lines of communication.

Another inhibiting factor was the marshals' lack of willingness to co-operate with each other, whether through self-interest or conflicts of personality. Some resented even being sent to the Peninsula; Macdonald, for example, was unhappy commanding the Army of Catalonia as he objected to the war itself, and 'the dishonesty – or what in high places is called policy – which caused the invasion of the country', expressed admiration for the 'noble and courageous resistance of its inhabitants' and found his task 'as odious as it was exhausting. The enemy were ubiquitous, and yet I could find them nowhere'[14]. Lejeune recalled: 'Marshal Soult was especially bitter at having to command men of equal rank with himself, and said he was often very much worried by being obliged to show so much consideration for them. "Of course," he said, "I feel greatly flattered at having Marshals de Treviso [Mortier] and Belluno [Victor] under my orders, but I should much prefer generals on whose passive obedience I could rely"'[15].

Such factors were not confined to relations between commanders of the highest rank or of individual armies. When Massena led the Army of Portugal he was heartily disliked by all four of his corps commanders (Ney, Reynier, Junot and Montbrun), a problem which culminated in Ney's insubordination in March 1811. Despite Ney's military talents, Massena could not permit such erosion of his authority, and dismissed

Ney from command of his corps; such was the dissatisfaction that Ney was urged to depose Massena and name himself army commander, a move which might have received widespread support, but which drastic step he declined to take. When Marmont took command of the Army of Portugal from Massena, he acted upon Napoleon's advice and replaced the corps structure with a divisional system, almost all the previous corps and divisional generals being sent back to France (only two divisional commanders were retained, two corps commanders departed immediately, Reynier soon after, and only the cavalry leader Montbrun remained any appreciable time). The divisions were led henceforth by those who had previously commanded brigades, so that Marmont was able fully to exercise his authority over subordinates who were very much his juniors, and unlike Massena was not beset by the problem of commanding those of high rank and seniority.

The absence of a single supreme commander with clear objectives was a problem compounded by Napoleon's own directions. Although for a considerable part of the Peninsular War the emperor was not occupied with campaigning elsewhere, after his original brief foray into Spain he never returned in person, but continued to issue orders from afar. Such might be given without the knowledge of local conditions and complicated by the time taken to cover the distances involved, with the danger of communications being interrupted and orders being overtaken by circumstances even before they had been received. The potential hazards were demonstrated in late 1811 and early 1812, when Suchet's successes with the Army of Aragon caused Napoleon to order the detachment of part of the Army of Portugal to support Suchet's operations against Valencia. Thus weakened, Marmont was unable to prevent Wellington's capture of Ciudad Rodrigo; while the force intended to support Suchet arrived too late to assist in the capture of Valencia, and its commander (Montbrun) declined to accept Suchet's advice and return immediately to Marmont, wasting ten days in a fruitless attempt to capture Alicante, which in Marmont's opinion was only attempted as a way of gaining laurels for a general who wished to prove himself in an independent command.

The position was made worse a short time later by Napoleon's instructions concerning Badajoz. Marmont realised that Wellington would probably attack that city, but Napoleon told him not to worry over its fate but instead to prepare for an advance into northern Portugal, which would deflect Wellington from making an attempt on Badajoz. Presumably from a lack of knowledge of local conditions, Napoleon overlooked the fact that Marmont could not operate in northern Portugal for long for want of supplies (that region being a virtual wasteland); but then, after Marmont had reluctantly made the necessary preparations to carry out Napoleon's instructions, the emperor issued contradictory orders which made Marmont responsible for Badajoz and authorised him to march to its relief if he thought it necessary. By the time these orders were received it was too late for Marmont to support the city, and while it may not be accurate to lay upon Napoleon all the blame for the loss of the border fortresses, it does exemplify the hazards of attempting to exert command from so great a distance.

Misleading reports and intelligence were also a problem in such circumstances. Napoleon's own dispatches were notoriously inaccurate, in underestimating his own losses and exaggerating his successes, which led to the colloquialism 'to lie like a bulletin' and attracted remarks from his enemies such as the description of his reports being 'a tinsel web of sophistry'[16]; but some of these distortions were deliberate attempts at misinformation with a strategic objective, to undermine enemy morale. There was less excuse for misleading reports from Napoleon's subordinates, and he appears to have found the official accounts in British newspapers not only a source of intelligence but at times more accurate than the reports he received from his own commanders. An example is his note to Berthier in June 1811: 'I send you the English account of the action at Fuente [sic] de Oñoro. Send a copy to the Dukes of Ragusa [Marmont] and of Istria [Bessières]. You may have copied even what is scratched out, that they may know the whole'[17]. Evidently this was preferred to the report from Napoleon's own commander at the action, Massena.

If lack of accurate intelligence complicated the orders sent by Napoleon to the Peninsula, then so did the logistic situation, of which at times he cannot have been fully aware. Despite the French army's ability in foraging, the system of supply was sometimes quite insufficient to permit the employment of large forces for protracted periods in some regions, as discovered by the troops who sat outside the Lines of Torres Vedras, unable to penetrate them and gradually withering away. Shortage of food on campaign had to be endured at times by all armies, but some had a more effective commissariat than others, and French troops in the Peninsula often went hungry, with operations inhibited by the threat of starvation. Local difficulties in the procuring of victuals apart, there were also other failings in the system of supply if the attitude expressed to one British officer was to be found elsewhere. Captured at San Sebastian, when he enquired how the French managed to feed their soldiers in the field, he was shown a biscuit which represented a soldier's daily ration, and told that: '"sometimes twenty are delivered to each individual, who is given to understand that he has no claims upon the commissariat for the number of days corresponding with the number of biscuit he receives". I observed that it was not possible for the soldier to carry them. "We know that very well; but then he has no claim upon the government for that period, and we do not inquire how he lives in the interim!"'[18].

Shortage of food was not the worst aspect of the French army's trials in Spain, however, but the nature of the war itself. Although operations against the British were conducted with the relative humanity which should have characterised 'civilised' warfare according to the tenets pertaining among the many who believed in a code of martial honour, the war against the Spanish and Portuguese population was very different, and Belmas' remark concerning the state of Zaragosa after a siege of unparallelled ferocity, 'a horror to behold'[19] might well serve as a comment on the French war in Spain in general. Whereas both British and French were campaigning in a foreign country, the natives of the Peninsula could hardly have been expected to regard the occupation and despoilation of their homeland with equanimity, and reacted accordingly, so that much of the conflict between them and the French was a horrifying catalogue of atrocity and reprisal. The level of inhumanity appalled even the most hardened campaigners, and many would have agreed with the officer quoted above, who, after conversing with many of his French counterparts, recalled that 'they detailed acts committed by their soldiers in Spain, so revolting to human nature, that I dare not commit them to paper; the reader would be disgusted with the recital, and my veracity impeached; and equally incredulous should I have been, had not the narrators declared they had witnessed the scenes which they described'[20].

To explain the horrors inflicted upon the French, the hussar Albert de Rocca stated that the Spanish people 'were animated solely by religious patriotism; they had no practical knowledge of discipline, or the laws of war . . . they had but one sentiment, to revenge, by every possible means, the wrongs that the French had done to their country'[21]. Under such circumstances, excesses were perhaps not surprising, but no less monstrous; Charles François, for example, saw a French hospital in which 400 men had been hacked to pieces and fifty three buried alive; and a French soldier who was the only survivor of some 1,200 invalids who had been butchered and mutilated, had his ears cut off and went mad as a consequence of what he had seen. Lejeune wrote of guerrillas exhibiting the 'cruelty and treachery'[22] of wild beasts, having personally witnessed the slaughter of wounded French prisoners by followers of 'El Médico', the sight and sounds of which remained a vivid and revolting memory even after the passage of thirty five years. To such barbarity the French responded. Jean-Baptiste Barrès recalled an incident in March 1810 on the Elza river, when a few grenadiers and a woman sutler fell behind their unit, were ambushed and murdered 'with refinements of cruelty'[23], a fate not unusual for small detachments of French troops in hostile territory. As a reprisal, the commander of the battalion to which these unfortunates belonged marched on the village in which they had been killed, burned it to the ground, herded together all the menfolk and began to shoot them one by one until they identified the killers. Four were executed before the fifth pointed out the guilty, who were then killed.

However necessary such actions may have been considered, they filled many with horror. Marbot, having found two French soldiers killed on the road and an officer murdered in the most dreadful fashion, was faced with having to execute two of the perpetrators. He moved off so as not to have to witness the deed; the two troopers who furnished his escort had no such qualms and completed the task while exclaiming to their victims, 'You don't know the Chamborant!', the old name of their regiment, the 2nd Hussars[24].

Of course such horrors were not universal, but where they did occur they were the cause of adverse comments on the French, and indeed were sometimes reported with incredulity: 'The people of England, I am certain, will not believe the horrible and infernal manner in which the French have behaved . . . nothing that ever I have read or heard of any where since the beginning of the world, has equalled their excesses'[25]; 'It is impossible to describe the scenes of horror of which I have been an eye-witness . . . it is hard for any body to believe that human nature could be guilty of such enormous or wanton wickedness'[26]; 'Human nature sickens at the objects of misery which have appeared in this scene of spoilation . . . a party of our dragoons found three Friars hanging to a tree by three of the branches, which had been cut off and sharpened, and then the unhappy men were suspended by the insertion of the sharp points in their throats. They were daubed over with some black substance like pitch, as if to preserve the bodies *in terrorem* to the affrighted Portuguese. We might mention a vast number of other circumstances, with which we have been favoured, but nature sickens at the recital'[27].

Nevertheless, there must be sympathy with the opinion of Elzéar Blaze, who wrote of the guerrillas: 'they frequently carried their reprisals to the most revolting barbarity. On several occasions they flayed alive the prisoners whom the fortune of war had thrown into their hands; many of those miserable wretches were sawed asunder between two planks; one of my friends was buried alive in the ground, all but his head, which served as a mark for the savages to play at bowls. One might fill volumes with the atrocities committed on both sides in this graceless war; but I can affirm, without fear of being contradicted by any one, that we were always less cruel than the Spaniards'[28].

Reprisals in kind can only have increased the animosity between the contending parties. At Oporto, for example, where Benjamin D'Urban described the French conduct as 'altogether unworthy of a civilised Nation. Attila might have blushed at having ordered the atrocities perpetrated'[29], such was the popular hatred of the one-armed French general, Louis Loison (nicknamed *Maneta*, 'one-arm') that his compatriot Maximilien Foy was almost murdered by a mob in March 1809, saving his life by holding up two hands to show that he was not Loison! Further antagonism was caused by the widespread looting in which some of the senior French commanders led the way. Among the most culpable, for example, was François Etienne Kellermann, the hero of Marengo, who not only plundered but held rich Spaniards to ransom; de Gonneville remarked of Kellermann's later piety in building a church near his house outside Paris, that: 'It is very likely that both house and church were the result of exactions committed in Spain'[30].

In addition to the interception of couriers and dispatches by guerrillas forming an important source of intelligence for the Anglo-Portuguese and Spanish armies, the protection of lines of communication absorbed the efforts of huge numbers of French troops. Some areas were so dangerous that the constant threat of assassination, ambush and the terrible fate which might befall those captured must have had a considerable effect in undermining French morale. As Blaze noted, 'By harassing us incessantly, [the guerrillas] fatigued our men, who fell ill: they occupied half the army in protecting couriers and very frequently a battalion was not sufficient to escort a letter . . . The guerrillas made it their study not to be found when we looked for them; to pounce upon us like vultures when we least expected them; and it must be confessed that they completely performed their task'[31]. Hostility to the French was also revealed in the smallest ways, and affected even the commonest pleasantries which made life bearable; it was reported, for example, that a French regiment (evidently the 21st *Léger*) went to great efforts to prepare a ballroom for the entertainment of the local people, even painting the walls with regimental symbols and an inscription 'El Grand Napoleon'; but no Spaniards would attend, all the ladies claiming that they had recently been bled in the foot, so that the French officers had to dance with each other![32]

Such factors all combined to make service in the Peninsula thoroughly unpopular and unpleasant for the French troops, and gave rise to such expressions as the lines of graffiti which stated: 'This war in Spain means death for the men, ruin for the officers, a fortune for the generals'[33]. Many grumbled loudly, like Lapisse's division when struggling through mountains in a snow storm, even in Napoleon's presence; they 'gave loud expression to the most sinister designs against the Emperor's person, stirring up each other to fire a shot at him, and bandying accusations of cowardice for not doing it. He heard it all as plainly as we did, and seemed as if he did not care a bit for it'[34]; but on finding food, shelter and wine these mutinous expressions turned to cheers of adulation when he appeared again. Desertion was always a problem, but rarely did objections to service in the Peninsula approach open mutiny. This was mooted in 1809 in the so-called 'Argenton conspiracy', named after the adjutant of the 18th Dragoons, in which a number of discontented officers, amid rumours that Soult was about to declare himself king of Portugal, made tentative proposals for a widespread revolt, even contacting their enemies. (Argenton spoke about the matter with Wellesley in person.) Although they might have found sympathy for a protest against continuing an unpopular war, their plan of insurrection against Napoleon had no chance of success and appears not to have had serious support outside the circle of intriguers in the Peninsula; but its very existence presumably is a reflection of the discontent prevalent among those engaged in an unpopular and savage war in which there was little opportunity for reward.

The war in Spain was an endless drain upon Napoleon's resources, drafts of men and *matériel* being consumed continuously, not only French but troops from allied states, the Confederation of the Rhine, Italy and Poland. Expensive though it was, in both financial and human terms, the maintenance of the war attained its greatest significance when Napoleon chose to embark again on campaigns in the east. The attempt to wage war on two fronts was never feasible, and the conflicting demand for military resources, which actually denuded the French armies in Spain of some of their best units, made a successful outcome of the Peninsular War quite impossible, at least once it became evident that Napoleon's campaigns in Russia and later Germany were not going to succeed. Even under the changed conditions, however, no new strategy was adopted until too late. Marshal Jourdan, Joseph's chief of staff, suggested that the occupation of territory be sacrificed in order to assemble a more mobile army to oppose Wellington's forces; but Napoleon insisted that Joseph relinquish none of the areas over which the French could claim control. (Conversely, it is interesting to speculate on what might have been the consequences for Napoleon's own campaigns in the east if he had had available under his own command the almost 262,000 men who in mid-October 1812 were employed in Spain, many of them experienced veterans; even though at that time more than thirteen per cent of them were sick in hospital.)

Not until after Vittoria was an attempt made on the radical reorganisation necessary for the army in Spain. In view of the collapsing situation, Soult was sent back to the Peninsula finally to assemble the French forces into a unified command; but even then, and presumably in view of that commander's successes, Suchet's Army of Aragon remained independent, so that there was still not complete co-ordination of effort. Napoleon now attempted a political settlement, proposing that Ferdinand be released from confinement and restored to the Spanish throne, with even the offer of ex-king Joseph's eldest daughter as a bride by way of cementing a Franco-Spanish alliance. The latter was declined by Ferdinand, but the other terms were ostensibly accepted, most significantly a repudiation of the British alliance and an undertaking to ensure the removal of British forces from Spanish territory; but although Ferdinand assented to the resulting Treaty of Valençay, he had surely no intention of respecting it. In the event, the Spanish authorities frustrated Napoleon's plan; when the proposals were presented to them, the Regency declared that by an existing decree, any documents signed by the king in captivity would be regarded as negotiated under duress and thus null and void, and the Liberal majority in the Cortes added the stipulation that Ferdinand should sign the Constitution of 1811 before he would be permitted to ascend the throne. The Treaty thus proved unavailing, but Napoleon was so convinced that it would succeed that he began the withdrawal of troops from the armies of Soult and Suchet, the last thing required by the French commanders in their situation. It is interesting, however, that even Wellington seems to have been uncertain about the reception of the Treaty of Valençay, and he speculated on what might have occurred had Napoleon adopted this approach earlier. In January 1814 he reported to Earl Bathurst: 'I have long suspected that Buonaparte would adopt this expedient; and if he had had less pride, and more common sense, and could have carried his measure into execution as he ought to have done, it would have succeeded. I am not certain that it will not succeed now: that is to say, so much of the misery felt in Spain is justly attributed to the vices and constitution of the Government, that I think there must be many who would desire to put an end to them even by the sanction of this treaty of peace. If Buonaparte had at once withdrawn his garrisons from Catalonia and Valencia (which in all probability he must lose at all events), and had sent Ferdinand to the frontier, or into Spain (and he must be as useless a personage in France as he would probably be in Spain), I think it can scarcely be doubted that the peace would have been made, or, at all events, the prosecution of the war would have been so difficult as to render it almost impracticable, and great success hopeless'[35].

When neither Napoleon's hopes nor Wellington's fears were realised, the war continued to its conclusion. In December 1813 Napoleon wrote to Joseph: 'I do not want Spain either to keep or to give away. I will have nothing more to do with that country, except live in peace with it, and have the use of my army'[36]. Sadly for Napoleon, this realisation of the prospects of involvement in Spain came too late for it to have any effects upon his fortunes. Many of the French soldiers who had survived the war might well have agreed with de Rocca, who remarked about his final departure from Spain with a convoy of sick and wounded: 'I was glad, at any price, to quit an unjust and inglorious war, where the sentiments of my heart continually disavowed the evil my arm was condemned to do'[37].

Notes

1   De Gonneville, A.O.Le H., *Recollections of Colonel De Gonneville*, trans C.M. Yonge, London 1875, I p. 243.

2   Las Cases, E.A.D.M.J., *Memoirs of the Life, Exile and Conversations of the Emperor Napoleon*, London 1836, II pp. 134–5.

3   Lejeune, L.F., *Memoirs of Baron Lejeune*, trans. Mrs A. Bell, London 1897, I pp. 73–4.

4   Ussher, Captain Sir Thomas, 'Narrative of the Embarkation and Conveyance of Napoleon from Frejus to Elba, in the *Undaunted* Frigate, with Personal Anecdotes and Opinions of the ex-Emperor on the Voyage and after his Occupation of that Island', in *United Service Journal*, 1840, III p. 152.

5   Las Cases, *Memoirs* II pp. 135–6.

6   *ibid*. p. 134.

7   *ibid*. p. 296.

8   *ibid*. pp. 297–8.

9   *ibid*. p. 296.

10 *Cobbett's Weekly Political Register*, 9 November 1811 (unpaginated: column 581)

11 *The News*, 8 October 1809.

12 Marbot, J.B.A.M., *The Memoirs of Baron de Marbot*, trans. A.J. Butler, London 1913, I p. 257.

13 This translation taken from *The Confidential Correspondence of Napoleon Bonaparte with his Brother Joseph, sometime King of Spain*, London 1855, II pp. 46–7.

14 Macdonald, J.E.J.A., *Recollections of Marshal Macdonald*, ed. C. Rousset, trans. S.L. Simeon, London 1892, II p. 16.

15 Lejeune, *Memoirs* II p. 58.

16 *Newcastle Courant*, 4 September 1813.

17 *Confidential Correspondence*, II pp. 184–5.

18 Jones, Lt-Col. H., 'Narrative of Seven Weeks' Captivity in St Sebastian', in *United Service Journal*, 1841, I p. 195.

19 Belmas, J., *Journaux des Sièges faits ou soutenus par les français dans la Péninsule, de 1807 à 1814*, Paris 1836, II p. 323.

20 Jones, 'Narrative' p. 195.

21 De Rocca, A.J.M., *Memoirs of the War of the French in Spain*, London 1815, pp. 47–8 (modern edition entitled *In the Peninsula with a French Hussar*, London 1990, pp. 39–40).

22 Lejeune, *Memoirs* II p. 75.

23 Barrès, J. -B., *Memoirs of a Napoleonic Officer*, ed. M. Barrès, trans. B. Miall, London 1925, p. 136.
24 Marbot, *Memoirs* II p. 266.
25 *The Courier*, 20 April 1811.
26 *Gentleman's Magazine*, April 1811, p. 384.
27 *The Courier*, 25 April 1811.
28 Blaze, E., *Lights and Shades of Military life*, ed. Sir Charles Napier, London 1850; orig. titled *La Vie Militaire sous le premier empire ou Moeurs de Garnison, du Bivouac et de la Caserne*, Paris 1837, and reprinted as *Life in Napoleon's Army: The Memoirs of Captain Elzéar Blaze*, London 1995, pp. 58–9.
29 D'Urban, Sir Benjamin, *The Peninsular Journal of Major-General Sir Benjamin D'Urban, 1808–1817*, ed. I.J. Rousseau, London 1930, p. 81.
30 De Gonneville, *Recollections* I p. 251.
31 Blaze, *Lights and Shades*, p. 58.
32 *Edinburgh Evening Courant*, 12 October 1812.
33 Parquin, C., *Charles Parquin: Napoleon's Army*, trans. & ed. B.T. Jones, London 1969, p. 126.
34 De Gonneville, *Recollections* I p. 190.
35 Wellington, Duke of, *Dispatches of Field Marshal the Duke of Wellington*, ed. J. Gurwood, London 1834–8, XI pp. 433–4.
36 *Confidential Correspondence*, II pp. 255–6.
37 De Rocca, *Memoirs* p. 170.

CHAPTER III

Siege warfare in the Peninsula, 1808–14

David Chandler

'Make few sieges and fight plenty of battles,' the French Marshal Condé was advised by the great Turenne in the 17th century; 'When you are master of the countryside, the villages will give us the towns.' This sage advice was largely ignored for much of the 18th century, wars of sieges and chess board manoeuvre taking precedence over the seeking of major battles until the time of Frederick the Great, although there were some exceptional commanders – Marlborough, Prince Eugene and Charles XII amongst them – who habitually sought out what Clausewitz would later term 'the bloody solution of the crisis' when circumstances permitted.

It is often claimed that the French Revolutionary and Napoleonic Wars saw a radical change in these attitudes – and that the large-scale engagement became the norm rather than the exception. This is certainly true of those campaigns conducted by Napoleon himself after 1796–7. The nine-month siege of Mantua (May 1796 – February 1797), twice broken off and as many times resumed, totally disillusioned 'the little corporal' on the desirability of major sieges as important focal points in campaigns. And it was only relatively rarely thereafter – as, for instance, at the sieges of Genoa in 1800, Danzig in 1807, or the blockade of Hamburg in 1813–14 – that this form of warfare played a central role, and more often than not it was at the insistence of France's foes. An analysis of comparative statistics for the years 1680–1748 and 1749–1815 reveals that the former period held 167 major sieges to 144 engagements, whilst the latter contained 289 of the former to 568 of the latter. (See G. Bodart, *Militär-Historisches Kriegs-Lexicon 1618–1905*, Leipzig 1908) Thus the respective totals drop from near parity in the first seventy-year period to a ratio of 2:1 in favour of battle-action in the second. The trend against time-consuming and expensive, elaborate sieges is apparent from these figures, and the Earl of Orrery's comment in the late 1670s that '. . . we make warre more like Foxes than Lyons; and you have twenty sieges for one battel' had to a large extent given way to Napoleon's dictum that '. . . I see only one thing, namely the enemy's main body. I try to crush it, confident that secondary matters will then settle themselves.'

One important exception to this general rule was the war in the Peninsula, where there were fifteen sieges and nineteen significant battles over the main struggle's seven-year period.* Three main reasons for this variation from the general European trend may be suggested. First, the towns and cities of Portugal and Spain were often important centres of population, and local government and fiscal control, and their relative sparsity in basically inhospitable and thinly populated countries made their possession – and denial to the enemy – a matter of strategic importance.

Secondly, Arthur Wellesley, later successively Earl, Marquess and Duke of Wellington, was, for all his well-deserved reputation as a tactician and commander of genius, essentially an 18th-century commander in his broad strategic concepts (save in his appreciation of the central significance of the guerrilla struggle). Unlike Napoleon, whose dynamic and unscrupulous strategic concepts were more akin to the *Blitzkrieg* campaigns of 1939, 1940 and 1941, 'the Peer' was essentially cautious and administration-conscious. He knew when he had to accept great risks, but rarely courted them. Like Montgomery, who refused to be hustled into premature offensives in the Western Desert in 1942, Wellington knew how to wait until all was ready before seizing the initiative. He then advanced with considerable caution, always ensuring that his triple-system of supply (namely the river-boats and ox-drawn convoys to the rear, the intermediate mule trains and the forward divisional trains and regimental transport) was in good working order. But to secure these vital communications, he needed to take many a town that Napoleon would have merely contained or even ignored, and his inability to undertake costly stormings of such places (for his military resources in terms of both men and equipment were always inferior to those of his opponents, at least in the quantitative sense) made inevitable his frequent recourse to siege warfare. 'Safe rather than sorry' was Wellington's guiding maxim.

And thirdly, good roads were few and far between in the Peninsula, and navigable rivers even rarer. The unhindered use of those available for the army's line of advance or rear communications rendered imperative the control of many towns, placed as they were around the main river bridges or, even more significantly, athwart the vital passes crossing the rugged and inhospitable regions dividing Portugal from Spain.

---

* Sir William Napier lists only ten 'made or sustained sieges' in his celebrated *History*, but seems to have ignored sieges undertaken by the French, and to have discounted such major operations as the three sieges of Saragossa in which British forces were not engaged.

The basic military geography of the Spanish-Portuguese frontier areas is of importance for any understanding of siege warfare in the Peninsular War. There were, essentially, four routes linking the two countries – two based upon major rivers and two on land-based passes. The Douro river, the northernmost passageway over the frontier region, ran through difficult country without benefit of major roads, was difficult to navigate in its central and upper reaches, and so did not provide a very suitable line of advance for either army. Far to the south, the broad waters of the mighty Tagus were a very different proposition, and this river figured considerably in these campaigns. It provided the most direct route between Lisbon and distant Madrid and good roads were linked with it. However, it too had practical disadvantages. For the Allies, advancing from their Lisbon base area, there was always the problem of moving upstream (as was also the case for them, of course, with the westward-flowing Douro) against the currents. Furthermore, the town of Alcantara formed a major block to the east of the Spanish frontier.

For the French, the river posed equal problems – principally linked to their lack of a naval or river force capable of challenging the Royal Navy whose flotillas of gunboats and other craft exercised almost unquestioned control of the Tagus's southerly reaches, guaranteeing safe passage for the convoys of barges carrying war materials for Wellington's army. In effect, therefore, the Tagus provided a strong defensive bulwark guarding the approaches to Lisbon from the direction of Cadiz and Badajoz, and an important supply lifeline for the Allies in many of their campaigns.

Most military operations, however, centred on the two land corridors. The more northerly of these ran past Almeida on the Portuguese side of the frontier through a hilly and inhospitable area towards Ciudad Rodrigo in Spain. The south corridor was similarly dominated by the corresponding fortresses of Elvas and Badajoz. To use the passes freely involved having possession of these key fortresses – and here lies one major reason for the important sieges associated with these place names. Until the final phase of the campaigns (when interest swung away to the distant Pyrenees where San Sebastian, Pamplona, Figueras and Perpignan played similar roles as blocks on the two main highways linking Spain with France) these four frontier towns, two Spanish and two Portuguese, played a determinant part in the fortunes of successive campaigns. From 1813, when Wellington switched his main communications from Cuidad Rodrigo to Santander and (later) the ports near San Sebastian – using the flexibility provided by the Royal Navy and the merchant convoys to link Lisbon with the war front by sea – the importance of the two corridors was reduced. But from 1809 to 1812 they figure prominently in every campaign, whether Allied-or French-initiated.

These then, were the main reasons why the Peninsular War contained proportionately more sieges than other campaigns in war-torn Europe at this time. Mention must also be made of many 'last-ditch' stands by Spanish patriots in such cities as Saragossa, Barcelona and Gerona, whose massive convents and churches, winding, narrow lanes and streets, forced the French to have recourse to blockades and formal sieges in their attempts to gain a real mastery over central-north and north-east Spain. But these operations are not the main subject of this chapter, although the central significance of popular resistance in such places, associated with the even more vital guerrilla struggle in the countryside, must be kept constantly in mind if the campaigns of the Anglo-Portuguese armies of Wellington and Beresford are to be studied with any real understanding. For it was the combination of the need to mount continuous counter-insurgency operations with the requirement to mass large field armies to meet the various Allied forays that posed an insoluble strategic problem for the French.

To contain the guerrillas they must scatter to dominate the country-side; to face Wellington they had to concentrate their forces, and thus relax much of their local grip. This factor, together with the inadequate French higher command arrangements, accounts for the cost and ultimate collapse of the French war effort in the Peninsula. 'If I thought it would cost 30,000 men I would not undertake it,' Napoleon had boasted in 1808. This was possibly his gravest miscalculation. By April 1814 the 'Spanish Ulcer' would have accounted for over 250,000 French casualties – and only slightly more than a quarter of these were directly attributable to battle and siege losses. Disease and assassination accounted for the remainder in approximately equal proportions. But if the popular war posed the greater strain on the French, it is important to appreciate that, without Wellington's disruptive presence in the Peninsula, the guerrilla struggle might well have been contained by the 300,000 French troops available before 1812. Each feature in the struggle had its own part to play – all were interdependent – and this is equally true of Wellington's sieges which tied down French as well as Allied forces for considerable periods of time, thus aiding the spread of the guerrilla struggle.

The techniques of siege warfare had altered little over a century and a half, and Louis XIV's great master of siegecraft in both its defensive and offensive aspects, Sébastien le Prêtre, Seigneur de Vauban, would have been as at home in the trenches before Badajoz or Burgos as in those before Mons, Tournai or Lille in his own generation. But if the techniques were largely unaltered, certain attitudes and conventions had changed considerably, most notably perhaps the attitude of the French garrison commanders who saw their duty to be to offer resistance to the last man and round rather than comply with the more gentlemanly attitudes of the 17th and 18th centuries, which permitted a defender to capitulate under certain circumstances without any loss of martial honour.

Sieges can be divided into three main types – containments, blockades and regular. A containment involved leaving a force, often cavalry and light infantry, to observe a town or minor fortress which was not important enough to warrant a full-scale siege. The observing force's role was to watch the garrison, and intercept it if it attempted break out. A blockade was a rather more elaborate affair, the purpose being to deny the enemy easy access to or egress from the place concerned. Thus, parties had to be posted to block all roads and tracks leading into the town, booms or other obstacles laid across rivers flowing through the place to interrupt any boat or barge traffic, and patrols sent out to watch the general countryside. Such a blockade would rarely be wholly effective: individuals or even small parties could still, at some risk, make their way into or out of the town by avoiding the roads and dodging patrols, but logistically the place was isolated.

A blockade was always the preliminary step to the establishment of a regular siege. Such an operation involved an all-out attempt to capture the town concerned – either by starvation or by assault following the failure of attempts to negotiate a capitulation. These regular sieges might last for considerable periods of time, involve large numbers of men, guns and other equipment, and were often costly in terms of a besieger's casualties – the ravages of disease in insanitary trenches creating as significant a hazard to human life as the risks of a local or general storming or the day-by-day wastage of occasional casualties.

Before describing the stage-by-stage conduct of a Peninsular siege, it is necessary to consider the nature of the defences to be overcome and the courses open to a defending garrison for the prosecution of a vigorous defence. In a very real sense, the advantage often lay with the defence, providing the garrison was sufficiently strong and had supplies adequate for the needs of both the soldiers and (rather less importantly but still a factor to be taken into account) for any civilian population within the town. Naturally, it was also necessary for the defences to be in a well-repaired condition. Finally, there needed to be at least some prospect of relief by a friendly force – a field army capable of marching within range of the siege of sufficient strength to drive away the covering forces and then compel the abandonment of the siege works by the besieging parties. Only rarely would all these conditions be met, but even a combination of some of them could make for a doughty defence – always providing the garrison's heart was in its task.

During the Peninsular struggle, French garrisons generally enjoyed high morale, although the abrupt conclusion of the second siege of Burgos after only two full days of operations in June 1813 forms an example of the contrary case. Allied garrisons had a more variable record: Almeida was surrendered prematurely to Marshal Ney by Brigadier-General Cox on 28 August 1810 after only 12 days, but the explosion of the main magazine the previous day was a contributory factor. On the other hand, an Allied garrison of 25,000 men (including 9,000 British and Portuguese troops) proved capable of holding Cadiz for two and a half years, though for much of that time the French were only strong enough to impose a blockade rather than conduct a regular siege, and the garrison also enjoyed the inestimable advantage of periodic contact with the outside world through the agency of the Royal Navy, which was never completely denied access to the port.

From time immemorial, fortifications have been designed to comply with certain principles. First, they must afford protection from enemy fire for both the garrison and the townsfolk, and make any attempted assault extremely hazardous for the attacker. Secondly the actual defences must be designed to make the greatest possible use of the ground upon which they are built, and with a view to keeping the attacker – particularly his artillery – at a distance. Thirdly, they must offer the defenders good fields of fire in all directions, of an enfilade nature wherever possible. Fourthly, they should be sufficiently strong to keep the besiegers at bay until a friendly relief force can be organised and brought up to raise the siege – in other words, the defences must be capable of winning time. And, lastly, they should be designed to permit the garrison to wage an active defence, by means of sally-ports and other contrivances, as a means both to win time and to regain some measure of the initiative from the foe.

As artillery became more powerful in destructive power and longer in range, so the design of fortifications adapted itself to new circumstances. To minimise the effect of direct or plunging shot, defences tended to sink into the ground rather than to rise above it, and to rely more on wide and deep ditches, protecting deeply constructed bastions and other defences, with carefully worked out lines of fire, than on the towering walls of earlier times. The more powerful the guns became, the more intricate became the defences intended to keep them at a distance. Thus, it was customary to find successive lines of defence stretching out from a fortress or town. Their full complexities cannot be described here, but the main features deserve a mention.

By the early 18th century, the outermost defence works often comprised strong forts or outworks defending important topographical features guarding the approaches to the town. At Badajoz there was Fort San Cristobal beyond the Guadiana river, and Fort Picurina on the Sierra di

Viento, the high ground on the southern side of the town. Such defences had to be taken, or at least masked, by a besieger before he could get to grips with the main fortifications beyond.

The outer line of the main defence trace would comprise the glacis, an area of levelled ground up to 200 yards wide, affording an attacker no cover whatsoever from either sight or fire. On the inner side of this was built the 'covered way' – a system of pallisades and fire-positions protecting a roadway running the whole way round the fortress, which afforded the garrison the chance to move their forces from one sector to another with maximum speed as need arose. Beyond the covered way came the first ditch perhaps fifty feet deep and as many wide, with sharpened stakes set in the bottom if it was not water-filled, protecting the scarp wall of sundry ravelins, demi-lunes and other defences set in the middle of the ditch complex to provide the defenders with fire-platforms, and at the same time afford a measure of physical protection for the main bastion-trace beyond.

Beyond these ravelins would extend the main ditch, perhaps sixty feet or more wide and thirty feet deep, wet or dry according to circumstances. In its counterscarp (or outer) wall were inset inward-looking galleries with loopholes dominating the foot of the ditch and the scarp (or inner) side of the ditch. Set into some ravelins and other works, near the foot of the ditch, would be caponiers – firing positions designed to sweep whole lengths of the moats transversely. Then, beyond these daunting defences, loomed the vertical scarp wall, and, above this, the massive stone-faced bastions and curtain walls linking them. Bastions usually presented four sloping faces into the ditch, and were massively constructed. The stonework faced up to sixty feet of packed rubble and earth, its cohesion further improved by planting coarse grass and willow trees so that their roots might bind the earth more firmly. Atop these bastions were the artillery platforms, provided with great embrasures for the guns. Along the crest of the bastion trace ran a sentry-walk, often provided with occasional 'pepper-pot' sentry boxes. Behind the bastions large earthen ramps provided a way up to the town within, and access to the curtain walls was similarly provided by stairways. Within these defences would be *places des armes* and parade grounds where the garrison could gather. Very often, an inner line of defences would be provided within this complex – either designed along similar lines or incorporating older town-walls – as along the northern sector of Badajoz. Finally, every important fortress would be provided with a citadel or castle, a self-contained, defensive entity set into part of the main trace of 'enceinte', which provided a garrison with a last refuge in the event of their being forced to give up the main defences and town. Roads entering the town would be dominated by special *têtes-du-pont* and barbicans, and provided with draw-bridges and various forms of barricades.

All in all these defences, taken together, constituted a formidable series of obstacles to a would-be attacker providing the garrison was well supplied and in good heart. Moreover, if he knew his business, a determined defender would not allow himself to be restricted to a passive defence. Series of mines of varying sizes would be prepared in advance of any siege beneath the most obvious approaches – often under the glacis and sometimes even beneath ravelins and other defence works. Tunnels would connect these mines to the main defences, and the stacked gunpowder barrels could be ignited from within the bastion by means of fuses and powder trails. Next, a defender could use the numerous narrow sally-ports to send out strong raiding parties to attack the besieger's works, blow up his batteries and drive back his trench-garrisons, inflicting as much mayhem as possible on both men and material before retiring again within the walls. Such measures were employed by the defence at both Ciudad Rodrigo and Badajoz as well as many another Peninsular siege.

Thus, on the foggy night of 16 January 1812, a sudden sortie by 500 Frenchmen from Ciudad Rodrigo managed to surprise the besiegers at the moment when a hand-over was in process, and wreaked no little damage before being repulsed. Even when a major breach had been made in the main defences, a defender could rapidly place mines beneath it, *chevaux-de frise* (balks of timber set with spikes and sword blades) and greased planks atop it, steepen the outer scarps by careful digging, and lastly devise extemporised series of defences inside the breach – all of which made a general storm through the breach a daunting prospect for a besieging army to face. Of course, in the more gentlemanly times of the 18th century, such all-out storms were rare, for the conventions of war declared that a defender who had held out for forty-eight days, and who had had a 'practicable' breach blown in his main defences (i.e. one whose out fall of rubble formed a sufficiently gentle slope to enable an attacking soldier to climb up without having to use his hands), was fully entitled to open negotiations with the attacking commander and arrange a mutually agreeable capitulation on the best terms he could procure. This was not the case in most Peninsular sieges, however, for defending commanders, imbued with loyalty to Napoleon and a fear of his wrath, saw their duty to be to hold out to almost the last – with effects at Badajoz that we shall recount later.

Turning to consider the role of the besieger, we again find a tale of preconceived courses of action dictated by the types of defences to be overcome. All sieges, on both the attacking and defending sides, contained an element of ritualised conduct going back to the days of Vauban and beyond. The decision to take a particular place having been made after careful strategic consideration of the options available, the attacking commander, after assembling all available information about the target and having accumulated all the necessary stores and equipment (including the massive siege artillery pieces), marched towards his objective. A considerable distance away, his force would divide into two, one part continuing towards the goal with the convoys and impedimenta, the second marching to a pre-designated covering position, from which it would be able to intercept any attempt by an enemy force to relieve or reinforce the beleaguered garrison.

Not a few battles of the Peninsular War came about as a result of operations centring on significant sieges. General Graham's victory at Barrosa on 5 March 1811 gravely impeded the French operations against Cadiz, and at the same time prevented Marshal Soult from taking advantage of the abrupt surrender of Badajoz to French arms on the 11th. The following year, when Marshal Beresford attempted to regain Badajoz for the Allies, it was the approach of Soult's army of 25,000 men and fifty guns on 13 May that induced Beresford to call off the first siege and mass his total of 37,000 men (fewer than one third of them British) to meet the French advance at Albuera. A month later, Wellington massed all 44,000 of his troops around Badajoz, now re-besieged, but was again forced to call off the attempt on 19 June because of his lack of proper siege equipment and engineers, and above all the approach of Soult and Marmont at the head of 60,000 men. Similarly, the battle of Fuentes de Oñoro on 3 and 5 May 1811 was closely linked to the Allied blockade and siege of Almeida, and in 1813, the whole series of engagements, jointly known as the Battle of the Pyrenees (July–August) were made necessary to thwart Soult's triple attempt to interfere with the lengthy siege of San Sebastian, which, with one fifteen day interruption, lasted from 9 July to 8 September – a total of seventy seven days. This, the longest siege ever undertaken by Wellington, required a force of 62,000 men to cover the operations against Soult's army totalling 79,000 men; the actual conduct of the siege itself was entrusted to Graham and 10,000 men, who faced General Rey and his garrison of 3,000 French troops. Thus, the interrelation and interaction between sieges and field operations can clearly be established.

The timetable of a 'regular' siege obviously varied considerably according to particular circumstances, for each was a unique operation. But the following broad stages can be defined. First, the besieging force would establish a 'blockade' by cutting all means of regular access to or egress from the objective. This was a task often entrusted to the cavalry and irregular forces of Spaniards or Portuguese. At this juncture, a formal summons to the enemy governor, inviting him to surrender with no further ado, might be sent into the town under a flag of truce, but this 18th-century convention was falling into disuse by the 1800s. Next, the commander of the siege forces would close in with his main forces, and completely isolate the target. It was no longer the practice to establish lines of circumvallation or contravallation all around the town as in earlier times; but large numbers of sentry cordons and outposts supported by larger formations would be established. That these were not completely foolproof was demonstrated at Almeida on 10 May 1811, when General Brennier, to Wellington's undisguised fury, successfully evacuated 900 men of his garrison through the British lines by night, and 'lived to fight another day'.

Whilst the blockade was in process of being thickened up into a regular siege, the commanding general, accompanied by his engineer, artillery and other staff experts, would complete a minute examination of the target, seeking out the best points to attack. State of the ground, type of sub-soil rock, the water situation – these, as well as the strength of the actual enemy fortifications, were key considerations. Often past history could be of assistance, information on previously successful sieges being carefully screened. Information provided by enemy captives or deserters would also be assimilated, and at last the decision taken. It was obviously impossible to attack the entire perimeter; on the other hand, it was important to keep the enemy guessing, so habitually at least two points of attack would be designated. The engineers and gunners would make their calculations, final decisions would be taken, and the orders issued.

The time had now come to 'open the trenches'. Under cover of night, engineer officers would crawl forward to tape out the main outlines of the work to be performed. Behind them, the first work parties – soldiers supplemented by large numbers of rounded-up peasantry – would begin to wield pick and shovel to dig the 'first parallel'. This, a large trench, faced on the enemy-looking side by previously prepared gabbions (large vertical hollow cylinders of branches into which the earth would be shovelled) and fascines (smaller bundles of sticks used to fill the gaps between gabbions), was usually dug some 600 yards out from the main enemy line of defences – a reasonably safe distance from direct artillery fire. By dawn, if all had gone well, this first trench, with its protective bank of earth flung forwards from the interior, would be sufficiently deep to protect the work parties. These would be relieved at frequent intervals to keep the work going steadily forward. While this work was going on, and of course it would be repeated at the site of the second selected 'attack', other parties were busily preparing the first battery positions into which the howitzers and heavy siege mortars (if available) would be sited, ready at first light to begin an intermittent bombardment of the enemy positions, dropping shells behind fortifications in attempts to dismount his guns, kill his garrison, and unsettle the townspeople by setting fire to houses and other buildings in the main town itself. Enemy fire, of course, would be concentrated against the besiegers' growing earthworks and battery positions in an attempt to delay the former and neutralise the latter.

Once the first parallel was well on the way to completion, a number of zig-zagging approach trenches would begin to be dug forward from it towards the designated site for the second parallel – often some 400 yards from the enemy's main defences. These approaches could not be dug directly forward for fear of the havoc a well-placed enemy cannon might wreak, sending shot screaming straight down the line of a trench. The point of maximum danger was the 'sap-head', where two or three men were working at a time. They would be protected by a movable mantelet, but every time it was necessary to move this forward a yard or two, the enemy artillery would be presented with a fleeting but tempting target. In due time, however, the line of the second parallel would be reached, and this would be dug out in the same way as the first. Meanwhile, a trench-garrison (as opposed to the work parties) would occupy the completed works, ready to defend them should the enemy decide to try a sortie. Then, the second completed, the whole rigmarole of approach trenches and the rest would be repeated a third time, and the third parallel established – which had to be extremely well constructed as it often occupied part of the enemy's glacis, a mere hundred yards or so from his forward positions.

This was a time when maximum enemy activity could be expected, as the defenders tried to put back the progress of the siege by sorties, raids, ceaseless bombardments and mining. To minimise the risk of the last, counter-mines would be driven forward by the besiegers, searching out the enemy's tunnels, and it was not unknown for horrible subterranean fights to take place by the light of sputtering torches, and cases were known when whole mining parties were buried alive. Nor were these dangers, and those presented by enemy shot, shell and musket-balls, the only perils faced by a besieging army. Disease was as feared an opponent as the enemy garrison or a relieving army. Trenches were very quickly insanitary places, and as often as not were flooded into muddy morasses by rainfall or a high water table. Conditions within them were frequently appalling, as at the first siege of Burgos in 1812 when the Allies were time and again flooded out by bad storms. Death, or at least incapacitation, from disease was the fare of many a soldier and impressed peasant worker in the sieges of the 18th and early 19th centuries.

Of course, it might well prove necessary to eliminate forward enemy positions before the main parallels could be established, so a whole series of subsidiary siege operations, including small-scale stormings, would be proceeding at the same time as the main trenches were being dug. At Ciudad Rodrigo, French advanced positions on the Greater Teson, particularly Fort Renaud, had to be taken by a *coup de main* in a night attack on 8 January 1812 before the first parallel could be seriously begun the following day. All such operations tended to increase the period of time taken by a siege.

As the trenches crept inexorably closer, the garrison might be expected to launch large-scale sorties in more attempts to wreak damage and thus win invaluable time. After losing control of the Lesser Teson, General Barrié launched 500 men against Wellington's trenches at 11 am on 14 January, and inflicted considerable mayhem before being driven back within the main defences. All such incidents added to the casualties and general inconveniences of mounting a regular siege.

In the fullness of time, however, the series of parallels and approaches would be complete, and the attackers firmly situated on the enemy's glacis. The danger of mines exploding under their feet obviously increased, but the besiegers, at last scenting the possibility of success, now redoubled their efforts to push sap-heads forward to the very edge of the ditch, and to establish the great breaching battery in a position from which it could begin to batter a breach, or series of breaches, in the main line of defences. Obviously, heavy metal was required for this task, 36-pounders or larger pieces being the norm. Such guns were very difficult to move, and would customarily be brought up by barge when practicable to the nearest convenient point before being painfully dragged overland to their prepared battery positions. Sometimes, an army just did not possess adequate resources of either skilled manpower or artillery for these tasks. The Allied second siege of Badajoz (24 May to 19 June 1811) foundered due to a combination of both deficiencies. Although the besiegers overcame the impenetrable rock surfaces of the north-east approaches to the town by building fortications and parallels of wool bales, the only heavy artillery available were century-old Portuguese iron guns which soon developed 'muzzle-droop', and became wholly unserviceable, whilst the total number of sappers present totalled just three sergeants, as many corporals and as many privates of the Royal Engineers. A year later, Wellington ensured that there was proper provision of both heavy guns and experts.

Once established, the breaching batteries fired almost incessantly, and the cumulative effect of ceaseless pounding would be to crumble away the face of the defences until a breach had been made faced by a gradual slope of debris. When the breach was deemed 'practicable,' the siege would enter its last major stage. But here the difference between the conventions of 18th-century warfare à la Vauban and the contemporary shift in attitude becomes very apparent. To mount a major storming through the breach, however extensive, against a determined defence, using all the methods mentioned earlier, was often prohibitively costly in terms of human life. This had been repugnant during the 'Age of Reason', and accordingly major stormings had been very rare (although minor ones against outposts, ravelins, etc. were frequently mounted). Instead, in the interests of conserving human life, it had become recognised that when a full-scale assault through a major breach was imminent, the defending commander was entitled to 'beat the chamade,' call a truce, and negotiate a capitulation on the best terms he could obtain. Negotiated surrenders of this type were not wholly unknown in the Peninsular War, but they had become the exception rather than the rule owing to the far stricter attitude of French commanders, who were imbued with their duty to defend their fortresses to the last man and round on behalf of l'Empereur. Hence the need for the major assaults at Ciudad Rodrigo in the early hours of 19 January 1812, the even more notorious one at Badajoz on 6 April, the bloody battles (ultimately unsuccessful) to storm Burgos castle in the autumn of the same year, and to assault the defences of San Sebastian (eventually successfully) on 31 August 1813.

These stormings were terribly costly. That of Ciudad Rodrigo was comparatively slight, with 568 Allied casualties, but to capture the great breach of Badajoz cost Wellington 2,500 men (out of 4,760 during the whole siege) in the space of two hours – a feat that needed more than forty separate attacks. San Sebastian's 'blood-list' was only slightly less – 3,376 men killed and wounded on 31 August out of a total of 3,700 casualties sustained between the 8th of that month and the final surrender of the castle garrison on 8 September after sixty-three days of 'open trenches'. Of course, the defenders also suffered heavily, but not on the same scale.

The shedding of blood on this scale had been avoided whenever possible in earlier generations. To discourage defenders from fighting to the bitter end, conventions had evolved which allowed an attacker, if he was put to the trouble and concomitant losses of mounting a major, and successful, assault, certain 'privileges' (or rather leave to commit atrocities) when he finally took possession of the town. Thus, the lives of the garrison could be deemed to be held forfeit, and certain 'soldiers' rights' of pillage, rape and arson were the compensation offered to the rank and file for their effort and sacrifice.

It was folk memories of these conventions, designed to avoid the need for costly stormings, and handed down from one generation of private soldier to the next, that account for the terrible excesses perpetrated by

British and Allied soldiery on several occasions in the Peninsula. At Ciudad Rodrigo the troops got out of hand for almost a day within the town; although no Spanish civilians were killed, there was much looting and drinking, and three serious fires were caused before Picton grimly restored order. At Badajoz, the situation was infinitely worse. After the agony sustained in the breaches, the troops went wild for three days, and even Wellington's presence could not restore discipline. Fearful excesses were perpetrated against the Spanish inhabitants – whom, technically, the Allies had come to liberate from French tyranny – and there are no clear estimates of how many were butchered and raped. Officers could not restore order, and even executions and floggings of recalcitrants did nothing to check the orgy, which only burnt itself out through sheer exhaustion after seventy two hours following the sending in of unaffected troops forcibly to suppress disorder.

Although less celebrated, the scenes that followed the capture of San Sebastian were in some ways even worse. There the chaos lasted five days, and following the culminating conflagration, there remained only a dozen houses standing in the town. 'With the exception of ten or twelve fortunate buildings,' wrote an officer, 'there is nothing left of San Sebastian but the walls of its houses, and they are falling every instant.' Tales such as these must destroy any comfortable, romantic illusions about the nature of Peninsular campaigning. The British army, like any other in history, has its grim record of Ouradours and My Lais, and the fact that the atrocities were committed in hot blood does little to palliate the nature of these crimes against humanity.

It is interesting to note that at Ciudad Rodrigo, and San Sebastian, the garrisons fared better than the inhabitants. At Rodrigo, General Barié was allowed to surrender at the head of the 1,407 survivors of his once 2,000-strong garrison; at Badajoz, General Phillipon and his garrison, which had retreated into the citadel of San Cristobal at the height of the assault, was similarly granted reasonable terms on 8 April when the Allied fury abated; whilst at San Sebastian, General Rey was even allowed to march out with the honours of war on 8 September 1813. Such are the (in some ways strange) inconsistencies of warfare as waged in the context of Peninsular sieges. But it all goes to show that there is all too much truth in the dictum of General William Tecumseh Sherman of US Civil War fame and notoriety, to the effect that 'war is hell'. The passage of time mercifully tends to tone down or even obliterate many bitter memories, but they should not be totally forgotten. The atrocities apart, it is noteworthy that the Allied army lost more troops prosecuting the sieges of both Badajoz and San Sebastian than Wellington's army lost in any Peninsular battle other than Talavera and Albuera. Sieges, therefore, were exceedingly costly affairs. Nevertheless, they make a fascinating subject for study – and also a rewarding one for the devotee of military history once he has mastered the main forms and conventions that governed their conduct, and once he has come to understand the reasons that lay behind their terrible aftermaths.

To serve as an example of a major siege operation in the Peninsular War, there follows the chronology, from inception to completion, of the third siege of Badajoz (January-April 1812):

28 January: Wellington orders the siege train to move to Elvas.

late February: Wellington and 60,000 men march towards Badajoz and the surrounding area.

early March: the Allies detach Graham with 19,000 men to guard against any relief attempt from the south by Marshal Soult, and General Hill with 14,000 troops to watch (from Merida) any movements by Marshal Marmont to the north-east. These detachments, together with the 5th Division and some cavalry left near Ciudad Rodrigo, constituted the forces covering the siege.

17 March: Badajoz (defended by General Phillipon with 4,333 men and 150 guns, as well as 667 sick and servants), is closely invested. The first parallel is started on a stormy night 200 yards from Fort Picurina on San Miguel hill.

18 March: French fire destroys the British parapets, which are then rebuilt.

19 March: the French extend their positions to enfilade the flank of the British position; at 1pm a sortie from Fort Picurina is driven off with a loss of some 150 men on both sides. Colonel Fletcher, senior RE representative, is among the wounded.

22 March: Wellington extends the first parallel to the entire south-east side of Badajoz, at a range of 700 yards, and counters a French attempt to outflank his lines by opening trenches against Fort San Cristobal.

night of 22/23 March: a torrential rainstorm floods the trenches; British pontoon bridges over the Guadiana river are destroyed by the rising water.

24 March: the British complete the establishment of six batteries (twenty eight guns) in the first parallel.

25 March: British guns silence and breach Fort Picurina at 11am; after nightfall, it is stormed with a loss of some 250 men on both sides. A French sortie from Badajoz is repulsed.

26–29 March: the second parallel is dug; new batteries (one in Fort Picurina) are established.

30 March: twenty eight heavy guns start to pound the bastions of Santa Maria and Trinidad and the linking wall. Because of flooding, no mines can be fired.

March-April: elsewhere, Soult is stirring, but is successfully contained by General Graham's force; Marmont appears to be threatening a serious attack against Ciudad Rodrigo in the northern corridor. Wellington decides to clinch matters at Badajoz and orders general storming.

6 April: Wellington is informed that three breaches would be 'practicable' by dusk.

6 April: at 10pm a 'forlorn hope' of volunteers enters the breach and encounters murderous fire. A succession of forty separate assaults by the Light and 4th Divisions against two of the three breaches are beaten back with mounting losses. General Picton and the 3rd Division manage to escalade into Badajoz castle following an initial failure of this part of Wellington's diversionary tactics. At 11.30pm General Leith and the 5th Division, although ninety minutes late in reaching their objective, successfully enter the town from the north-west. Major Wilson with 1,000 men storms the Lunette of San Roche.

7 April: at 1am Picton and Leith attack the French holding the breach from the rear. French resistance collapses; Phillipon retires into Fort San Cristobal. At approximately 3am Badajoz falls into Allied hands. Phillipon surrenders Fort San Cristobal.

7–10 April: the sack of Badajoz.

Casualties
The Allies lose 3,350 during the assault (2,500 in the main breaches) out of

a total of 4,760 (including six generals wounded and four colonels killed) during the siege. The French suffer 1,350 killed and wounded, and 3,500 taken prisoner.

Strategic Effect
On news of the fall of Badajoz, Soult retreats back into Andalucia. Marmont heads for Salamanca, where Wellington follows him in due course. The Allies, with both corridors in their possession, can now safely take the offensive, especially as large numbers of French troops are being withdrawn from Spain to serve at the imminent invasion of Russia.

CHAPTER IV

Vermin, Scorpions and Mosquitoes: The Rheinbund in the Peninsula

John H Gill

The grinding war in the Iberian Peninsula not only absorbed thousands of French, Italian and Neapolitan soldiers from 1808 through 1814, it also became the battleground upon which the mettle of dozens of German contingents was tested. Besiegers of Gerona, besieged at Badajoz, instrumental in victories such as Medellin and participants in the disaster at Vittoria, Napoleon's allies from the Confederation of the Rhine (Rheinbund) played a secondary but significant role in this cruel conflict.[1] Their variegated battalions adding to the colour, confusion and complexity of French orders of battle, more than 35,000 Germans eventually found their way to Spain, but their place in the history of the Peninsular War is often overlooked.[2] A brief chapter can hardly pretend to trace the activities of contingents from at least eighteen sovereign states as well as several independent formations – totalling some thirty-three battalions and eleven squadrons in addition to artillery batteries and miscellaneous detachments – through five years of combat, but it is hoped that the following will serve as a general introduction to this little known dimension of the Napoleonic experience in Spain and Portugal.

Founded in 1806, the Rheinbund provided Napoleon with a means to expand his influence in central Germany at the expense of the Habsburg and Hohenzollern monarchies. Although he originally intended the confederation as a foundation for political, social, economic, judicial, and military institutions, only the latter received real emphasis and most of the other planned features never progressed beyond the concept stage. According to the 'constitutional act' signed by France and the other fifteen original members, each state in the Rheinbund committed itself to providing a contingent for the common defence in case of crisis or war. These ranged in size from the 200,000 Frenchmen promised by Napoleon as the 'Protector' of the confederation to the twenty nine owed by the Prince von der Leyen's miniature monarchy. By 1808,

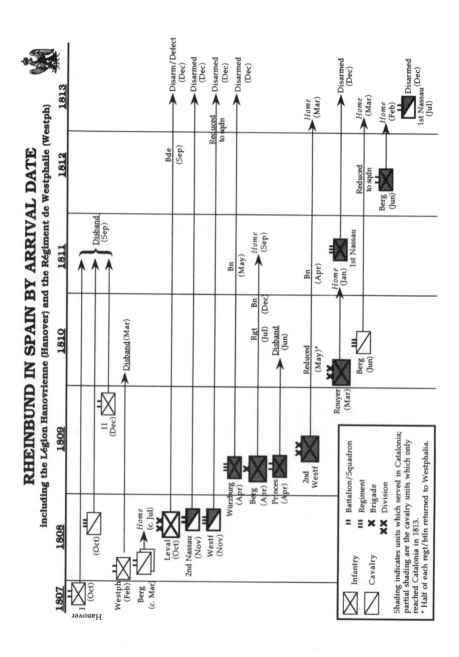

RHEINBUND IN SPAIN BY ARRIVAL DATE

including the Légion Hanovrienne (Hanover) and the Régiment de Westphalie (Westph) when the Rheinbund reached its maximum size of thirty six German members, many of these contingents had already experienced combat under France's eagles and Napoleon had no hesitation in calling on them to augment the force he was sending to Spain.

Spain, however, was not Napoleon's only concern in the autumn of 1808: in addition to the collapsing situation in Iberia, the Emperor faced a potential war with Austria in central Europe. Owing to their proximity to the hastily rearming Habsburg Empire, therefore, the largest Rheinbund states, Bavaria, Saxony and Württemberg, were exempted from the Imperial demand to assemble contingents for Spain. The north German princes who had only recently joined the Confederation (Oldenburg and the two Mecklenburgs) were likewise left alone. In their case, however, the likely reason was that their 'armies' were in such a state of decrepitude that they could hardly be expected to field contingents for foreign service. The rest had no option but to submit to Napoleon's summons and by the autumn of 1808, thousands of Rheinbund troops were on the road for Perpignan or Bayonne in Pyrenean France.

With the exception of Andalucia, German troops eventually served in almost every corner of the Iberian Peninsula. Viewed from the broadest vantage, however, the Rheinbund contingents fought in two principal theatres of war – central Spain and Catalonia – and this division offers the most convenient approach to their history.

The first large contingent of Confederation troops to enter Spain (some non-Rheinbund formations will be addressed later) marched in from Bayonne in October 1808. These were contributions from Baden, Hesse-Darmstadt, Nassau and Frankfurt which had been combined with the Dutch contingent to form the so-called 'Division Allemande' under Général de Division (GD) Jean Leval.[3] Though often dispersed in small detachments, most of these Rheinbund units would continue to serve together with honour throughout the Peninsular War.[4]

Leval's Division, including its 5,700 Germans (see box overleaf), was initially designated the 2nd Division of Marshal François Lefebvre's IV Corps and the marshal held the customary reviews to inspect his new troops. He found a number of organisational oddities. Most glaring was the intermixing of green and blue uniform coats in the Hessian Gross- und Erbprinz Regiment. This resulted from the peculiarities of Hessian infantry organisation where the regimental equivalent was called a 'brigade' and consisted of two musketeer battalions clothed in blue and a single fusilier (light infantry) battalion in green. Before departing for Spain, however, the regiment had been reorganised along French lines into two battalions of six companies each (including the standard grenadier and voltigeur companies). The unfortunate outcome was a hopeless intermingling of green and blue coats that irked Lefebvre.[5] Like the Hessian regiment, the Baden 4th Infantry was organised according to the French pattern and it too had to cope with unusual uniform difficulties. When summoned to provide a contingent for Spain, the Grand Duchy had elected to send the 1st Battalion of the 4th Regiment (deep red facings) and the 2nd Battalion of the 3rd (white distinctions). Early in 1809, these two were redesignated as the new 4th Infantry (the corresponding battalions back in Baden became the 3rd), but the strange mismatch between battalion facings probably lasted until new uniforms were issued in 1810.[6]

Leval's men participated in a number of small combats and major battles through late 1808 and into the summer of 1809, the Baden and Nassau troops quickly earning especially good reputations for professional competence and tactical skill.[7] Lefebvre honoured them by selecting a battalion from each regiment as his personal guard after observing their performance at Durango on 31 October. He also included the voltigeurs from these two contingents in the two-battalion advance guard regiment he formed in mid-November and placed the new regiment's mixed French-German battalion under Baden's respected Major Ludwig von Grolman.[8] The Baden and Nassau troops received

---

LEVAL'S DIVISION IN SPRING/SUMMER 1809

Infantry (brigading changed repeatedly and is not reflected here)
  combined voltigeur battalion
  Nassau 2nd Infantry Regt
  Baden 4th Infantry Regt
  Hessian Gross- und Erbprinz Regt
  Frankfurt Battalion
  Dutch I/2 Infantry Regt
  Dutch II/4 Infantry Regt

Artillery:
  Baden Battery
  Dutch Battery
  Hessian Half-Battery

Note: Only the 2nd Battalion of the Hessian regiment was present at Talavera, the 1st Battalion being in Segovia. In addition, the Westphalian 1st Chevauxlegers were with Merlin's Brigade, the 3rd Dutch Hussars with Milhaud.

---

welcome Imperial recompense during a review on 10 December, as Napoleon dispensed medals, promotions and plaudits with his unique facility.

The Hessians, on the other hand, initially had problems. In addition to expressing displeasure at the calico appearance of the reorganised battalions, Lefebvre and other French generals were dissatisfied with the regiment's combat performance, its ignorance of French drill and its behaviour towards the local population. To make matters worse, there was a considerable degree of personal friction between the old marshal and some of the Hessian officers, particularly the regimental commander, Oberst von Ledebur.[9] Nor did it help matters that Leval was almost captured when a Hessian voltigeur company retreated precipitously before a sudden Spanish attack near Durango on 27 October. Cursing, the general recovered from his narrow escape and called to the Baden regiment: 'Show these dogs that good troops are here'; and the Badeners happily chased off the encroaching Spaniards.[10] With all these irritations and annoyances, the Hessian contingent quickly acquired a poor reputation, leading Napoleon to comment in the 17th Bulletin of the Army of Spain that 'the Hesse-Darmstadt Regiment has not sustained the reputation of that country's troops'.[11] He also wrote directly and plainly to Grand Duke Ludwig X of Hesse: 'The Hessian is a good and brave soldier. If Your Grace will give them commanders of merit . . . they will retrieve the reputation they have earned for many centuries.' While the Badeners and Nassauers enjoyed promotions and decorations, therefore, the Hessians received only obloquy. To restore Hessian honour, the regiment's much-loved former commander, General-Major (GM) Georg von Schäffer, was sent to Spain and von Ledebur was recalled 'for reasons of health'. The Hessian infantrymen were much encouraged by Schäffer's arrival in March 1809 and the change also had a salutary effect for the small Hessian artillery detachment which had appealed in vain to Ledebur for administrative support.[12]

The Frankfurt Battalion was likewise neglected. Annoyed at finding the battalion with only seven officers and 200 men present in the ranks during the 10 December review, Napoleon refused to award a single medal (moreover, the battalion had been assigned to rear area duties and thus had little opportunity to distinguish itself in combat). As Grolman noted, the disgruntled Frankfurt men 'vowed to avenge themselves through bravery' and they, along with their Hessian comrades, soon did so.[13]

Detached to Marshal Victor's I Corps during February 1809, the Germans left a good impression with their French commanders by their steadiness at Meza de Ibor, Valdecannas, and Medellin.[14] After their superb advance at Meza de Ibor (17 March 1809), for example, GM Konrad von Schäffer and his Nassauers were proud when Victor said 'Nassau decided the battle'.[15] Oberst-Leutnant Welsch and his Frankfurt troops basked in similar verbal praise. The French commanders were also pleased with the Germans in the following day's action at Valdecannas: 'Yesterday you saw Nassau, today you see Baden,' Leval told Victor, and the marshal reported that Leval's Division had 'attacked with extraordinary impetuosity' and had 'chased them [the enemy] from every position'.[16] Formed into squares and interspersed between blocks of French cavalry, the Germans bore the brunt of the infantry fighting at Medellin (28 March). The Nassau regiment's steadiness earned it the nickname 'the moving citadel', and Leval told Hesse's GM von Schäffer that he and his brigade 'had decided the affair'.[17] Victor was again generous with his praise, writing that Leval's men had 'demonstrated the greatest bravery'. Similarly, a more junior French observer, Lieutenant Albert de Rocca of the 2nd Hussars, commented that the Germans, left alone in the midst of the battlefield against markedly superior numbers, 'vigorously resisted every effort of the enemy' to overwhelm them.[18]

Despite their contribution to the victory, the Germans were assigned the 'ghastly task' of helping to inter the thousands of Spanish dead. While a Baden soldier congratulated himself on finding large sums of money on the Spaniards, the men of the Frankfurt Battalion took this opportunity to replace their worn-out breeches with brown cloth from their deceased foes.[19] Combined with new coats of requisitioned and appropriated blue fabric, the Frankfurters thus effected a complete change in uniform from their original white breeches and coats trimmed in red to baggy brown trousers and blue coats (still sporting red distinctions). Furthermore, at some point in their peregrinations, they managed to dispose of their old bicornes and adopted French-style shakos. This new uniform was also instituted among the troops back in Frankfurt and the Grand Duchy's men would march to Russia in blue coats and shakos.

New clothing was badly needed. As early as November 1808, the Baden commander, Colonel Heinrich von Porbeck, had complained that 'Our uniforms are tearing to pieces, especially those of the common soldiers, and we shall soon find ourselves all in tatters'. Grolman recorded that the Baden troops arriving for their 10 December review by Napoleon 'looked dreadful after the arduous mountain marches, most were without shoes'.[20] The situation was no better the following year: 'Our boots are in shreds,' wrote Porbeck, and 'the gunners' coats are torn to bits, the endless bivouacking has ruined them completely . . . the helmets are unbearable because of their weight and unsuitability for the soldiers in the Spanish heat, they shrink and cannot be removed from the soldiers' heads'. Expediency and inventiveness kept utter nakedness at bay, but before long the only uniform item that united the Baden contingent was the dark blue fabric of their coats.[21] The other contingents resorted to similar measures: in May 1809, for instance, the Hessian artillerymen trimmed the long tattered tails of their uniform coats to improve their appearance.[22]

Back with IV Corps (now under GD Horace Sébastiani), the German Division stood in the front ranks at Talavera de la Reyna in July. This engagement also had a sartorial dimension for one of the German contingents. As noted by an officer in Baden's 4th Infantry, the musicians of his regiment somehow managed to gather up a number of helmets formerly worn by the unfortunate 23rd Light Dragoons, thereby allowing the Baden bandsmen to wear helmets (however maligned by their commander) long after their comrades had switched to shakos.[23] In other respects, however, Talavera was a less happy experience. Placed in the centre of the French line, Leval's men attempted to advance through thick olive groves against Campbell's battalions but could make no headway and suffered bloody repulse.[24] From a strength of some 4,200, the battle cost the division over 1,000 casualties, including the courageous Colonel von Porbeck.[25] Despite the outcome, French accounts of the struggle were full of praise for the Germans: Sébastiani reported that they 'had covered themselves with glory' and made especial mention of the 'brave' Porbeck and the Hessians.[26]

The weakened division, now known officially as the 'Division de la Confédération de la Rhin', also received accolades from its French commanders for its role in the victories at Almonacid (11 August) and Ocaña (19 November). The German Division 'displayed great valour' at Ocaña wrote Marshal Mortier, 'The German regiments rivalled all in ardour and devotion'.[27] Following Ocaña, the Germans were assigned to escort the numerous Spanish prisoners back across the Pyrenees, many French sharing Albert de Rocca's opinion that 'their national character and strict discipline rendered them vigilant and inflexible' when dealing with captives as compared to the more relaxed attitude of the French soldiery.[28] The Germans themselves were less than pleased with this task. Hesse's GM von Schäffer, for example, found prisoner escort demeaning; infuriated at this and the lack of official recognition after Ocaña, he wrote 'This assignment is the final blow to the German Division. I request to be relieved' (his request was denied).[29] Escort and garrison duties filled the remainder of 1809 and most of the following three years as well, although much of the division took part in GD Louis Montbrun's expedition to Murcia in December 1811.

Two months later, the Hessians departed the division's ranks to become part of the garrison of Badajoz.[30] During the siege of that fortress city, they participated in the defence of the outer works, the 19 March sortie, and the bitter fighting at the main breach and in the castle on the night of 6/7 April 1812.[31] Of 910 Hessian infantry and artillerymen who entered the fortress in February, 444 surrendered and were transported to Lisbon. They were poorly treated. Robbed, stripped naked, beaten and thrown into a flooded ditch, one officer was rescued by a Brunswick soldier; an artillery sergeant was appalled that he and his comrades were 'thoroughly plundered and, under the accompaniment of blows from fists and musket butts, robbed of every piece of clothing of any value whatsoever'. Abuses, indignities and privations continued during the journey into Portugal. In part, this was an effort to induce the Hessians to enter English service, and some responded with alacrity to the recruiting teams that soon appeared to offer an escape from the endless misery. Still suffering from maltreatment and the rigours of the siege, the remainder were transported to England and spent the next two years in confinement; a mere 183 returned to their homeland in June 1814.[32] With the fall of Badajoz, various small Hessian detachments totalling about 245 men were gathered up and returned to Darmstadt in time to participate in the gruelling 1813 campaign in Saxony.

The remaining contingents, Nassau, Baden and Frankfurt, now constituted a brigade in GD Jean Darmagnac's Division of the Army of the Centre. Under Baden's GM Karl von Neuenstein, they were heavily engaged at Vittoria (21 June 1813), particularly in the struggle for La Hermandad. Lieutenant Leonhard Rückert of the Baden artillery recalled that the British columns advanced against the German Brigade 'like a hurricane and developed a fire which soon enveloped our entire division in powder smoke'.[33] Losses in this whirlwind of destruction mounted to more than 500 dead and wounded from a strength of 2,678, and the Germans recoiled in disorder to rally on their French supports. The brigade maintained its cohesion, however, and fought valiantly in several rearguard scuffles that day and during the long retreat back to France.[34] Now numbering barely 2,000 soldiers under arms, the German Brigade was assigned to GD Eugène Villatte's Reserve Division when Soult reorganised the army in July; it gained a last small, but otiose, success under French command along the banks of the Bidassoa on 31 August.[35] Napoleon's star was fast failing, however, and as Soult withdrew towards Bayonne, Colonel August von Kruse, commander of the 2nd Nassau, received instructions from his sovereign to defect to the English at the first safe opportunity.[36] Consulting secretly with his fellow Rheinbund commanders (Captain Damboer of Frankfurt and Major Hennig of Baden) and establishing clandestine contact with old acquaintances in the King's German Legion, Kruse bided his time for several weeks. His chance finally came on 10 December during the combat on the Nive and, leaving its baggage and some 340 men behind (approximately 190 in Bayonne and 250 in various French hospitals), the 2nd Nassau marched into the British lines and announced its shift in allegiance. Acting on his own initiative (he had no instructions), Captain Damboer led the Frankfurt Battalion across the lines with the Nassauers, but the Badeners (now only a battalion) remained with their French allies and were disarmed the following day.[37]

At the other end of the Pyrenees, two Rheinbund cavalry units were also disarmed in early December 1813: the lone surviving squadron of the Westphalian 1st Chevauxlegers and two squadrons of Nassau Reitende Jäger. These troopers had joined Marshal Gabriel Suchet's forces in the autumn of that year after long service in central Spain, often in the company of the Division Allemande. The Westphalian regiment had departed home in mid-September 1808 with 550 men in three squadrons, but suffered considerable desertion en route to the Peninsula and only counted some 400 troopers in the ranks when it crossed the Pyrenees in November.[38] Nonetheless, the light horsemen earned a reasonably good reputation for their participation in many of the large engagements of 1809 as part of I and IV Corps, particularly for their contribution to the destruction of the 23rd Light Dragoons at Talavera. A different episode in 1809 illustrates the oppressive cruelty of the contest between the occupying forces and the population in the Spanish war. In late February, a detachment of chevauxlegers numbering between twenty and twenty five men was sent to a small town called Arenas to gather supplies. Invited to dine by the inhabitants, the Westphalians were ambushed by insurgents, disarmed, tortured abominably and finally killed. In revenge, Leval's Division conducted a punitive expedition which culminated in Leval giving the town up to plunder. Dreadful scenes ensued in the streets as German infantry and French dragoons indulged in a drunken fury of murder and destruction. The horrid incident ended with Arenas disappearing in a welter of flames. This small example of the grim Iberian conflict was typical of the experiences endured by the Westphalians (and their countrymen) for the next four years. Armed with lances in 1812, the regiment slowly melted away and was reduced to a single squadron the following year before being transferred to Suchet (the cadres returned to

Westphalia to help reconstruct the kingdom's cavalry after the Russian disaster).

The 125 men of the 2nd Squadron of the Nassau Reitende Jägers crossed the Pyrenees to reach Burgos on 13 November 1808 and served with great distinction in central and northern Spain for the next five years. Dressed in fur colpacks with green dolmans and loose brown trousers, they exuded the casual dash of competent professionals. As commander in Burgos in early 1809, GD Paul Thiébault could not praise them enough: 'They are, in effect, a corps d'élite or, more exactly, a small band of heroes'.[39] Serving with the German Division from 1809 into 1813, the Jägers missed Talavera but participated in numerous other actions with the 2nd Nassau Infantry and other Rheinbund troops, including Montbrun's expedition into Murcia and the battle of Vittoria. The 1st Squadron joined its compatriots near Bayonne in early July of 1813, but in October both were reassigned to Catalonia where they were disarmed at the end of the year.[40]

In Catalonia, the closing scenes between the French and their German allies were very different from the story of defection farther north. Suchet lamented the loss of the German troops, reporting that as recently as 1 December, he had employed the Westphalian light horsemen and the elite companies of the 1st Nassau Infantry as his advance guard: 'they served with great zeal and not a single soldier deserted'. When GB Louis Ordonneau told the Westphalians they were to be disarmed, they reportedly wept bitterly and cried 'Just show us the enemy and see if we have not decided to lay down our lives for the Emperor!' The squadron commander, Major von Plessen, and one of his officers offered their services to France; Suchet recommended them, describing Plessen as 'a fine officer of a brilliant valour'. The reaction of the Nassau Jägers was similar. Major von Oberkampf was 'most distraught' and told his erstwhile allies: 'for five years I have served in your ranks; I have received flattering testimony of my conduct and of that of my regiment, and I desire an enduring proof by obtaining the cross of an officer in the Legion of Honour.' Suchet treated the Germans with 'the dignity these brave soldiers have earned' and sadly carried out his orders.[41]

On joining Suchet in late 1813, the Nassau and Westphalian troopers found a few small remnants of the thousands of Rheinbund soldiers who had served in Catalonia during the preceding four years. Napoleon viewed the province as nearly isolated from the remainder of Spain, a place of secondary importance where his Italian, Neapolitan, and German contingents could be employed in place of French troops. As a result, over 11,000 Rheinbund soldiers crossed the mountains from Perpignan in early 1809. Most would never return.

The largest of these contingents was the 2nd Westphalian Division under GD Joseph Morio, one of King Jerome's feckless cronies, whom Napoleon regarded as 'a sort of lunatic whom I despise'.[42] The division was composed of the 1st Light Infantry Battalion and the 2nd, 3rd, and 4th Infantry Regiments, all organised on the French pattern with two battalions per regiment, each battalion comprising four line and two elite companies. Two foot batteries provided artillery support.[43] Losing some deserters en route, the division entered Catalonia in May 1809 and was assigned to GD Jean Verdier who was charged with besieging the fortress city of Gerona.[44]

Arriving before the city, the Westphalians found a brigade of Rheinbund troops already in the trenches. This was Général de Brigade (GB) François Amey's command, a mixed force consisting of the Würzburg Infantry Regiment (1,717 men in two battalions), the Berg Brigade (1st and 2nd Infantry Regiments, two battalions each, with 1,358 and 1,343 effectives respectively), and the ephemeral Bataillon des Princes. There was also a detachment of approximately fifty Berg artillerymen assigned to the siege artillery.[45] Departing their homelands in December 1808, the Würzburg and Berg troops had crossed into Spain on 1 and 12 April 1809 respectively. Like many of the other contingents, the Berg troops altered their uniforms en route to Spain: passing through Paris between December 1808 and January 1809, each man had to replace the 'J' (Joachim) on his shako and giberne with an 'N' (Napoleon) when their former grand duke, Marshal Joachim Murat, left Berg to assume the royal throne of Naples. Also like most of the other Rheinbund contingents, Berg and Würzburg organisation matched that of the French infantry: each battalion was composed of one grenadier, one voltigeur and four fusilier companies.

The Bataillon des Princes, on the other hand, was doubtless one of the most colourful formations of the entire war. Composed of one company each from six different principalities (Schwarzburg-Sondershausen, Schwarzburg-Rudolstadt, Lippe-Detmold, Schaumburg-Lippe, Reuss, and Waldeck), it assembled as a battalion for the first time on 10 December 1808 in Metz under Major August von Brokenburg of Schwarzburg-Rudolstadt. The battalion departed for the Spanish border the following January, spent a month in Perpignan and finally crossed over the Pyrenees on 14 April 1809 with 812 men in its ranks. Exhausted by outpost and escort duty, small skirmishes and illness, however, its strength steadily declined. Still numbering 700 on 1 June, by 1 September it was down to 200 effectives (the two Schwarzburg companies were now commanded by sergeants), and 12 October found it with only fifty seven men fit for duty. With small numbers returned to the ranks, its strength fluctuated between forty and a hundred for the remainder of its brief existence. Although its combat history is not without successes, small size, limited training, differences in drill amongst the constituent companies and rancorous squabbles between the company commanders and their nominal battalion commander made the Bataillon des Princes one of the least effective Rheinbund units.[46] On 5 June 1810, a little over a year after its arrival in Spain, it was broken up in Gerona and its few survivors (184 men) distributed to the 5th and 6th Rheinbund Regiments of GD Rouyer's Division.[47]

In the meantime, the Berg, Würzburg, and Westphalian troops played an important role in the long siege of Gerona. Life in the trenches before the fortress was a miserable experience. As a Berg veteran wrote: 'Grass and weeds were cooked; every living animal, often even dead ones which had already begun to decay, was greedily consumed. The battery 'l'Impériale' was robbed of its sandbags to provide wrappings for [our] feet and, to make the misery complete, innumerable vermin, scorpions, mosquitoes, and insects of all types tortured us and left us not a moment's peace'.[48] In addition to enduring the many privations attendant upon operations conducted in a desolate area with inadequate logistical support, the elite companies of the German units made up about one third of the assaulting force that attempted to storm the Montjuich fort on 7 July 1809. They suffered accordingly. Oberst Eduard Legras of the 2nd Westphalian Infantry told his expectant officers 'Well, gentlemen, here is the occasion to win your Cross of Honour!' but the dreadful scenes before the breach recall those described by British veterans of Badajoz. Westphalian Lieutenant Franz Morgenstern remembered: 'The ditch was not even partly filled, either with earth or with fascines, and, as we climbed down, we made the distressing discovery that there were only a few, widely separated ladders along the wall under the breach, and that the ladders were too short by a man's height . . . At the base of the ladders, we were received with every conceivable means of destruction: grenades, showers of burning pitch and oil, huge, plunging blocks of stone and exploding sacks of powder'.[49] The Westphalians lost 219 and the four élite companies of the Würzburg Regiment thirty four dead and 152 wounded in the assault.[50]

Casualties in the abortive storm, the steady drain of quotidian siege duty and, above all, the ravages of disease reduced the strength of most Rheinbund battalions by half between June and September. The situation of the 2nd Westphalian was even worse: from a strength of 1,009 on 1 June, it was down to 340 by 15 September. The other contingents were in a similar state. Nonetheless, Berg and Würzburg troops participated in the storming of Gerona's walls on 19 September. Despite considerable courage and heavy casualites, however, they were unable to maintain themselves in the breach. An eyewitness recalled: 'A strong detachment of

Berg troops hung on in the breach by Los Allemaños until total darkness fell; one by one all the officers were killed or wounded because they did not want to abandon their comrades who had broken into the city'.[51] The four Berg battalions lost 261 men (total casualties among the attackers were 1,600), including the able commander of the 1st Infantry, Oberst Mouff, and three more painful months would pass before the city finally succumbed to starvation.[52]

The siege of Gerona wrecked the Berg, Würzburg and Westphalian contingents. Despite the arrival of replacements, their first and only major combat operation in the Peninsula had left all of them well below fifty per cent strength (over half the men of the two Berg regiments were hospitalised; the artillery detachment only had four soldiers fit for duty) and all three were reduced in size during the next two years.[53] The Westphalian Division, in particular, never really recovered from the assault on Montjuich; when the city capitulated in December it could only muster some 1,500 men under arms.[54] By the spring of 1811, both the Westphalian Division and the Würzburg Regiment had been reduced to small battalions (approximately 500 and 420 men respectively). And that autumn, the last survivors of the Berg Brigade, redesignated first as a regiment and then as a battalion in 1810

THE RHEINBUND IN CATALONIA (MAY 1809)

German Brigade: GB Amey (French)
  Würzburg Infantry Regt: Oberst Gebsattel
  Berg Brigade: Oberst Geither
    1st Infantry Regt
    2nd Infantry Regt
    (Berg artillery detachment with siege park)
  Bataillon des Princes: Major von Brokenburg

Westphalian Division: GD Morio
  Brigade: GB Boerner
    2nd Infantry Regt
    4th Infantry Regt
  Brigade: Adjutant Commandant von Ochs
    3rd Infantry Regt
    1st Light Battalion
  two foot batteries

Note: 1st Chevauxlegers were officially part of the division but never served with it.

(July and December respectively), departed Spain to be rebuilt for the Russian campaign. The 'battalion', officially still the 1st Battalion, 1st Infantry, had only 248 men under arms in August 1811 and numbered a meagre 120 when it finally returned to Düsseldorf on 22 November that year.[55] The Westphalian Battalion, down to about 300 effectives under Major Winkel, suffered a similar fate, returning to the kingdom with the remaining gunners (minus guns) in March 1813 just in time for the harrowing campaign in central Germany.[56] One other Berg infantry unit, the 2nd Battalion, 3rd Infantry, also served in Catalonia, but its tenure was brief (June 1812 to February 1813) and its combats minor.[57] By the summer of 1813, therefore, only the Würzburg Battalion remained of the original Rheinbund troops that had marched across the Pyrenees for Gerona four years earlier.[58]

Another German infantry unit was also still in Catalonia in mid-1813. This was the 1st Nassau Infantry (two battalions) which had arrived with GD Marie-François Rouyer's Division of miscellaneous Rheinbund contingents in March of 1810.[59] Rouyer's command, an effort to make effective use of tiny German contingents, consisted of four Rheinbund regiments: 2nd (1st Nassau), 4th (Saxon Duchies), 5th (Anhalt and Lippe), and 6th (the two Schwarzburgs, Reuss, Waldeck). Sent off to Spain after its participation on the fringes of the 1809 campaign against Austria, the division suffered heavily from desertion when the men learned of their destination; the 4th Rheinbund, a good unit which had performed well in the Tyrol, lost 200 men in a single night before crossing the border into France.[60] Still, Rouyer counted some 4,700 men in his ranks when

---

ROUYER'S DIVISION IN CATALONIA (MARCH 1810)

Brigade: GB François Schwarz (French)
  1st Nassau Infantry Regt
  4th Rheinbund Regt (Saxon Duchies)
    Light Battalion (Weimar and Hildburghausen)
    Line Battalion (Gotha, Coburg and Meiningen)

Brigade: Oberst Friedrich von Chambaud (Anhalt)
  5th Rheinbund Regt
    1st Battalion (Anhalt)
    2nd Battalion (Lippe)
  6th Rheinbund Regt
    1st Battalion (the two Schwarzburgs)
    2nd Battalion (Reuss and Waldeck)

he reached Barcelona to assume garrison duties. Almost immediately, however, the 1st Nassau Regiment (1,600) and elements of the 4th Rheinbund (600) were sent off on an expedition to Manresa under French GB François Schwarz. Although they reached the town with little difficulty, the Germans soon found themselves surrounded by Spanish insurgents and cut off from all succour. Several days of incessant skirmishing exhausted the force's food and ammunition supplies, leaving Schwarz with no option but to abandon his vehicles and retreat across wild mountain tracks under constant harassment from the guerrillas. Schwarz and his men finally regained Barcelona on 5 April having lost 929 men from an initial strength of 2,200. Furthermore, an additional 140 of the division's men, Anhalters from the 1st Battalion, 5th Rheinbund, had been lost when guerrillas ambushed and destroyed a relief column en route to Manresa.[61]

After the Manresa fiasco, the Nassauers remained in Barcelona to recuperate while their comrades moved north to assume garrison duties in Gerona and other parts of the province.[62] Despite reinforcements from Germany, the division's strength was steadily diminished by sickness and encounters with the guerrillas. In a particularly spectacular disaster, the 5th and 6th Regiments, guarding the coast near La Bisbal in September 1810, were virtually annihilated by a brilliantly executed Anglo-Spanish raid that cost the two weakened regiments over 1,100 casualties.[63] Eviscerated by disease and battle losses, the grateful 'division' finally departed Catalonia in January 1811. The 1st Nassau, left behind in Barcelona, slowly rebuilt itself with replacements and convalescents, but the other three regiments, who had crossed the Pyrenees with over 3,000 men under arms, could barely muster 500 dispirited effectives when they returned to Perpignan.

The Nassauers continued to serve the French with distinction, accepting warm praise (and the most difficult assignments) from the French governor, GD Maurice Mathieu.[64] Thanks to considerable reinforcement, the regiment maintained its combat effectiveness throughout its sojourn in Catalonia and numbered 1,748 when finally disarmed at Barcelona in December 1813. Nassau, however, could focus all its efforts on Spain, it had no troops in other theatres. The manpower reserves of the Grand Duchy of Würzburg, on the other hand, were repeatedly drained to support the invasion of Russia and then the post-catastrophe reconstruction of the Grande Armée. As a result, the Würzburg Battalion in Catalonia received few replacements and only counted 280 men on its rolls when it laid down its arms. As with the Westphalian Chevauxlegers and Nassau Jäger, there were numerous expressions of loyalty to the French cause and Napoleon. Voltigeur Lanz of the 1st Nassau wanted only to stay with the French 18th Léger. Similarly, Oberst Friedrich Meder, the regimental commander, refused British offers to defect and cast his lot with the French; curiously, although the British delivered a letter from Oberst von Kruse urging him to change sides, Meder never received instructions from his sovereign and thus decided to ignore Kruse's plea.[65] Entering French service, he was killed near Barcelona in February 1814 and posthumously promoted to Général de Brigade.

Like Rouyer's men, the Berg Lancer Regiment arrived in Spain after its brief participation in the war against Austria. This, however, was the second time Berg troopers had ridden into Iberia. In the spring of 1808, when Murat, then Grand Duke of Berg, went to assume his duties as Napoleon's 'Lieutenant in Spain', he took with him two squadrons of his duchy's cavalry regiment. Then known as Chevauxlegers and clad in pale-yellow uniforms with rose trim (in accordance with Murat's rather garish tastes), they left that summer when their grand duke went off to assume the throne of Naples.[66] They returned in June 1810 dressed in handsome dark green, armed with lances and 700 strong (another 85 in hospital).[67] Based in Burgos and (after June 1812) in Vittoria, the regiment served with the Guard cavalry of the Army of the North for the next three years, participating in innumerable small actions against the Spanish insurgents. Under Oberst von Goltstein ('an incomparable man, full of zeal and devotion' in the words of the provincial governor, GD Jean Dorsenne), they earned a fine reputation for their 'outstanding courage', tactical skill and ability with their difficult weapon. 'The cavalry under Count Goltstein performed marvels', wrote GD François Roguet after an engagement in August 1810.[68] The regiment fought at Fuentes de Oñoro and participated in the September 1811 combats around Ciudad Rodrigo as part of Marmont's command.[69] With detachments totalling some 500 men returning to Berg the following year to form the basis for a new cavalry regiment, the regiment was drastically reduced in size, a situation exacerbated by endless, exhausting expeditions in small detachments which badly eroded the unit's strength (particularly in horses). Nonetheless, though left with little more than 100 men scattered in several garrisons, the remnant in Spain remained active, playing an important role in the discomfiture of Anson's Brigade at Villadrigo in October 1812. Its renown intact, the last elements of the regiment (105 troopers) thankfully departed Spain in March 1813.[70]

Although they were not Rheinbund troops, two other German units deserve mention: the Légion Hanovrienne and the Régiment de Westphalie. Originally organised in 1803, the Hanoverian Legion included a 'light' infantry regiment dressed in red and a regiment of Chasseurs-à-Cheval with a green uniform very similar to that of their French counterparts. Part of the Legion's infantry, a battalion about 800 strong, entered Spain for the first time in October 1807 as part of GD Jean-Pierre Travot's 3rd Division in GD Jean Andoche Junot's 1er Corps d'Observation de la Gironde. It took part in the dreadful march to Portugal but was assigned to garrison Santarem and thus missed the major engagements against the British expeditionary force. Evacuated with the rest of Junot's troops, the battalion (450 men) returned to the Peninsula in late December 1808 under the regimental commander, Colonel Charles Striffler, as part of GD Etienne Heudelet's Division in Junot's VIII Corps.[71] The division was almost immediately transferred to Marshal Jean-de-Dieu Soult's II Corps, however, and the Hanoverians, now down to 242 officers and men under arms (15 January 1809), found themselves chasing Sir John Moore's army through the cruel Spanish winter to Corunna. After Corunna, the battalion took part in Soult's fruitless foray into Portugal but was badly diminished by desertion.

In December 1809, a second battalion was dispatched to Iberia with GD Louis Loison's newly formed 1st Reserve Division of the Army of Spain. Tidying up his order of battle, however, Napoleon placed both battalions under Loison in January 1810, and assigned the division to Marshal Ney's VI Corps for Marshal André Massena's invasion of Portugal.[72] The Hanoverians augmented the artillery during the sieges of Ciudad Rodrigo and Almeida, performing arduous manual labour in return for small but valued compensations: 'we received a 30 sous daily supplement which was paid out to us punctually each day, in addition a glass of wine and, with breakfast, a glass of good brandy'.[73] The French, however, complained about their poor morale and high desertion rate.[74] The Legion infantry subsequently fought at Busaco (losing 217 dead and wounded) and Fuentes de Oñoro.[75] In the latter struggle, they formed part of the force that stormed the village of Fuentes on the first day and, according to Jean-Baptiste Marbot, suffered severely from the fire of French troops who were confused by the Hanoverians' red coats.[76] Fuentes was the regiment's last battle. Always prone to desertion, the entire Legion was disbanded in August 1811 and its veterans redistributed to the new 127th, 128th, and 129th Régiments de Ligne as well as the 3rd Berg Infantry and the Régiment de Prusse.[77]

Unlike the infantry component, the Legion's two-squadron cavalry regiment (770 strong) did not arrive in the Peninsula until the autumn of 1808. Initially assigned to I Corps, by December the chasseurs had been transferred to II Corps and participated in the Corunna campaign and Marshal Soult's unfortunate invasion of Portugal under GD Jean Francheschi-Delonne's command.[78] The following year, still with II Corps, they suffered a second gruelling campaign in Portugal, this time in GB Pierre Soult's Cavalry Division (345 strong on 15 September 1810).[79] When the Legion was broken up in 1811, the troopers went to fill the ranks of the 1st Hussars and 9th Lancers. The regiment's commander for most of its existence was Colonel Charles Joseph Evers, a Belgian who had served in French light horse units from 1792 to 1803 when he was named to command the Hanoverians. Evers returned to France in April 1810 owing to poor health, but was promoted to général de brigade in March 1812 and served briefly in the Russian campaign before being captured in Königsberg in January 1813.[80]

The Régiment de Westphalie was another short-lived unit. In December 1806, Napoleon authorised Hereditary Prince Carl von Hohenzollern-Sigmaringen to raise a light infantry regiment of four battalions organised after the French pattern and paid from the French treasury.[81] Recruitment in north-central Germany, however, proceeded slowly and in October 1807 the 3rd and 4th battalions were merged into the 1st and 2nd to produce enough men for one field battalion. The over-strength 1st Battalion duly marched off for Bayonne in the latter part of the year while the 2nd remained behind in northern France as a depot. Entering Spain in February 1808 with 1,078 men, the battalion participated in the occupation of Spain as part of GD Louis Musnier's 1st Division in Marshal Bon Adrien Moncey's Corps d'Observation des Côtes de l'Océan.[82] Prince Carl, dissatisfied with an employment that left him 'no longer at the side of the greatest man in the world', soon went off to join Murat's staff in Madrid, leaving the battalion's senior officer, Chef de Bataillon Schenk, in command.[83] Schenk thus led the battalion during Marshal Moncey's expedition to Valencia (June to July 1808) and was among those wounded in the abortive storm of the city on 28 June. The battalion spent most of its remaining existence on wearing garrison duty in north-central Spain, and, by late October, when Hereditary Prince Friedrich von Hohenzollern-Hechingen assumed command, its strength had fallen to 572 men. In January 1809, the 1st Battalion was redesignated as the 'Bataillon de Westphalie' (which causes considerable confusion between this formation and the remnants of Morio's Westphalian Division), but remained in French service as an independent unit while the 2nd Battalion returned to Westphalia to be incorporated into King Jerome's army. Napoleon encountered the Bataillon de Westphalie in Valladolid that month and, disturbed by the poor state of its clothing and equipment, ordered that it be provided with 400 complete new uniforms.[84] Perhaps

1. Carlos IV (1748-1819), King of Spain. Dominated by his wife, the 'toothless and incontestably ugly' Maria-Luisa, and her lover, Manuel Godoy, it was Carlos' feud with his son, Ferdinand VII, that led to Napoleon's intervention and, ultimately, the outbreak of the war in Spain.

2. Ferdinand VII (1784-1833), Prince of the Asturias. Napoleon, whose support Ferdinand had sought, tired of the bickering between Carlos and his weak and hapless son, had the latter sent under Guard to the Château of Valençay, where he was to remain until 1814.

3. Joseph Bonaparte (1768-1844), King of Spain. Never happy in his appointment, Joseph nevertheless proved a benevolent if reluctant ruler of Spain. He was no great military commander and was recalled to France after his crushing defeat at Vittoria on 21 June 1813.

4. Sir Arthur Wellesley (1769-1852), 1st Duke of Wellington. The dominant figure of the Peninsular War, Wellington commanded the Anglo-Portuguese army throughout the war, save for a brief spell when he returned to England for the inquiry into the Convention of Cintra.

5. Sir John Moore (1761-1809). Commanded the British army in the Peninsula during its ill-fated Corunna campaign in the winter of 1808-9. He was mortally wounded at the battle of Corunna on 16 January 1809, the British victory which enabled the army to escape the clutches of the pursuing French and return to England.

6. André Massena, Prince of Essling (1758-1817). Commanded the Army of Portugal and was Wellington's most dogged opponent. His failure before the Lines of Torres Vedras, his subsequent costly retreat and his defeat at Fuentes de Oñoro led to his recall by Napoleon in 1811.

7. Marshal Nicolas Soult, Duke of Dalmatia (1769-1851). Generally recognised as a good organiser of troops rather than a brilliant battlefield commander, Soult led the pursuit of Moore during the Corunna campaign. Expelled from Portugal by Wellesley in 1809, he was recalled and subsequently served in Germany. He returned to the Peninsula in 1812 and, following the French disaster at Vittoria in 1813, was made Commander-in Chief in Spain, a post he held until the end of the war in April 1814.

8. The role of the Spanish guerrillas in the Peninsula was later acknowledged by Wellington to have been one of the main factors in the Allied victory over the French. Here, General Franceschi-Delonne is ambushed and taken by 'El Capuchino' and his men near Toro in May 1809. He died of fever whilst in captivity in 1810.

9. 'Assassination'. The French laboured under a great disadvantage with every hill and rock seemingly concealing a guerrilla. It was fatal to wander too far from camp, straggle on the march or fall asleep on piquet duty, whilst despatches sent to France travelled under strong cavalry escorts in order to ensure their safe delivery.

10. Berg Infantry Officer, probably 2nd Regiment. A good illustration of a standard infantry officer in field dress during the Peninsular War. This junior officer has adapted to the exigencies of campaigning in Spain by acquiring brown trousers, a haversack and a walking stick. In addition, German officers in Spain seem to have favoured pistols carried in large holsters slung over the shoulder.

11. Nassau Infantryman, 1810. Nassau's soldiers regularly earned praise for their appearance and good discipline as well as their tactical competence.

13. Baden Artillery Officer and Gunner, 1810-13. These figures provide a good contrast to the infantrymen, showing the gunner with covered shako and haversack and the officer's bicorne. Note also the officer's pistol holster.

12. Berg Infantryman, 1809. This illustration shows one of Baden's infantry soldiers early in the campaign. He still wears the large, heavy 'Raupenhelm' (crested helmet), but has procured trousers of Spanish brown cloth. Although the helmet was later replaced by a shako this uniform remained essentially unchanged for the duration of the war.

14. 'Campagne en Espagne, 1809.' French infantry in action in a smoke-filled house in Spain.

15. A lancer and infantryman of the Polish Vistula Legion which served in the Peninsula from 1808 until 1814. Their greatest exploits were the charge at Somosierra in November 1808 and the destruction of Colborne's brigade at the battle of Albuera in May 1811.

16. The Fusilier Brigade advances in line at the battle of Albuera, 16 May 1811. One of the great episodes of the war, the Fusiliers' charge turned the tide of battle in favour of the Allies.

17. The 5th (Northumberland) Fusiliers demonstrating that infantry, even in line, were capable of attacking cavalry. This painting by Simkin shows the 5th engaging in such an attack at El Bodon on 25 September 1811. The 5th won the distinction of wearing white plumes in their caps following an action against the French at St Lucia in 1778.

18. 'A British Soldier taking two French officers at the Battle of the Pyrenees.'

19. The Tower of Belem, Lisbon. French prisoners were housed here prior to being transferred to England.

20. Portchester Castle. Many French prisoners, captured in the Peninsula and elsewhere, were kept here. The castle and its prisoners are the subject of a set of paintings by Captain Durrant, a British officer who served at Portchester during the Napoleonic Wars.

21. Fraternisation in the Peninsula. British light dragoons exchange news and views with French cavalry at the outposts. Such exchanges were commonplace in the Peninsula.

22. French infantry under fire from British Royal Horse Artillery. Note the baggy, striped trousers worn by the man on the right and by the man falling back in the centre.

this recent experience with the battalion led him to accede when the Prince requested permission to form a new 2nd Battalion in March 1809. Napoleon insisted, however, that the battalion retain its German character and refused to allow recruiting among prisoners of war of other nationalities.[85] In the event, these plans for expansion came to naught and an order disbanding the entire organisation was issued in March 1810: in September, its active members were absorbed into the infantry of the Hanoverian Legion and whatever new recruits the Prince had been able to collect were drafted into Westphalian service.[86]

Finally, it remains to account for the least known of those Rheinbund soldiers who served in the Peninsula: several detachments of train troops from Würzburg, Bavaria and (possibly) Saxony. In early July 1809, near the end of the war against Austria, General Junot picked up some twenty-five Würzburg train troops as he passed through their capital en route to his embarrassing defeat at Gefrees. As might be expected, the Würzburgers stayed with Junot for the remainder of the Austrian war and were still under his command (now designated VIII Corps) in October when the peace treaty was signed. Linked to Junot's small contingent of Berg troops, the Würzburgers, through a series of misunderstandings, were dragged off to Spain and Portugal in November with the rest of VIII Corps. There they remained until 1811, when a meagre eight of the original detachment finally returned to their home fires.[87]

The case of the Bavarians is slightly different. In 1808, the French demanded 150 Bavarians for use as replacements in French train battalions. After some negotiating, some deserting and some returning of deserters, about sixty six Bavarians duly joined the 3rd Train Battalion and went off with it to the Pyrenees. They continued to serve in the ranks of this French unit through 1814 (even after the other German troops had been disarmed), and a fortunate twenty seven of them finally made their way back to Bavaria. There are hints that 100 Saxons might have shared this fate but the details of their odyssey are unknown.[88]

In reviewing the participation of the Rheinbund troops in Iberia,

---

SAMPLE STRENGTHS AND CASUALTIES

	Autumn 1808	Repls	Cadres	December 1813	Losses
Frankfurt Battalion	853	500	300	284/71	800
Würzburg Regt	1,717	258	52	280	1,645

Note: 'Cadres' refers to troops sent back to Germany to help construct new units.

several general points are worthy of consideration. First, although their overall numbers were usually small, their presence was often crucial, particularly in 1809 when they played important roles in many of the large struggles in central Spain and provided about one third of the besieging forces at Gerona. Second, although some were weak or unreliable, many of the German units performed very well in the Peninsula, earning the respect and trust of their French allies. As Victor said of Leval's Division: '[it] has shown ardour and courage to which I cannot pay adequate tribute. Its officers and men are worthy to be allies of France'.[89] Even in the prevailing wretchedness of the siege of Gerona, the troops committed to the two assaults did all that could be expected of soldiers and Verdier's sniping comment that 'the troops cannot be trusted' seems a shallow attempt to excuse his own failings.[90] Third, as with France itself, the Spanish war was for the Rheinbund a frightful experience that not only decimated solid military units which could have been employed elsewhere, but also accentuated the bitter resentment which many Germans were beginning to develop toward the alliance with Napoleon. War against Prussia or Austria might be explicable and the troops could be expected to come home with their honour and most of their lives intact, but the Iberian experience was one of unrelenting misery, spilling German blood to no apparent purpose. Small wonder then, that the Reuss troops of the Bataillon des Princes were stricken with dismay when the newspapers announced that their countrymen in Rouyer's Division were headed for the Pyrenees.[91]

Notes

1 The present chapter is based on an article published in Issue 17 of *The Age of Napoleon* and a talk given to the Napoleonic Association in November 1994. The author gratefully acknowledges the courtesy and gracious assistance of Mr Richard Partridge and Mr Paul Chamberlain for (respectively) permitting use of the article and arranging the talk. I would also thank the following institutions for their kind and prompt assistance: Militärgeschichtliches Forschungsamt, Badische Landesbibliothek, Universitäts- und Landesbibliothek Düsseldorf, Hessische Landes- und Hochschulbibliothek, Universitäts- und Landesbibliothek Münster, Niedersächsisches Landesbibliothek.

2 This number is an approximate total for the *original* strengths of the units committed to the Iberian Peninsula and does not include the thousands sent as replacements; if the poorly recorded replacements were added, the total would nearly double.

3 Other units sometimes served as part of the division. As one example, a battalion of the Garde de Paris was included in its order of battle for part of 1809. In addition, the Westphalian Chevauxlegers and Nassau Reitende Jäger were occasionally assigned to the division.

4   The histories of the Baden and Hessian artillery detachments (a battery of eight pieces and a half-battery of four respectively) are especially complex and too detailed to recount here. It is interesting to note, however, that the two contingents were often treated as a combined unit (with Hessians serving Baden pieces, for example). See Fritz Beck, Karl von Hahn and Heinrich von Hahn, *Geschichte des Grossherzoglich Artilleriekorps*, Berlin, 1912, pp. 142ff.

5   August Keim, *Geschichte des 4. Grossherzoglich Hessischen Infanterie-Regiments (Prinz Karl) Nr. 118 und seiner Stämme*, Berlin, 1879, pp. 135–8.

6   The facings of the 3rd Regiment were finally standardised in 1810; it seems likely the same applied to the 4th Regiment in Spain.

7   Four pieces from the Baden artillery battery were detached to Marshal Ney's corps from October to December 1808.

8   See Grolman's pithy, insightful and entertaining memoirs ('Aus dem Tagebuche eines deutschen Offiziers über seinen Feldzug in Spanien 1808') in Friedrich M. Kircheisen, ed., *Memoiren aus dem spanischen Freiheitskampfe 1808–1811*, Hamburg, 1908.

9   Keim, p. 138.

10   Grolman, p. 40.

11   See Camille Sauzey, *Les Allemands sous les Aigles Françaises*, Paris, 1987–8, VI, pp. 160–63. Napoleon to Ludwig X, 15 January 1809, *Correspondence*, no. 14,719.

12   Beck/Hahn, p. 145.

13   Grolman, p. 81; Sauzey,. I, p. 24.

14   They also made an organisational change, collecting the voltigeur companies of the Baden, Hessian and Nassau regiments to form a combined voltigeur battalion under Grolman, an innovation that was maintained through at least the battle of Talavera (Grolman, p. 95).

15   Wilhelm Isenbart, *Geschichte des 2. Nassauischen Infanterie-Regiments Nr. 88*, Berlin, 1903, p. 50.

16   Sauzey, I, pp. 28–29;. VI, pp. 174–8.

17   During a royal review, General Jean Dessolles declaimed to King Joseph; 'Sire! Here is Colonel Kruse who commanded the moving citadel on the plains of Medellin!' (Isenbart, p. 53). For Hesse, see, Keim, p. 146. The presence of two General Schäffers (one Nassau, one Hessian), both brigade commanders, provides innumerable opportunities for confusion.

18   Victor cited in Sauzey, VI, pp. 177–82. Albert de Rocca, *In the Peninsula with a French Hussar*, London, 1990, pp. 77–83.

19   Quote and Badener's recollections from Sabina Hermes and Joachim Niemeyer, *Unter dem Greifen*, Rastatt, 1984, p. 57.

20   Grolman, p. 80.

21   Porbeck quotes in Paul Sauer, *Napoleons Adler über Württemberg, Baden und Hohenzollern*, Stuttgart, 1987, pp. 257–8.

22   They gratefully received new uniforms in the autumn of 1810. Beck/Hahn, p. 146.

23   Cited in Sauzey, II, p. 118.

24   According to Franz Rigel, an officer in the Baden 4th Infantry, the German Division advanced in the following fashion: Dutch and Badeners in the centre deployed in line, the Hessian and Frankfurt battalions on the left and the Nassau Regiment on the right, all in squares, 10 guns in the intervals, and the combined voltigeur battalion deployed across the front; owing to the difficult terrain, the Nassauers deployed into line as they

approached the British line (Franz Xavier Rigel, *Der siebenjährige Kampf auf der Pyrenäischen Halbinsel*, Rastatt, 1819, II, p. 301). Note that only the 2nd Battalion of the Hessian Regiment was present for the battle, the 1st was detached in Segovia.

25 Von Porbeck had been appointed the regiment's 'Inhaber' (patron) at the beginning of July; General-Major Karl von Neuenstein become the new Inhaber in October 1809.

26 In Sauzey, II, pp. 118–19 and VI, pp. 190–1.

27 Mortier's report to Napoleon in Sauzey, I, p. 38.

28 Rocca, p. 83.

29 In less than perfect health, Von Schäffer had previously requested permission to return to Germany, but had been asked to stay on to care for his old regiment. He finally went home in mid-1810. Keim, p. 177.

30 The thirty nine artillerymen left their guns behind in a depot and were distributed among the fortresses' pieces individually, often as gun commanders. Beck/Hahn, pp. 155–6.

31 A small controversy surrounds the performance of the Hessians at Badajoz with some French blaming their allies for the fall of the fortress. See Keim, p. 209ff. for a thorough review and rebuttal of these insinuations.

32 Keim, pp. 225–8, Beck/Hahn, pp. 155–9. See also August Schaumann, a commissary with the KGL, who met a number Hessian officers in Lisbon (*On the Road with Wellington*, New York, 1925, p. 349; with thanks to Major Bob Burnham, USA (retd), who helped me locate this recondite source). Figures from Sauzey, VI, pp. 221–33.

33 Rückert's diary in Friedrich von Weech, *Badische Truppen in Spanien 1810–1813*, Karlsruhe, 1892, pp. 40–1.

34 Oman gives German losses at Vittoria as 620 (including ten from the Nassau cavalry); the Nassau Regiment lost another 76–80 at Yrurzun during the retreat. See Oman, Runkel and Sauzey.

35 During the reorganisation, GM Neuenstein and the 2nd Battalion (cadre strength) of the Baden Regiment returned home; similarly, Major Vogt led cadres of three companies of the Frankfurt Battalion back to Germany. Strengths as of 1 August 1813 after these departures (present under arms/hospital): 2nd Nassau Regiment (1,035/402), Baden 1st Battalion (564/69), Frankfurt Battalion (three companies with 310/57). From Sauzey, I, p. 65; II, p. 147; VI, p. 243.

36 Kruse, who led the Nassau troops in the Waterloo campaign, was also serving as the brigade commander, replacing von Neuenstein. Strengths as of 10 December 1813 (present under arms/hospital): 2nd Nassau Regiment (1,016/282), Baden Battalion (483/26), Frankfurt Battalion (284/71), Baden artillery and train (155/20). Note that the Baden artillery and train troops were with Darmagnac's Division. From Sauzey, VI, p. 251.

37 Details of this curious incident vary. Using good sources, Sauzey writes that the Badeners refused to defect until they had specific directions from their grand duke (instructions to this effect had been sent, but never reached the battalion, Sauer, p. 259); this interpretation is also found in Hermes/Niemeyer. Moreover, this version is in accord with the reminiscences of Francis Larpent, who met with Kruse and other German officers immediately after their defection (*The Private Journal of F. S. Larpent*, London, 1853, pp. 191–201). Oman, however, whose list of sources includes Sauzey, says that Henning was the only Baden officer aware of the conspiracy and that he was absent on the day of the defection

(owing to a wound) with the result that the Baden troops stayed with the French while their colleagues marched away (Oman, VI). For Nassau, see Isenbart, pp. 120ff.

38 Fritz Lünsmann (*Die Armee des Königreichs Westfalen*, Berlin, 1935, p. 281) gives the regiment a strength of 390 when it arrived in Spain, but unit strength reports dated 15 November 1808 list over 400 (in Balagny, III).

39 This quote from Thiébault is only one of many instances where he praises the Nassau troops (see his *Memoirs*, Felling, 1994, II, pp. 245–74).

40 The two squadrons, under Major von Oberkampf, reached Gerona on 19 November, when disarmed a month later, they were 243 strong. Information on the Nassau cavalry from Philip von Rössler, *Die Geschichte der Herzoglich Nassauischen Truppe*, Wiesbaden, 1863, pp. 48–55 and Sauzey, VI.

41 Details from Suchet's 21 December 1813 Order of the Day (in Alfred Roessler, *Geschichte des Königlich Preussischen 1. Nassauischen Infanterie-Regiments Nr. 87*, Berlin, 1882, pp. 98–9) and report to Clarke, 26 December 1813, in Sauzey, VI, pp. 278–81. See also Suchet's *Memoirs of the War in Spain*, Felling, 1986, II, pp. 358–9.

42 Napoleon to Jerome, 11 February 1809 (*New Letters of Napoleon I*, Lady Mary Loyd, trans., New York, 1897, p. 117). In late 1811, Jerome proposed Morio to command the Westphalian Corps destined for the Russian campaign; this gaffe led Napoleon to comment that Morio was 'utterly incapable of commanding your corps' (to Jerome, 17 December 1811, *Correspondence*, no. 18,341).

43 The division reported a strength of 7,572 in march 1809 en route to Spain ('Etat de Situation des Troupes Westphaliennes', Archives de la Guerre, Armée d'Allemagne, C2/509).

44 Between Westphalia and Metz, the 2nd Infantry lost thirteen deserters, the 4th fifty six (unit reports for March 1809 in Archives de la Guerre, Armée d'Allemagne, C2/520; 1st Light Battalion did not report any desertion; there is no report for the 3rd Infantry).

45 Berg infantry strengths are from 1 April 1809 situation report in Archives de la Guerre, C8/362; an additional 116 and 101 men were listed in hospital for the 1st and 2nd Regiments respectively. These files also contain almost the only available information on the Berg artillery troops who fought in Spain. The strength of the artillery detachment fluctuated between twenty and fifty. Information kindly provided by Dr John Morgan, University of Alabama, from his extensive research into French operations in Catalonia.

46 Although the battalion commander's memoirs paint a very rosy picture of his abilities and his unit's accomplishments, letters written by Georg Barkhausen, one of the company commanders, offer a dramatically different record of persons and events. See August von Brokenburg (the battalion commander), 'Erinnerungen aus den Jahren 1808 bis 1811', *Beliage z. Schwarzb.-Rudolstädtischen Landeszeitung*, September 1906; and George Barkhausen, *Tagebuch eines Rheinbund-Offiziers*, Wiesbaden, 1900.

47 For this odd battalion, see Fiebig, 'Das Bataillon des Princes', *Zeitschift für Heeres- und Uniformkunde*, Heft 61/63, 1934; and Wilhelm Oesterhaus, *Geschichte der Fürstlich Lippischen Truppen in den Jahren 1807–1815*, Detmold, 1907.

48 P. Zimmermann, *Erinnerungen aus den Feldzügen der bergischen Truppen in Spanien und Russland*, Düsseldorf, 1842, p. 35.

49 Franz Morgenstern, *Kriegserinnerungen*, H. Meier, ed., Wolfenbuettel, 1912, pp. 21, 23.

50 Meier, p. 26; Joseph Schuster, *Das Grossherzoglich Würzburgische Infanterie-Regiment in Spanien 1808–1813*, Munich, 1909, p. 8.
51 Quoted in W. Neff, *Geschichte des Infanterie-Regiments von Goeben*, Berlin, 1890, p. 9.
52 Figures for June to September are from Oman; Berg losses from Neff, p. 9.
53 Berg figures from 1 January 1810 situation report (Archives de la Guerre, C8/362) provided by Dr Morgan.
54 The biography of Westphalian GB Adam von Ochs (based on his diaries) comments 'After the significant losses in assault on Montjuich, the Westphalian Division began to lose its cohesion' (Leopold von Hohenhausen, *Biographie des Generals von Ochs*, Cassel, 1827, pp. 185, 196).
55 Berg battalion's August strength from a 1 August 1811 situation report (Archives de la Guerre, C8/370) provided by Dr Morgan. Other data from Zimmermann.
56 Hellrung, 'Die Organisation der Westphälischen Armee', *Minerva*, December 1840. For the Berg troops, see especially Zimmermann, pp. 53ff.
57 Departing Germany in November 1809 after the war with Austria, the 3rd Infantry had spent several years on garrison duty along France's channel coast. Gradually wasting away, the 1st Battalion gave up most of its men to the 2nd in July 1811 and returned to Berg in cadre strength. The 2nd Battalion remained on the French coast until March 1812, when it was shipped to Bordeaux; it marched into Spain near Puigcerda on 12 June 1812 under the regimental commander, Major Moers (assigned to GB Jean Beuermann's Brigade). Looping through France, it marched into Catalonia in August and spent several months visiting the battlefields its German comrades had fought over (Gerona, Barcelona, Manresa) before recrossing the Pyrenees in February (P. Zimmermann, *Erinnerungen aus den Feldzügen der bergischen Truppen in Spanien und Russland*, Düsseldorf, 1840, pp. 49–52).
58 For the Westphalian, Würzburg and Berg contingents, see: Lünsmann, Schuster, Zimmermann and Karl Schröder, *Zwischen Französischer Revolution und Preussens Gloria*, Eitorf, 1989; as well as the memoirs and regimental histories listed above.
59 The Rheinbund numeration of Nassau and Würzburg regiments is a matter of some confusion. According to Napoleon's *Correspondence* (eg, 14793, 21 February 1809), the 2nd Nassau (formed first) was the 1st Rheinbund and the 1st Nassau (formed later) the 2nd Rheinbund, while the Würzburg Regiment was to be designated the 3rd Rheinbund. Some sources, however, make the Würzburg formation the 1st Rheinbund Regiment and allot the numbers 2 and 3 to the Nassau units. Although I am convinced the *Correspondence* version is accurate, for the purposes of this piece, I have used the national rather than Rheinbund designations to minimize confusion.
60 L. von Seebach, *Geschichte der Feldzüge*, Weimar, 1838, p. 274.
61 Sauzey gives a detailed account of the expedition (see VI).
62 Note that Nassau's units also included the tiny contingents from Hohenzollern-Hechingen, Hohenzollern-Sigmaringen and Isenburg. They were completely integrated into the regiments and wore the same uniforms as the Nassau natives. By a contract arrangement, Nassau provided troops on behalf of Aremburg, Liechtenstein, Hohengeroldseck, and the two Salm principalities (that is, instead of providing soldiers, these princes paid subsidies to Nassau).
63 This catastrophe figures prominently in the accounts of Lippe participants as

well as the histories of the Anhalt Battalion: see Klessmann and Barkhausen. At the time, the thin brigade was under the command of GB Schwarz, the same officer who had led the Manresa expedition.

64 Roessler, pp. 72, 77, 94.

65 Roessler, p. 95.

66 Only one squadron accompanied Murat into Spain, the other remained behind (partly unmounted) in Bayonne. The men of these two squadrons were sent in three directions when Murat moved to Naples: most of the officers stayed with Murat and entered Neapolitan service, some men were incorporated into the Chasseurs-à-Cheval of the Guard, some men returned to Berg to form a new cavalry regiment.

67 In the interim, the regiment had been transformed from yellow-clad chevauxlegers to green chasseurs; they acquired their lances in Paris in the autumn of 1809 and received training in their use from the Polish Lancers of the Guard. Upon arriving in Spain, therefore, they were the 'Chevauxlegers-Lanciers de Berg' attached to the Guard cavalry. Strength from Armand von Ardenne, *Bergische Lanziers, Westfälische Husaren Nr. 11*, Berlin: Mittler & Sohn, 1877, p. 14.

68 Ardenne, pp. 19–22 (quotes on courage from GD François Roguet's reports of the regiment's performance in several actions during the late summer and autumn of 1810).

69 The strength of the regiment at Fuentes is not clear. Berg and Polish lancers marched together and numbered about 340 troopers (Oman, V), but existing accounts do not differentiate between the two nationalities.

70 Friedrich Herrmann, 'Bergische Reiter', *Zeitschrift für Heereskunde*, 287, 1980; and Zimmermann, pp. 94ff.

71 General information on the Hanoverian Legion derived from Dominique Balagny, *Campagne de l'Empereur Napoléon en Espagne*, Paris, 1902–6 (I, p. 42), Colonel John R. Elting (*Swords Around a Throne*, New York, 1988 and *Napoleonic Uniforms*, New York, 1993), Alphonse Grasset, *La Guerre d'Espagne*, Paris, 1914–32 (I, pp. 431–38) and Alain Pigeard, *L'Armée Napoléonienne*, Paris, 1993 (p. 454). Details of assignment, strength and losses from annexes in Balagny and Oman. With many thanks to John Elting for numerous recondite citations from *Ordres et Apostilles de Napoléon*, Arthur Chuquet, ed., Paris, 1911–12. Note that the infantry was authorized a standard and, apparently, an eagle (see Jean Regnault, *Les Aigles Impériales*, Paris, 1967, p. 31).

72 Relevant correspondence: Napoleon to Clarke, 28 November 1809; to Berthier, 15 December 1809, 11 January 1810, 31 January 1810, and 12 February 1810 (in *Correspondence*, nos. 16,027, 16,055, 16,131, 16,190, 16,245); also Napoleon to Clarke, 30 October 1809, in Napoleon I, *Unpublished Correspondence of Napoleon I Preserved in the War Archives*, Ernest Picard and Louis Tuetey, eds., New York, 1913, III, pp. 298–91.

73 Johann Mämpel quoted in Hermann Berdrow, ed., *Vor 1813*, Leipzig, 1933, p. 111.

74 D. D. Horward, *Napoleon and Iberia*, Tallahassee, 1984, p. 284 (Eble to Massena, 21 August 1810).

75 During the course of the campaign, the strength of the two infantry battalions diminished from approximately 1,150 (15 September 1810) to 722 (15 March 1811); figures from Oman.

76 Marbot, Jean Baptiste, Baron de, *The Memoirs of Baron de Marbot*, London, 1905, II, p. 463.

77 Grasset cites losses recorded in the unit's records as a clear indication of the desertion problem (I, p. 436); Oman points out that the KGL accepted over 160 deserters from the Legion during the first Portugal expedition alone.

78 Although they were transferred to GB César Debelle's Brigade in February 1809, the chasseurs were not with his command during the disastrous skirmish at Sahagun on 21 December 1808. The two French cavalry regiments in that engagement were the 8th Dragoons and the 1st Provisional (or Auxilliary) Chasseurs. Some of the French troopers may have been of German origin (as Captain Alexander Gordon of the 15th Hussars indicates), and the 8th Dragoons had recently come from Hanover, but they were not members of the Hanoverian Legion cavalry regiment (see Alexander Gordon, *A Cavalry Officer in the Corunna Campaign 1808–1809*, Felling, 1990, pp. 111, 115; see also the excellent description of this affray in Balagny, III, pp. 522–8, 695–6).

79 Strength figure from appendix in Jean Jacques Pelet, *The French Campaign in Portugal*, Donald D. Horward, ed., Minneapolis, 1973.

80 Georges Six, *Dictionnaire Biographique des Généraux & Amiraux de la Révolution et de l'Empire*, Paris, 1974, I, pp. 433–4.

81 As light infantry, the regiment's elite companies were carabiniers and voltigeurs (Major von Runkel, 'Zur Geschichte der Besatzung der Burg Hohenzollern und der Truppen der Fürsten von Hohenzollern', *Mittheilungen des Vereins für Geschichte und Altertumskunde in Hohenzollern*, 1899/1900, pp. 104–6). The regiment was authorized a standard, but Napoleon denied the Prince's petition for an eagle (Regnault, p. 107).

82 Balagny states that detachments from the battalion participated in Junot's invasion of Portugal (I, pp. 44–5).

83 Prince Carl's attitude and quote from Fritz Kallenberg, 'Die Fürstentümer Hohenzollern im Zeitalter der Französischen Revolution und Napoleons', *Zeitschrift für die Geschichte des Oberrheins*, III, 1963, p. 424.

84 Balagny, V, p.367. Nor did Napoleon forget: on 3 March 1809, he wrote to Berthier asking whether the battalion had been reclothed as directed (Napoleon I, *Lettres Inédités*, Léonce de Brotonne, ed., Paris, 1898, p. 173).

85 Decisions of 8 and 22 March 1809 in *War Archives*, II, pp. 760, 830.

86 Most of the information on the Régiment de Westphalie is taken from Runkel, pp. 103–11, and Pigeard, pp. 454, 479–80; supplemented by data from Balagny, Grasset, Foy (Maximilien Foy, *History of the War in the Peninsula*, Felling, 1989), Elting, and Martinien (A. Martinien, *Tableaux par Corps et par batailles des Officiers Tués et Blessés*, Paris, 1984). Pigeard implies that, although the order for disbandment was dated March 1810, the men were not actually merged into the Hanoverian Legion until September that year. Note that Runkel and others state that the battalion was dissolved in the autumn of 1809; Napoleon was still referring to it in January 1810 (to Berthier, *Correspondence*, no. 16,131, 11 January 1810).

87 Although Helmes says the number of Würzburgers was twenty two (Hermann Helmes, 'Die Würzburger Truppen vor Hundert Jahren', *Archiv des historischen Vereins für Unterfranken und Aschaffenburg*, 55, 1913), Junot's Chief of Staff, GB Pierre Boyer recorded the number as twenty six in the VIII Corps' report for 15 August 1809 and twenty five enlisted personnel in his 10 November 1809 itinerary for the march to Paris (Archives de la Guerre, Armée d'Allemagne, C2/508 and C2/520).

88 Rudolf von Xylander, *Geschichte des 1. Feldartillerie-Regiments*, Berlin, 1909, pp. 118–20.

89   Quoted in Sauzey, I.
90   Verdier's corps commander, GD Gouvion Saint-Cyr, was certainly of this
     opinion; he called his subordinate's assessment 'unjust'. Both cited in Oman's
     account of the siege.
91   Benno von Hagen, *Das Reussische Militär in den Kriegsjahren* 1806–15, Gera,
     1904, p. 12.

CHAPTER V

'Heroes or Villains' revisited: fresh thoughts on la guerrilla

Charles Esdaile

Some years ago the author of this paper published an article entitled 'The Spanish guerrillas: heroes or villains'.[1] Relatively short and written for a popular journal, it yet had a serious purpose, namely to point to the need for a major re-evaluation of the nature and effect of the guerrilla war that assailed the French in Spain between 1808 and 1814. In no sense intended as a definitive statement on the subject, the article nevertheless made a number of suggestions that have in certain circles proved controversial.[2] Whilst recognising the overall importance of the contribution made by the guerrillas to the war against Napoleon, it suggested that the *partidas* weakened the regular Spanish army by encouraging desertion, that their military capabilities were at best limited, that popular attitudes to the guerrilla struggle were extremely ambivalent, and that the latter was closely linked with social disorder and outright banditry. In view of the criticism and, in some cases, misunderstanding, that such arguments have provoked, together with the growing academic interest in the War of Independence, it would therefore be as well for the article to be revisited.

Before we go any further, however, it is worth noting that there is nothing especially controversial about questioning our assumptions about *la guerrilla*. On the contrary, even a cursory examination of the original sources suggests that the phenomenon was one which gave rise to much criticism, discussion and argument, there being in the first place a clear realisation in some quarters that it was futile to trust to the guerrillas for Spain's salvation. Let us take as an example a pamphlet that was published in Cadíz in 1810:

> As a method of waging war, popular insurrection is almost always
> . . . far more costly than the use of regular forces. When protected by
> a regular army, at the right moment the former can reinforce the latter,
> but otherwise the only result is momentary success avenged later with

great sacrifice . . . Is it still doubted that the kingdom is lost if we do not raise large armies? Let us suppose that Spain becomes the tomb of twenty thousand French soldiers every year . . . An annual draft of fifteen or twenty thousand men would be enough to put paid to such a plan. Napoleon has necessarily to subjugate Spain or lose his reputation . . . and, now that the north [i.e. Austria] is quiet . . . it would not be difficult for him to send . . . 100,000.

Nor was this an end to the argument:

It is held . . . that our arms cannot match those of the enemy when both sides are fighting in large forces. From here stems the foolish idea that instead of increasing our armies, we should rely solely on the use of *partidas* and the defence of towns [i.e. by the people-in-arms, as at Zaragosa in 1808–9] when the war that we are waging on the contrary demands large armies that are capable of imposing themselves on the enemy . . . It is true that Madrid was defended heroically by its own people, that La Mancha has devoured many Frenchmen without the aid of any troops, and that the enemy was expelled from Galicia by the peasantry alone. Nevertheless, Madrid is occupied by the enemy and La Mancha in reality controlled by them, whilst Galicia would also fall into their hands if there was not a large army to protect it. Little by little the French extend their dominions whilst we celebrate a riot in some village or an attack by some guerrilla band.[3]

Lest it be thought that these views are in some way infuenced by social or political prejudice, it should be noted that such doubts were also shared by many British observers. Thus:

There are points where it is of infinite consequence to the cause that there should be armies for, useful and important as the services of the guerrillas are, that is not enough, let them be ever so much spread over the face of the country. They can never stop the march of a considerable body of the enemy and protect a country as Blake has lately done in Murcia, and O'Donnell has so successfully done in Catalonia.[4]

So obvious is this point that it hardly seems worth expanding upon. Nevertheless, it would perhaps here be of value to reinforce it by a brief consideration of the course of the war. The fact is that until 1812 the Allies were losing the war in the Peninsula. Throughout occupied Spain the steadily growing numbers of guerrillas undoubtedly made themselves a considerable nuisance, a German officer who was stationed in Navarre remarking that the position of the invaders was akin to that of the fabled lion who was tortured to death by a flea.[5] Yet, for all that, there was no check to the tide of French expansion. With the Anglo-Portuguese army of the Duke of Wellington firmly bottled up in Portugal – and, indeed, for some months confined to the vicinity of Lisbon – from August 1809 to January 1812, there was nothing to stop the French from concentrating their considerable resources on Patriot Spain. Commencing in January 1810, the French occupied the whole of Andalucía (with the exception, of course, of the impregnable island-city of Cadíz) and Asturias, the whole of such territory as the Patriot forces still held in León and Extremadura, a large part of what was left to them in Catalonia, and the northern half of the Levante. Army after army was lost and with them fortress after fortress, in terms of regular warfare the Spanish cause being reduced to a state of complete prostration. To quote the commander of the battered regular army that clung to a precarious existence in the interior of Catalonia until the very end of the war:

> In the state in which Catalonia is currently to be found, every kind of assistance is necessary if the army is to take the offensive . . . Barely able to put 7,000 men into the field . . . and badly clothed and supplied, it has been able to protect only the most remote parts of the country from the enemy, and even then only with the greatest difficulty, whilst it has had to leave all the most wealthy and productive parts of the country in their hands. Confined to this system since the fall of Tarragona . . . we have lost all the resources and young men of those districts, the French having shut them up behind a . . . field force far superior to anything that we can oppose to it . . .[6]

With the French on the offensive in this fashion, continue to fight and to grow in numbers though the guerrillas did, they could do little to delay the process of disaster – a desperate attempt by Joaquin Blake to make use of them to slow down the invasion of Valencia in the autumn of 1811 achieved no success whatsoever – whilst they may even have accelerated it. We here return to one of the more controversial claims of 'Heroes or villains', but in fact nothing has emerged in recent years to contradict the arguments which it advanced in this respect – above all that they undermined the regular army, the only force with any hope of stopping the French – by encouraging desertion. The reasons for such desertion were simple: as one Spanish officer put it, they offered 'more freedom and less discipline'.[7]

But touched on in 'Heroes or villains', the question of desertion may be gone into in somewhat greater depth. In the first place, we now have considerable evidence that the hostility to conscription that was so rampant in the Spain of the *antiguo regimen* continued unabated into the War of Independence. In Galicia, for example, young men rushed to get married so as to avoid the *sorteo*; in Asturias so great was the number of those who fled, that in April 1810 the provincial *junta* had to order that a close watch be set on the passes through the Cantabrian mountains; and in Jaén not only was there frantic competition to secure places in one of the various 'home-guard' units raised to defend the capital, but the province as a whole was plagued for the entire period that it remained in Patriot hands by bands of young men who, having fled conscription, had had no option but to turn to banditry in order to survive.[8] Forced into the ranks by methods of conscription that were generally characterised by a greater or lesser degree of corruption and injustice, the soldiery soon found that life in the army had little to recommend it. Not only were food, clothing and pay all in short supply, but disease was rampant and defeat incessant, not to mention generally very bloody. By contrast, the guerrillas, whose supposed achievements the Patriot press was making ever more widely known, offered multiple advantages, including freer discipline, a better chance of survival, greater rewards – not for nothing were the *partidas*, again as argued by 'Heroes or villains', associated with pillage – and, perhaps above all, the chance to remain in the *patria chica*. With desertion easy – the average Spanish soldier was for much of the war dressed in a manner that differed little from the peasantry, whilst discipline on the march and in camp was notoriously lax – the guerrillas therefore deprived the regular army of the services of thousands of veteran soldiers. To quote just two examples of such cases, we have Josep Bosoms, a Catalan infantryman turned bandit who escaped from jail to become a guerrilla, and José Fombella, an Asturian cavalryman who established himself at the head of a group of fellow deserters in the Cantabrian mountains.[9] Nor were such cases isolated, every defeat seeing hundreds of men scattering into the hills to join existing bands or form new ones of their own, as, for example, occurred in Jaén following the French occupation of January 1810.[10]

Given that the regular armies had by reason of this constant haemorrhage to fill their ranks with ever larger numbers of miserable conscripts, and thereby to dilute their quality still further, there seems little reason to modify the argument advanced in 'Heroes or villains': like it or not, the guerrillas most certainly undermined the Spanish army in both quantity and quality in the period 1809–12. Nor can it be pretended that the guerrillas could successfuly take their place, for, if they could not protect territory against the advance of the French armies, they could not win it back either: until the end of the war, it was very rare for a *partida* to have any hope of defeating a French column, let alone of taking a fortified town (to be fair, Espoz y Mina on several occasions did both in the period 1812–13, but he was very much the exception rather than the rule). And, plague the French incessantly though they did, the guerrillas did not do so to the extent that they forced them to evacuate any part of their conquests, still less persuade them to give up the Peninsular War as a futile endeavour. Indeed, it cannot even be argued that they were a foe which it was impossible to eradicate. In Aragón, in particular, the intelligent occupation policies pursued by the French commander, Marshal Suchet, secured a considerable degree of pacification, whilst even in Navarre it was repeatedly shown that the guerrillas could be suffocated provided sufficient regular troops were deployed against them.[11] Unpleasant though such an admission might be, it therefore has to be recognised, that, so long as the French managed to confine Wellington's army to Portugal, the life of *la guerrilla* must have been finite once the seemingly inevitable *quietus* had been administered to the cause of regular resistance. With the last Spanish army out of the way and Wellington helpless to do much more than look on, the French could then have turned on the guerrillas and dealt with them once and for all (and that this could have been done there is no doubt, as witness the unhappy fate of the both the Tyrolean revolt of 1809 and the guerrilla insurrection that raged in Calabria between 1806 and 1811). All that was required was an endless stream of replacements and reinforcements, and these the French continued to receive in abundance until the middle of 1811 (a more unified command structure would also have helped, but it seems unlikely that its absence would have saved the guerrillas in the end). And, with the guerrillas gone, Wellington would ultimately have been faced with an invasion of Portugal so overwhelming that even he would have been hard put to it to maintain his position.

That the matter did not work out in this fashion was not the fault of the guerrillas. Much as they may have caused endless difficulties for the French generals, on occasion greatly benefited the operations of the Allies, helped to keep Spanish resistance alive, demoralised the occupation forces, increased war-weariness in France, or even seriously compromised the emperor himself, they did not cause Napoleon to abandon the struggle, or do more than slow down the pace of French conquest, and then but little. What saved the Allies was rather Napoleon's invasion of Russia in 1812, the demands of this campaign being such that it became impossible to send any further troops to Spain. With the French currently engaged in the conquest of Valencia, the result was fatal. So long as the guerrillas continued to resist, every fresh French conquest needed a powerful garrison, but, thus far, the 'wastage' inherent in this requirement had more or less been made up by the dispatch of fresh troops from France. However, with this supply suddenly cut off, the necessary troops somehow had to be found from the occupation forces' own resources, a variety of factors combining to persuade the French that these could be taken from the forces facing Wellington. In consequence, it was not long before a strong detachment was on its way eastwards – and Wellington prepared to launch an offensive that would change the course of the entire war.

If the propositions advanced in 'Heroes or villains' can thus be shown to be well founded with regard to the military role of *la guerrilla*, in other respects the article's arguments are deficient or even seriously misleading. One of its chief themes was the growing militarization of the guerrilla movement, much emphasis being placed on the role of army officers in the formation of many bands, the desire of civilian leaders such as Espoz y Mina to adopt the structures of the regular army, and the transformation of the more important *partidas* into 'flying columns' of regular troops. That this development occurred in some cases there is no doubt – indeed, fresh examples could be advanced of it such as the two new cavalry regiments formed in remote parts of Jaén in the course of 1811.[12] However, it was by no means universal even amongst the larger bands – despite heading a force that eventually numbered 3,500 men, the Valencian *cabecilla*, Agustín Nebot, otherwise known as 'El Fraile', seems to have made no attempt to give his men a regular appearance. Meanwhile, the adoption of military forms did not necessarily imply the transformation of a *partida* into a miniature army – by the end of 1812 Mina may in theory have commanded a division composed of several regiments, but the latter were rarely cantoned together and in practice resembled units of the regular army in little more than name.[13] In any case, what is very clear is that the more-or-less regularised *partidas* of such figures as Espoz y Mina, El Empecinado, Sánchez, Durán, Villacampa, Longa, Merino, and Porlier, were (except in Navarre, where Espoz y Mina succeeded in eliminating them) to the end of the war surrounded by a host of bands that were wholly irregular in nature and have therefore left us with little trace of their existence. Taking the case of Valencia, Ardit lists some nineteen such bands, whilst Carentona comes up with another fourteen in Asturias, and López Pérez nine more in Jaén.[14]

Clearly, then, guerrilla warfare genuinely was a far more widespread and diffuse phenomenon than a concentration on its more visible elements might lead us to expect, whilst it is clearly mistaken to think in terms of a concentration of the guerrillas into ever larger bands that, whilst packing a heavier punch, at the same time provided the French with a more identifiable target. Does this mean that it is also necessary to modify the author's original emphasis upon a growing division between the population on the one hand and the guerrillas on the other? To answer this question, however, it is first necessary to delve far more deeply into the question of what the guerrillas were actually fighting for, in which respect simplistic notions of *dios, rey y patria* are none too helpful (though the British officer who remarked of the Spanish peasantry that, 'had they been permitted to live in peace, it would have been a matter of the greatest indifference to them whether their king was Joseph, Ferdinand or the ghost of Don Quijote', was doubtless throwing the baby out with the proverbial bathwater[15]).

In 'Heroes or villains' the social context of the guerrillas was barely touched upon other than to suggest that they had strong links with banditry, this having been identified elsewhere as a primitive form of protest, and, indeed, means of survival, in societies where the bulk of the rural population were either landless labourers or tenant farmers with unfavourable leases or insufficient land on which to survive. For Marxist historians such links with movements of social and economic protest are axiomatic, a good example being the work undertaken by Ardit with regard to Valencia. As this shows, when war broke out against the French, Valencian society was already in crisis, the peasantry's resentment of the exceptionally heavy burden which *señorialismo* represented in Valencia having been fuelled by a series of metereological disasters and crop failures, and the catastrophic economic effects of Spain's involvement in the Revolutionary Wars on the side of France after 1796. When the government of Manuel de Godoy had made a praiseworthy but nonetheless ill-timed attempt to extend conscription for the militia to Valencia in 1801, the result had been a full-scale peasant uprising whose chief targets were the most obvious manifestations of the *señorial* system.[16] That such social violence extended into the War of Independence there is no doubt, Brian Hamnett having shown that the whole region was rocked by a series of anti-seigneurial disturbances that by 1813 had more or less attained the status of an armed revolt.[17] The problem is, however, that it is not easy conclusively to show that the Valencian guerrillas were motivated above all by hostility to the *señorios*. Certainly many of the local collaborators – the Marqués de Dos Aguas, the Marqués de Carros, the Marqués de Valera, the Marqués de Jura-Real, the Marqués de Sardanyola, the Marqués de Mirasol, the Marqués del Moral, the Marqués de Malferit and the Conde de Castellar – were prominent local feudatories. Certainly, too, several of the local guerrilla leaders can in one way or another be made to fit with the image of *la guerrilla* as a movement founded upon social revolution – for all his clerical background, Agustín Nebot was a convinced liberal; Gregorio Martínez and Pascual Giner had both been prominent in the rising of 1801; and Jaime Alfonso was a renowned local bandit; meanwhile, Nebot and Giner both fought as liberal guerrillas in the civil war of 1822–3. Yet there are also many contradictions: not only did Alfonso, at least four of the other eighteen Valencian *cabecillas* named by Ardit, and several of Nebot's chief lieutenants, all go on to take up arms for the absolutists, and, by implication, the cause of *senorialismo*, but Ardit is unable to offer a single shred of evidence of a guerrilla band acting in an overtly anti-feudal manner.[18]

If even the relatively well-documented Valencian example does not make a wholly convincing case for *la guerrilla* as a social conflict, for the rest of Spain the picture is even more fragmentary. That the period immediately preceding the French invasion of 1808 was a period of social tension there is no doubt. Setting aside the various calamities of which we have already spoken, Godoy's decision to embark on the sale of the lands of the Church to meet the needs of the war against Britain produced the destruction of numerous charitable foundations and a widespread rise in rents. With its cities filled with beggars and its countryside terrorised by bandits and bands of desperate vagrants, Spain was in a highly volatile condition, and the violence of the rising of 1808 needs no explanation. With the abortive accession to the throne of Ferdinand VII presented by its architects as the coming of a new golden age in which all ills would magically be swept away[19], it is hardly surprising that the rural masses suddenly sprang to life, and all the more so as the established authorities, whether military, municipal, judicial or ecclesiastical, and, by extension, the *señores*, were so often hostile to the uprising. Thus, from many parts of Spain we have evidence of a widespread refusal to pay the Church's tithes and of fierce attacks on the propertied classes, a good example of the latter being the murder of the successful merchant and proto-industrialist, the Marqués de Sargadelos, in Ribadeo on 2 February 1809.[20] Furthermore, setting aside the impoverishment consequent upon the war, and, in particular, the rapacious 'contributions' exacted by the French and Spanish armies (the British, by contrast, paid for all their supplies, although there is evidence that their troops were enthusiastic looters), there is little doubt that the structural conditions experienced by the Spanish peasantry altered gravely for the worse in the course of the war. Thus, the French on the one hand, and the liberals who dominated the *cortes* of Cadiz on the other, introduced a series of reforms – the sale of the lands of the Church and the municipalities, the abolition of all controls on rents and prices – that could not but seriously damage the interests of the rural lower classes; still worse, although the *cortes* abolished *señorialismo*, it left the estates of the nobility intact and allowed the *señores* effectively to convert most of their old dues into rents. Information on the precise effects of these changes is lacking (and it must further be recognised that in many cases they were only implemented on paper), but evidence from Guipúzcoa certainly shows that the peasantly experienced a process of rapid differentiation with over seventy-one per cent of the 27,000,000 reales' worth of communal property sold in the course of the war being acquired by barely fifteen per cent of the purchasers.[21]

That such developments gave rise to considerable social tension goes without saying – in Asturias, for example, the mere rumour that the provincial junta formed in the aftermath of the uprising intended to abolish a number of Bourbon measures which offered tenants a certain degree of protection produced a peasant uprising.[22] However, it nevertheless seems a little imprudent to proceed from here to the Marxist position that *la guerrilla* 'was based upon nothing other than a marginalised peasantry . . . launched by a disamorticising bourgeoisie upon an implacable process of proletarianization'.[23] Of course, the guerrillas drew a large part of their rank and file from landless labourers and more-or-less desperate peasants in Spain as a whole, whilst it may be argued that, had rural Spain not been in a state of crisis, *la guerrilla* would never have been so dramatic. Yet, if we look at the province of Navarre, we find a picture that is very different from that which one might expect. Thus, in this case – which deals, be it said, with the most imposing, successful and well organised guerrilla movement produced in the entire war – the picture which emerges is the very opposite of the one which a Marxist analysis would lead us to expect. As is well known, Navarre is divided into two very different regions in the shape of the (then) largely Basque-speaking *montaña* to the north, and the Castillian-speaking *ribera* to the south, of which the former is dominated by small peasant properties and the latter by great estates. Of the two, it was needless to say the *ribera* which experienced the greater social tensions: not only were the majority of the population already artisans, landless labourers, or tenant farmers with insufficient land to support a family, but the war years saw a sustained attempt on the part of the *pudientes* who dominated the municipalities to defend, or even improve, their position. Thus, councils such as those of Tudela, Corella and Olite passed the cost of French requisitioning on to the lower classes through substantial increases in indirect taxation, and sold off the commons and the lands of the Church to the local elites. However, far from finding that the *ribera* was a hotbed of guerrilla resistance, we find that it remained comparatively quiet with few of its inhabitants making their way to join Mina, whose chief support came rather from the homogenous and relatively prosperous *montaña*.[24]

Of course, none of this is to say that *la guerrilla* did not have strong links with social conditions. Taking the Navarrese example again, the peasants of the *montaña*, with their traditions of self-government and customary tenure, had much to fear from a 'bourgeois revolution' of whatever provenance, whether it be imposed from *josefino* Madrid or liberal Cadíz, and it therefore may well be possible to regard their rebellion as a counter-revolutionary movement akin to that of the Vendée – not for nothing did Espoz y Mina delay the ceremony whereby his troops were supposed to swear loyalty to the constitution of 1812 to the last possible minute, refuse to recognise the authority of Pedro Sainz de Baranda, the *jefe político* – civil governor – dispatched to Navarre following its liberation in the course of 1813, and in 1814 celebrate the restoration of absolutism by having the constitution symbolically 'executed' by a firing squad![25] Yet, whilst the Navarrese example may constitute a case where the guerrillas fought consciously to defend the social and economic aspects of the *antiguo régimen* because they happened to favour the peasantry, it is hard to find any concrete evidence of them trying to overthrow it where they did not. With regard to Galicia, for example, when the population rose in revolt against the invaders in January 1809 it invariably chose as its leaders prominent local notables, and that despite the fact that Galicia was a stronghold of *señorialismo*. By the same token, meanwhile, neither Ardit not Hamnett cite any instances of the various manifestations of *señorialismo* in Valencia being attacked by the guerrillas, the violence that they describe seemingly stemming rather from the local population.

It will here of course be argued that the guerrillas and the local population were one and the same, but in fact such a claim does not appear to be wholly tenable. We thus return to the argument advanced by 'Heroes or villains', and, in particular, the claim that the guerrillas became more or less divorced from the civilian population. That this development was not *ipso facto* the effect of militarization as the author then maintained is obvious, it being very clear that Mina's growing strength and organization did not prevent the population of the Navarrese *montaña* from maintaining very close links with his forces. But that is not to say that it did not take place. On the contrary, a more diffuse *guerrilla* can actually be seen to make it more likely. Marxist historians like Ardit have made much of the links between the guerrillas and the Spanish tradition of social banditry, but, whilst many bandits might have taken to the hills on account of poverty, desperation and even anger, they were by no means automatically transformed into 'Robin Hoods' who stole from the rich to give to the poor. The history of Spanish banditry is not devoid of such figures, but no evidence is known to the author of one that is associated with the Peninsular War. On the countrary, at least some of the infinity of irregular bands which came and went in the course of the conflict were never anything other than gangs of criminals who had from the start looked upon the struggle as an opportunity to prey on all and sundry, whether rich or poor, *afrancesado* or patriot. In this respect, Tone cites the case of one Antonio Temprano, a renegade monk who looted many villages round Madrid, but one might also refer back to the unsavoury figures of Bosoms and Fombella, of whom the latter was described as 'the captain of a band of . . . thieves and ne'er-do-wells at whose head he has . . . committed the greatest atrocities'.[26] Also worth mentioning here are the bands of deserters from every army who terrorised many parts of the Peninsula (it will be objected that such bands cannot be defined as *partidas*, but the fact that they were as happy to attack French targets as they were any other makes it hard to separate them from the general phenomenon).

Let us accept, however, that outright criminality was not the motive of the vast majority of the guerrillas, much though it might have been encouraged by such measures as the decree of 'land piracy' whereby the Junta Central ordained that the personal effects of the French and their sympathisers constituted legitimate prize. The problem was rather one of capacities and logistics. Given that in most cases the guerrillas very soon did come to lead a more-or-less permanent existence, they naturally could not grow their own food, but rather became increasingly dependent upon the resources of the local population. At first, perhaps, this was given willingly enough, but it was not long before French reprisals began to make the costs of such support prohibitively high. To retain the support of the population, the guerrillas had therefore to be able to offer them at least some measure of protection, but this the smaller *partidas* were incapable of doing (indeed, it was hard enough even for the larger ones) with the result that they tended to become more and more unpopular. Faced by growing hostility from the *pueblos* on which they depended, the dictates of survival left them with no option but to turn to the use of terror. Taking the case of Navarre once again as an example, at the instigation of the dictator of Zaragosa, José Palafox, in the summer of 1808 one Andrés Eguaguirre raised a flying column entitled the Fusileros de Navarra with the object of harassing the French lines of communications. However, so great were the French forces stationed in Navarre, that it was not long before Eguaguirre was being harried from valley to valley by the enemy. Thus prevented from establishing a stable relationship with the local inhabitants, he very soon to all intents and purposes became a bandit chieftain who kept his dwindling band of followers alive through sheer pillage and was constantly dodging the attempts of such towns as Leiza to turn him over to the invaders.[27]

Whether the case of Eguaguirre is typical of the evolution of the minor bands is hard to say. What is undeniable is that the evidence that contemporary observers made a very strong distinction between 'regular' and 'irregular' guerrillas is overwhelming. Let us cite a few examples from very different elements in the patriot camp. First of all, we have a young infantry officer sent to Catalonia from Andalucia:

> Every day I hate these people more and more: they have no other god than money, and for this they would sell the fatherland, their fathers, their saints and anything else that they could lay their hands on . . . The much-vaunted . . . Army of Catalonia is in its entirety no more than a gang of thieves who under the guise of *somatenes* enter the towns in a manner almost on a par with that of the French and sack all the houses . . . with rather more skill than they do.[28]

Next we can cite a representative of the old military hierarchy, the Duque del Parque, who in September 1809 complained that the guerrillas of Old Castile were fast becoming 'bands of highwaymen whom it will be necessary to shoot if they are to be brought under control'.[29] Following this, we have the testimony of representatives of the civil authorities, the Junta of Najera complaining that the guerrillas 'act as if they were the owners of the property of the nation, and, still more, that of the municipalities and private individuals, frequently making use of the shameful epithet "traitor" to satisfy their greed at the cost of the honour and subsistence of unfortunates who in the most unheard of fashion find themselves pillaged and stripped of their possessions without any proper trial'; and Navarre's representatives to the Junta Central that 'certain parties of guerrillas' were riding from village to village and seizing large numbers of mules, demanding supplies of food and clothing, and exacting exorbitant sums for their 'pay'.[30] Such complaints, meanwhile, are mirrored in the protests of private individuals, and in the reports dispatched to Wellington's headquarters by his extensive network of (generally, be it said, highly reliable) *confidentes*.[31] From British sources, meanwhile, we might quote Wellington's complaint that, following his liberation of Madrid in August 1812, the guerrillas were 'getting quietly into the large towns and amusing themselves or collecting plunder of a larger and more valuable description', and Sydenham's that they 'plundered many towns with as little mercy as the French, and, where the French preceded them, they generally carried off all which the French had left'.[32] Last but not least, even the liberals, who were for political reasons always eager to extol the guerrillas as the personification of their theory that the heroic Spanish people were fighting for their liberty, became concerned at the chaotic situation in the countryside: not only does the

Cádiz press from the end of 1812 become filled with complaints about the guerrillas, but within a year the *cortes* was moving to take repressive measures against them.[33]

Given that complaints of pillage, rapine and arbitrary behaviour were the natural refuge of all those in one way or another threatened by the guerrillas, whether they were army generals, property owners, officials of the *antiguo régimen*, or collaborators, *some* of this evidence must inevitably be regarded as suspect. Yet, for all that, it comes from so widespread a base that the picture that it presents is impossible to dismiss. As was maintained in 'Heroes or villains', the guerrillas very clearly did live off the population rather than amongst them, the growing antagonism that this produced being exacerbated by the fact that the violence engendered by the social resentments which they encapsulated was directed not just against the wealthy, but rather against all sections of society: there is, for example, no suggestion that there was anything selective about the sack of Tudela by the forces of Javier Mina (not to be confused with his distant relative, Francisco Espoz y Mina) in November 1809.[34] It is therefore hardly surprising that we must also revise our opinion with regard to the Spanish forces that were raised by the French to resist the guerrillas, whether as sedentary urban militias or as *cuerpos francos* that could help to hunt them down in the hills. Although this subject lacks the detailed study that it merits, it is probable that the number of these *jurados* was substantial, the Madrid militia alone eventually numbering some ten battalions.[35]

Broadly speaking, then, the concerns outlined in 'Heroes or villains' can be seen to have been well founded even if some of the details of the argument require revision. That said, however, the author would not wish to be accused of denying the importance of the Spanish guerrillas in the history of the Peninsular War. Not only has that never been his intention, but his findings do not contradict the traditional view that they posed immense problems for the French. Certainly the guerrillas were often as merciless towards the civilian population as they were towards the French; as in Navarre, the *partidas* were that much more effective where they managed to remain on reasonably friendly terms with the *pueblo*; but to argue that the various qualifications that must be made with regard to their nature and motivation undermine their military importance would be purblind in the extreme. With even a single gang of outright bandits being capable of causing the invaders immense trouble, it follows that the infinity of *partidas* scattered across the wilder areas of occupied Spain transformed it into a veritable morass, and all the more so as most of the bands were not devoid of at least some degree of patriotic feeling (the Valencian, Jaime Alfonso, may have been a bandit and have continued to act as a bandit, but he was nonetheless a dangerous enemy to the French and their supporters). Furthermore, if the militarization of the guerrillas was far more limited a process than was originally argued, this was all to the good, given the contemporary French opinion that, once organized into permanent formations, the guerrillas were actually far more vulnerable.[36]

None of this, of course, undermines the contentions that the guerrillas undermined regular resistance in Spain, or that they would not ultimately have been overcome had Napoleon not invaded Russia in 1812. However, the fact is that Napoleon did invade Russia, thereby opening the way for Allied victory in the Peninsular War, it being the final task of this paper to reassess the manner in which the guerrillas contributed to that victory. For British military historians the answer to this question has been bound up with their admiration for the heroic figure of the Duke of Wellington, not to mention their tendency to view every aspect of Spanish resistance in terms of the guerrilla war. In brief, their thesis, which has now become the standard orthodoxy, is that Wellington was only able to maintain his position in the Peninsula because the guerrillas neutralised the huge numerical superiority which the French enjoyed over his forces; that there was a constant inter-relationship between his operations and those of the *partidas* in that he struck repeatedly into Spain to relieve French pressure upon them; and that he based the great offensive of 1813 that finally liberated Spain primarily upon co-operation with their activities.[37]

However, such arguments are, to put it mildly, misleading. In the first place it is clear that the real foundation of Wellington's position in the Peninsula was the much maligned Spanish army given that its final defeat – as we have seen, imminent by 1812 – must have brought with it the eventual destruction of the guerrillas. In the second, the idea that the campaigns of 1809, 1811 and 1812 were mere forays designed to provide some relief to the guerrillas can only be described as a dishonest exercise to excuse failure, the fact being that Wellington was openly scornful of the idea that he should march across the frontier to take the pressure off even the Spanish regular armies, let alone the guerrillas.[38] And, in the third, as early as September 1808 the British commander had already come to the conclusion that it was foolhardy to base any plan of operations upon the contribution that might or might not be made by irregular forces acting inside Spain.[39] In short, it would therefore appear that it is necessary to look again at the position which the guerrillas occupied in Wellington's strategy.

To argue that Wellington was not aware of, or did not appreciate, the guerrillas would, of course, be foolish, his correspondence, on the contrary, being replete with references to *la guerrilla* that suggest that he believed that it was doing great damage to the invaders.[40] At the same time, there is little doubt that popular resistance played a most important role in his plans for the defence of Portugal in 1810, no fewer than twenty-eight regiments of Portuguese militia, not to mention the irregular levies known as the *ordenança*, being detailed to conduct a guerrilla war against the French rear. However, an analysis of Wellington's military thought suggests that he entertained a very great difference between the defence of Portugal and operations in the hinterland of Spain. In Portugal he never had to trust guerrillas, or anyone else, to tie down the French, given that the security of his forces was virtually guaranteed firstly by the almost impregnable fastness of the 'Lines of Torres Vedras', and secondly by the certainty that the Royal Navy could easily evacuate his forces should anything go wrong. However, in the vast distances and empty plains of Spain the situation was very different. The farther that Wellington advanced into the interior, the more at risk did his outnumbered forces become to a French counter-offensive, the implication being that, with every step which the British advanced, the more they became dependent upon Spanish aid: indeed, in 1808 under Sir John Moore, and then in 1809 under Wellington himself, British armies had almost been destroyed following an advance into central Spain. Useful though the guerrillas were, however, they simply could not offer the guarantees that Wellington needed: not only had the many direct contacts that the British had had with the guerrillas of the Cantabrian coast provided alarming evidence of the guerrillas' many military defects – their want of arms, discipline and training, the rivalries that beset their leadership, the incompetence of many of their chieftains, and their sheer unreliability – whilst the events of 1809 suggested that the French would be willing to abandon whole provinces to them in order to concentrate against the Anglo-Portuguese.[41]

Hardly surprisingly, then, Wellington never had any intention of trusting the guerrillas to tie down the French armies if and when the time came for him again to strike deep into Spain, his opinion remaining unchanged when opportunity finally offered at the beginning of 1812. It is certainly true that throughout 1812 the British took what steps they could to stir up guerrilla resistance, particularly in northern Spain, landing shipments of arms on the coast and dispatching a naval squadron under Sir Home Popham to assist the *partidas* in making attacks on French garrisons, that in February 1812 Wellington expressed the hope that the guerrillas would impede any French attempt to raise the siege of Badajoz, and, further, that he asked for their help in distracting the French during the campaign of Salamanca. Yet the fact remains that the majority of the diversionary operations that he planned to prevent an overwhelming enemy concentration against his invasion forces depended not upon the guerrillas, but on units of the regular Spanish armies based in Alicante, Cadíz, Galicia and the frontiers of Portugal. Of the guerrillas themselves, Wellington expected little. Thus:

> The guerrillas, although active and willing, and although their opera-
> tions in general occasion the greatest annoyance to the enemy, are so
> little disciplined that they can do nothing against the French troops
> unless the latter are very inferior in numbers . . .[42]

Nor did subsequent events do anything to boost the British commander's confidence in the guerrillas. As the tide of French conquest receded in the wake of the conquest of Ciudad Rodrigo and Badajoz and the victory of Salamanca – by September the French had either been driven from, or forced to evacuate, the whole of Asturias, Extremadura, Andalucía, León, and New Castile and the vast majority of Old Castile – the *partidas* of the liberated territories, as we have seen, for the most part did not follow up the French, but rather battened still more firmly upon the suffering inhabitants. Advancing to besiege the citadel of Burgos, Wellington then found himself threatened by an overwhelming enemy army whose concentration all the efforts of the guerrillas of northern and eastern Spain failed to detain, the result being yet another hasty retreat for the safety of the Portuguese frontier.

In Wellington's opinion, needless to say, the fault for this situation lay entirely with the Spaniards. Including, though it did, all the representatives of his unfortunate allies – 'I have never known the Spaniards do anything, much less do anything well.' – his scorn was particularly directed at the guerrillas, who were now reduced in his correspondence to 'a few rogues'.[43] With the passage of time, his position moderated slightly – by January 1813 he could admit that the *partidas* of the Basque country and Navarre were playing 'the very devil' with the French[44] – but never again was he prepared to trust to their efforts even to the limited extent that he had done in 1812. Accepting the command-in-chief of all the Spanish forces in the Peninsula in January 1813 (it had in fact been offered him the previous September, but Wellington had first insisted on referring the matter to London, and then engaged in some very hard bargaining before he would accept it), he concentrated on the restoration and revivification of the regulars. Insofar as his plans for the campaign of 1813 were concerned, meanwhile, he more or less ignored the guerrillas altogether, it being his intention to neutralise the French numerical superiority – still very great – with a combination of the Spanish regular armies, supposedly now much improved, and the Anglo-Sicilian expeditionary force that had landed at Alicante in the summer of 1812. If the guerrillas proved of some assistance, all well and good – the divisions of Villacampa and Durán, which were both nominally part of the Spanish Second Army, but, in practice, continued to operate as guerrillas in the interior, were in fact ordered to cut the communications of the French forces in the Levante with those in Old Castile – but, if they did not, then they could at least now do little harm.[44]

To reiterate, then, in 1813 Wellington initially planned to liberate Spain without relying on the Spanish guerrillas in the slightest: indeed, so far was he from including them in his plans that he does not seem to have made the slightest attempt to contact the many chieftains, such as Mina, who as yet remained outside the structure of the Spanish army. However, matters did not work out as he intended. To prepare its exhausted and skeletal forces for the role which Wellington intended for them, the Spanish government needed men and money, but in fact neither were forthcoming. Although the large expanse of liberated territory that had remained in Allied hands at the end of 1812 in theory offered both despite their devastation by years of war, in practice little could be done to exploit them. On the contrary, the interior of the country was in a state of complete anarchy with military service as unpopular as ever, much of the south gripped by an epidemic of yellow fever, the peasants in many areas in open revolt against the *señorios*, the countryside swarming with deserters, bandits and erstwhile participants in *la guerrilla*, the various opponents of the liberals stirring up traditionalist feeling, and the representatives of the government frequently unable to secure any recognition, let alone to exert any authority. Simultaneously denied the resources of Latin America, most of which was by now in a state of open rebellion, the Cadíz regime could barely feed or pay the forces already at its disposal, still less raise new ones, the troops that it did have being so lacking in footwear and transport that they could barely be moved. With the liberals desperate to retain as many forces as they could around Cadíz to defend themselves against their political opponents, and determined to restrict Wellington's power, of which they were deeply suspicious, the new generalissimo's plans could not but fail, the number of Spanish regulars that took part in the campaign of Vittoria being relatively limited.[45]

However, if Wellington's original scheme for the campaign of 1813 failed, in large part, be it said, due to the havoc wreaked by the guerrillas in the liberated areas of Spain, how are we to explain his triumph? With considerable irony, we must now return to the guerrillas. In order to drive back Wellington's offensive against Burgos in the autumn of 1812, the French had had to draw heavily upon the so-called 'Army of the North' – the garrisons of Cantabria, the Basque country and Navarre

– and, although most of the troops involved had returned to their posts fairly soon, some 3,000 men had then had to be withdrawn to France to help remedy the disastrous consequences of Napoleon's retreat from Moscow. By now very well organized, highly experienced, strong in numbers, and equipped with artillery pieces landed from British ships on the Cantabrian coast, the forces of Porlier, Longa and Mina had seized their opportunity to great effect. Establishing a number of liberated areas, they made regular travel along the main road from the French border to Miranda de Ebro – the umbilical cord of the bulk of the occupation forces – absolutely impossible, captured a number of French garrisons and forced the evacuation of several others, imposed a close blockade on such strongholds as Pamplona, and repeatedly defeated the enemy columns sent against them. Extremely annoyed, Napoleon ordered that the whole region be pacified forthwith, and, with extraordinary insouciance, authorised the commander of the Army of the North to draw such forces as he needed from the troops containing Wellington in León. Not surprisingly, however, the guerrillas proved a very tough nut to crack, inflicting a number of embarrassing reverses on the first troops sent against them, with the result that yet more reinforcements had to be called for from the west. Eventually no fewer than five of the six divisions facing Wellington were thus engaged, the result being, of course, that the British commander was enabled to launch his offensive notwithstanding the inability of most of the Spaniards to take the field. Furthermore, so deep had most of the troops who should have been blocking his advance become embroiled in the fruitless struggle with the guerrillas – fruitless in that, although some degree of French control was restored to Navarre, Mina merely fled eastwards into Aragón and stirred up fresh trouble there – that several divisions were still absent when the French finally chose to give battle at Vittoria.[47]

In the end, then, for all that Wellington had little faith in them, the guerrillas – or, at least, some of them – did play a vital role in the liberation of Spain from the Napoleonic imperium, and it is essential that this is given its proper emphasis. Yet, for all that the battle of Vittoria, with its dramatic consequences, could not have been won without the guerrillas, it remains clear that their role in the war as a whole requires considerable revision. Thus, more or less as argued in 'Heroes or villains', in the crucial period from the end of 1808 to the beginning of 1812, the guerrillas probably did inflict more harm than good on the Allied cause, for, by undermining the resistance of the regular army, they hastened the day when the French would have been able to turn overwhelming forces upon first them and then the army of the Duke of Wellington. With Wellington, and still more the guerrillas, able only to delay the march of events in Spain, it may be inferred that the Allied cause's salvation rested solely upon the fatal decision to go to war with Russia. However, if the arguments advanced in 'Heroes or villains' are in this respect justified, the same cannot be said for its tendency to 'depopularise' the guerrillas and to regard them as subject to an ever more general process of militarisation. Whilst some of the guerrillas did owe their origins to military initiatives, and some others seek for a variety of reasons to adopt military forms, it is abundantly clear that in origin and nature *la guerrilla* was above all a great popular convulsion that remained characterised by the band rather than the battalion. To recognise, this, however, is to encounter further difficulties in that it is abundantly clear that, as witness the immense hostility engendered by attempts at conscription, the Spanish people were by no means devoted to the war against the French *per se*. Whilst imminent threats to *la patria chica*, the experience of French occupation, and sheer desperation all undoubtedly fuelled resistance, this was very obviously closely related to various manifestations of social tension. Nevertheless the manner in which the relationship functioned is by no means clear, and it would be a brave historian indeed who would argue that *la guerrilla* of 1808–14 was a definite precursor of later agrarian revolt, whether in the form of Carlism or of anarchism. Rather than offering any firm conclusion, the author would therefore prefer to conclude this discussion by stressing the need for further work on the social history of this most complex of phenomena on the style of that pioneered by John Tone for Navarre and Manuel Ardit for Valencia, such studies being essential for a proper understanding of the place of *la guerrilla* in the history of Spain.

This paper was originally presented at the II Seminario Internacional sobre la Guerra de la Independencia, held in Madrid in October 1984. It was originally published in E. Martínez Ruiz (ed.), *II Seminario Internacional sobre la Guerra de la Independencia* (Madrid: Ministerio de Defensa, 1996), and is here reproduced with the permission of the Centro de Publicaciones del Ministerio de Defensa, in which respect the author is indebted to the good offices of Excmo. Sr. D. Leopoldo Stampa, and Sr. D. Jaime Serret Moreno-Gil.

Notes

1   C. J. Esdaile, 'The Spanish guerrillas: heroes or villains', *History Today*, XXXVIII, No. 4 (April, 1988), pp. 28–35.
2   For example, in his recent work on the guerrillas in Navarre, John Tone claims that 'Charles Esdaile could suggest in 1988 that the guerrillas were a military liability to the allies'; J. L. Tone, *The Fatal Knot: the Guerrilla War in Navarre and the Defeat of Napoleon in Spain* (Chapel Hill, 1994), p. 186.

3 Anon., *Medios de salvar el reino* (Cádiz, 1810), pp. 5–6, 8–9. In fact, even the feats of arms alluded to here are somewhat dubious, Madrid holding out for precisely one day, and Galicia arguably only being evacuated because of Wellington's invasion of Extremadura in the summer of 1809.
4 Graham to Bunbury, 27 September 1810, Public Record Office (hereafter PRO), WO 1/247, p. 629.
5 H. von Brandt, *The Two Minas and the Spanish Guerrillas* (London, 1825), p. 58.
6 Eroles to Wellington, 5 February 1813, University of Southampton, Wellington Papers (hereafter US WP) 1/366.
7 F. X. de Cabanes, *Historia de las operaciones del Ejército de Cataluña en la primera campaña de la guerra de la unsurpación, o sea de la independencia de España* (Tarragona, 1809), I, p. 48.
8 J. Patterson, *The Adventures of Captain John Patterson* (London, 1837), p. 216; F. Carantona Alvarez, *La guerra de la independencia en Asturias* (Oviedo, 1983), p. 148; M. López Pérez and I. Lara Martín-Portugués, *Entre la guerra y la paz: Jaén, 1808–1814* (Granada, 1993), pp. 249, 254.
9 J. Torras Elias, *La guerra de los agraviados* (Barcelona, 1967), 38–9; Carantona Alvarez, *Asturias*, p. 168; there is a discussion of the general problem of desertion in C. J. Esdaile, *The Spanish Army in the Peninsular War* (Manchester, 1988), pp. 140–1.
10 López Pérez, *Entre la guerra y la paz*, p. 395.
11 The progressive prostration of the Spanish army is discussed in Esdaile, *Spanish Army*, pp. 133–44, 159–65. There is an excellent discussion of the achievements of Marshal Suchet in D. W. Alexander, *Rod of Iron: French Occupation Policy in Aragón during the Peninsular War* (Wilmington, Delaware, 1985); for Navarre, see Tone, *Fatal Knot*, pp. 104–10, 121–4.
12 López Pérez, *Entre la guerra y la paz*, p. 397.
13 Tone, *Fatal Knot*, 117–19.
14 M. Ardit Lucas, *Revolución liberal y revuelta campesina: un ensayo sobre la desintegración del regimen feudal en el país valenciano, 1793–1840* (Barcelona, 1977), pp. 213–17; Carentona Alvarez, *Asturias*, 167–8; Lopez Perez, *Entre la guerra y la paz*, pp. 396–7.
15 J. Kincaid, *Adventures in the Rifle Brigade* (London, 1909), p. 86.
16 Ardit, *Revolución liberal y revuelta campesina*, pp. 77–87, 98–119.
17 B. Hamnett, *La politica española en una edad revolucionaria, 1790–1820* (Mexico City, 1985), p. 92; cf. also Ardit, *Revolución liberal y revuelta campesina*, pp. 219–25.
18 For these details, cf. Ardit, *Revolución liberal y revuelta campesina*, pp. 197–9, 213–17.
19 For an account of the millenarian aspects of 1808, cf. R. Herr, 'Good, evil and the revolt against Godoy', in R. Herr and H. Parker (eds.), *Ideas in History* (Durham, North Carolina, 1965), pp. 157–81.
20 Cf. J. Fontana Lazaro, *La quiebra de la monarquía absoluta, 1814–1820: la crisis del antiguo régimen en Espana* (Barcelona, 1971), pp. 159–60; X. Barreiro Fernández, *Historia de Galicia* (Vigo, 1981), IV, p. 242; J. L. Comellas (ed.), *Historia general de Espana y America, XII: del antiguo al nuevo régimen* (Madrid, 1981), p. 46; for the murder of Sargadelos, cf. F. Lanza Alvarez, *Ribadeo antiguo* (Madrid, 1933), pp. 316–18.
21 Comellas, *Historia general*, XII, p. 66.
22 R. Alvarez Valdés, *Memorias del levantamiento de Asturias en 1808*, ed M. Fuentes Acevedo (Oviedo, 1889), p. 41.

23 J. Pérez Garzón, *Milicia nacional y revolución burguesa: el protitipo madrileño* (Madrid, 1978), p. 80.
24 Tone, *Fatal Knot*, pp. 163–70.
25 J. M. Iribarren, *Espoz y Mina, el guerrillero* (Madrid, 1965), pp. 532–6.
26 Tone, *Fatal Knot*, p. 72; *cit.* Carantona Alvarez, *Asturias*, pp. 168–9.
27 Tone, *Fatal Knot*, pp. 65–6.
28 Letter of Francisco de Paula Guervos, 18 November 1808, Academia Real de Historia, 11–5–7:9003, No. 4; in this context it is also worth recalling the bitter words of Luis de Villalba, a regular officer who fought in the siege of Zaragosa, *viz*: 'The guerrillas who go by the name of 'patriots' should be exterminated: they are gangs of thieves with *carte blanche* to rob on the roads and plunder the villages'; *cit.* Esdaile, 'Heroes or villains', p. 30.
29 Del Parque a Cornel, 24 September 1809, Archivo Histórico Nacional (hereafter AHN), Estado 41C, No. 70; cf. also La Romana to Mahy, 25 July 1809, Servicio Histórico Militar, Archivo de la Guerra de la Independencia (hereafter SHM AGI), 5/8/2, No. 5; Del Parque to Mahy, 6 October 1809, SHM AGI 5/8/4, No. 17.
30 Junta of Najera to Junta Central, 30 November 1809, AHN Estado, 41E, p. 124; representation of Valera and Amética, 18 October 1809, AHN Estado, 41D, p. 78; cf. also Del Canto and Bonifaz to Junta Central, 4 December 1809, AHN Estado, 41E, p. 127.
31 E.g. 'Manifiesto de los leales castellanos', 9 November 1812, US. WP.1/364; Guillén to Wellington, 27 February 1813, US. WP.1/382; Escobeda to Wellington, 12 March 1813, US. WP.1/364.
32 Wellington to H. Wellesley, 23 August 1812, US. WP.1/347; Sydenham to H. Wellesey, 10 October 1812, US. WP. 1/361; cf. also Doyle to Cooke, 31 December 1808, PRO WO.1/227, 651–2.
33 E.g. *El Redactor General*, 2 April 1813, p. 2645, Hemeróteca Municipal de Madrid (hereafter HMM) 6/3; *El Conciso*, 1 April 1813, pp. 3–5, HMM AH2–5 (351); Pérez Garzón, *Milicia nacional*, pp. 80–4.
34 For this incident, cf. Tone, *Fatal Knot*, p. 76.
35 Considerable information on the *josefino* militia may be found in Pérez Garzón, *Milicia nacional*, 33–59; in private conversation with the author, the Spanish military historian, Juan José Sanudo, whose as yet unpublished research has found traces of an extraordinarily large number of *juramentado* anti-guerrilla units, has even suggested that at certain points there may have been more Spaniards in arms against the guerrillas than there were in service with them.
36 Cf. Esdaile, 'Heroes or villains', p. 34.
37 Cf. in particular their remarks in D. Chandler, 'Wellington at war: regular and irregular warfare', *International History Review*, XI, No. 1 (February, 1989), p. 9; D. Chandler, review of David Gates, *The Spanish Ulcer: a History of the Peninsular War* (London, 1986), *Times Literary Supplement*, 4 July 1986, p. 742; J. Weller, 'Wellington's use of guerrillas', *Journal of the Royal United Services Institution*, CVIII (May, 1963), pp. 155–6.
38 E.g. Wellington to H. Wellesley, 10 March 1812, US. WP.12/1/5.
39 Wellington to Castlereagh, 5 September 1808, US. WP.1/214.
40 E.g. Wellington to Liverpool, 11 and 19 April and 19 August 1810, PRO WO.1/244, pp. 62, 69–71; WO.1/245, pp. 357–8.
41 For British distrust of the guerrillas, cf. Walker to Liverpool, 18 September and 1 November 1810, PRO WO.1/261, 46–8, 115–16; Christian to Cotton, 26 August 1811, PRO WO.1/261, pp. 386–7.

42 Wellington to Liverpool, 18 June 1812, US. WP.12/1/5.
43 Wellington to Cooke, 25 November 1812, US. WP.1/351.
44 Wellington to Bathurst, 27 January 1813, US. WP.1/365.
45 Wellington's plans at this stage in the war may be examined in C. J. Esdaile, *The Duke of Wellington and the Command of the Spanish Army, 1812–14* (London, 1990), pp. 109–13, 132–3.
46 *Ibid.*, 114–34.
47 A detailed account of the role of the guerrillas in 1813 may be found in C. Oman, *A History of the Peninsular War* (Oxford, 1902–1930), VI, pp. 252–74; for a discussion of their part in Wellington's strategy, cf. C. J. Esdaile, 'The Duke of Wellington and the Spanish guerrillas: the campaign of 1813', *Consortium on Revolutionary Europe Proceedings*, 1991, pp. 298–306.

CHAPTER VI

'Carrying on the War as it should be': Fraternisation

Philip J Haythornthwaite

An aspect of the Peninsular War which might appear curious when compared with the ferocity with which battles were contested, is the number of contemporary accounts which describe fraternisation and at times friendly relations between the contending armies. Such relations were generally restricted to the British and French armies, both of which were campaigning in a foreign land; the Spanish and Portuguese, whose home was being ravaged by war, could hardly be expected to exhibit the same kind of civility towards their enemies. Amicable encounters between opposing troops were not restricted to the Peninsula, and were reported elsewhere; for example, the French *chasseur* Jacques Chevillet recalled sharing a drink and exchanging pleasantries with an Austrian hussar whom he met on an island in the Brenta river, near Vicenza, in 1809, the hussar recalling a victory over the French and Chevillet pointing to a captured Austrian belt that he was wearing, before they parted on the best of terms; and perhaps it is significant that in this case also, neither man was campaigning in his own homeland. It is in memoirs of the Peninsular War, however, that such events are reported in considerable numbers.

The pursuit of a system of what might be termed 'limited' warfare was often a practicality in the interests of both sides, for example in an unspoken truce to permit the recovery of wounded, or in the humane treatment of prisoners of war; but it also involved a perception of the nature of war. A contemporary opinion stated that he who perfected 'the art of destroying his fellow-creatures [with] no other end in view than to gratify the ambition of sovereigns, he was a monster of whom it may be said that it would have been happy for the world if he had been strangled at his birth; but if he did it only for the defence of persecuted virtue or for the punishment of insolent and overbearing atrocity, to put a curb on ambition or to restrain the unjust pretentions of violence, humanity ought to raise monuments to his honour'[1]. Similarly, the belief that to expend life without a specific tactical or strategic objective was indefensible was remarked upon by Frederick the Great: 'To shed the blood of soldiers when there is no occasion for it, is to lead them inhumanly to the slaughter'[2]. This was echoed in 1804: 'The lives of men are not to be thrown away upon attempts, the success of which is inadequate to compensate the loss of a single life. We had imagined, too, that it was not justifiable to take the lives of our enemies but for some object by which we should be in a better situation, and our enemy in a worse. Mere killing is not the purpose of war, and operations that terminate in mere unavailing slaughter, have been reprobated by all Moralists and Publicists'; but, the statement added, 'It is probable enough, however, that these principles are antiquated, and it is natural enough that they should be so among those who would make war merciless and destructive, in proportion as they make it contemptible and inglorious'[3].

The 'merciless and destructive' element occurred in the appalling cycle of atrocity and reprisal which was a feature of the 'irregular' warfare involving the French and the inhabitants of the Peninsula. This shocked most onlookers: '. . . the streets presented a scene of the most horrible nature – a scene that was at once calculated to harrow up every good feeling, and to make the blood run cold at the barbarities to which an unprincipled enemy is capable of having recourse to, for the purpose of spreading terror and desolation . . . horror and indignation at the appalling sight filled the bosoms of the allied troops with the desire of revenge'[4]. Nevertheless, apart from such uniquely dreadful sights, the combatants came to regard 'ordinary' destruction as commonplace. Writing of a deserted and devastated village, one witness remarked that the enemy was 'as reckless and careless of the mischief he had left behind as we [the villagers'] friends and allies were, who viewed this scene of havoc with the most perfect indifference; and yet, though callous from habit, the soldier is by no means cruel or hard-hearted; accustomed when on service to death in all its forms, he thinks not of the miseries his profession, "the profession of Kings and Princes", causes . . . nothing was to be seen but naked and blackened walls – not a soul had returned to his home – all was desolation and ruin. War, like the simoon of the desert, had swept over the spot, and left alone its scorched and fiery track behind. But why should I now moralize? At that time I thought as little about it as the meanest soldier in the ranks, or the brute beast that carried my baggage. My imagination dwelt only on the bliss of a good breakfast, and the comfort of a clean shirt . . .'[5].

If the concept of 'civilised' war was thus an impossible illusion, there were many contemporary objections to the infringement of what some regarded as the tenets of honour or a military code, even though these might be overtaken by the heat of battle. At Sahagun, Alexander Gordon saw a member of his squadron cut down a Frenchman who was trying to surrender: 'I hallooed to the fellow to spare him, but before I could reach the spot the villain had split the Frenchman's skull . . . It was fortunate for him that he got out of my reach, for, in the indignation I felt at his conduct, I should certainly have treated him in the same manner[6]. The man later admitted that he did not want to let the day pass without killing an enemy, and that that was his opportunity; but to their credit, his conduct also disgusted his comrades. John Cooper was similarly revolted when one of his battalion's sergeants came upon a soldier who had stumbled during a charge, and exclaiming 'I'll kill a Frenchman for once' deliberately shot him dead[7].

On occasion, even helpless wounded were not spared; although here, as elsewhere, the possession of rank could be an advantage. Harvey Jones recalled how he lay helpless in the breach at San Sebastian during an unsuccessful attack, when 'my attention . . . was aroused by an exclamation from the soldier lying next to me – "Oh, they are murdering us all!". Upon looking up, I perceived a number of French grenadiers, under a heavy fire of grape, sword in hand, stepping over the dead, and stabbing the wounded; my companion was treated in the same manner: the sword was withdrawn from his body, and reeking with his blood, was raised to give me the *coup de grâce*, when fortunately the uplifted arm was arrested by a smart little man a serjeant, who cried out, "*Oh, mon Colonel, êtes-vous blessé?*" (the serjeant must have mistaken my rank, from seeing a large gold bullion epaulette on my right shoulder, and the blue uniform, rendering it more conspicuous) and immediately ordered some of his men to move me into the town'[8]. (Having escaped this dreadful episode, Jones was then treated with the customary civility shown to a wounded enemy, even being kissed by the first French officer he met as he was being carried to hospital.)

Perhaps the best known incident of this nature involved Charles Napier, who was incapacitated by injury at Corunna; as he lay wounded his life was saved twice by a French drummer named Guibert who forcibly restrained an Italian soldier from stabbing Napier to death. The treatment Napier received subsequently, and the kindness bestowed upon him by Marshals Soult and Ney, caused him to hold them, and Napoleon, in the highest regard.

Such incidents epitomised the mutual respect and compassion for enemy wounded which was evident on many occasions, demonstrating the best aspect of the concept of military honour. An officer of the British 51st recalled how some of his battalion's wounded fell into the hands of the correspondingly numbered French regiment; 'pointing to the number

117

in their caps, they said they all belonged to the same regiment, and that our men should fare as their comrades. They fed them, dressed their wounds; nay, they did not even plunder their packs, and in the morning we found these soldiers whom the French, owing to their wounds, could not take away with them in their retreat, all speaking in the highest terms of the treatment they had received. This is the real chivalry of modern warfare, and robs it of half its horrors'[9].

Those taken prisoner did not all receive the very favoured treatment accorded, for example, to Charles Napier and to the great dandy Samuel Hobkirk of the British 43rd, who when captured at Arcangues in November 1813 was mistaken for a general from the richness of his uniform, and dined with Soult on the evening of his capture; but in many cases, especially the officers, prisoners escaped even robbery and insult. Louis Lejeune was treated 'with the considerable courtesy of true gentlemen'[10] by the British officers into whose custody he was delivered, with Sir William Lumley, Beresford, Portuguese officers and Castaños all showering him with kindness. Moyle Sherer was taken prisoner when a French officer 'beat up the muskets of his leading section, already levelled for my destruction; This noble fellow, with some speech about "un Français sait respecter les braves", embraced me, and bade an orderly conduct me to Count d'Erlon'. Some French soldiers saved Sherer from robbery by the 'rascally sculking stragglers, who are always the cowards and plunderers of an army'; and d'Erlon 'took off his hat instantly, and spoke to me in a manner the most delicate, and the most flattering, asking no questions, but complimenting highly the brave resistance which had been offered to him', and apologised that he had no spare horse for Sherer to ride. Going to the rear with other prisoners, 'None of the soldiers offered to insult us; many of the officers indeed saluted us, though here and there a decorated officer smoothed his mustachoes as he looked upon us, with an air of impatient brusquerie', and that was the worst he experienced[11].

Sherer was typical in expressing his respect for a brave enemy: '. . . in the French army, as in all others, the good hearts far outnumber the bad[12]; and the absence of hatred towards the foe was articulated by George Napier: 'there is never any personal animosity between soldiers opposed to each other in war . . . so it is, and I hope will always be the case. I should hate to fight out of personal malice or revenge, but have no objection to fight for *"fun and glory"*'[13]. Such sentiments could even apply in battle; the common revulsion against useless sacrifice of life was remarked upon by Jonathan Leach, who wrote bitterly of a French officer who ordered a hopeless attack at the Coa, 'a piece of unpardonable and unjustifiable butchery on the part of the man who ordered those brave grenadiers to be sacrificed, without the most remote prospect of success. They deserved a better fate, for no men could have behaved with more intrepidity'[14].

Such sentiments were not restricted to the higher ranks, who most commonly recorded them. A telling remark was made with regard to a noted raid mounted upon a French outpost in January 1814, before Bayonne, by the captain of the 11th Foot's grenadier company, Francis Gualey. Such raids were most unusual, but Gualey (who was himself a Frenchman) had received official sanction for his enterprise, and succeeded in surprising and capturing the French picquet, in the course of which sentries had to be overpowered. This skilful operation, however, was not regarded with admiration; a soldier of the 42nd recalled that 'The French and British outposts used to be very good friends before this night, but this cruel job annihilated all feeling of honour, and we were denounced savages. The taking of this piquet [sic], and the barbarous murder of the unfortunate sentinel, added nothing to the success of the war, while it covered its authors with disgrace'[15].

Moyle Sherer recounted a similar expression of regret when he overheard 'a section of our men speaking in terms of great admiration of the gallantry of a French officer, who, it seems, had made himself very conspicuous in a late skirmish in trying to bring on his men. "I was sorry to see him drop, poor fellow", said one. "Ah!" said another, "he came so close there was no missing him; I did for him!" "Did you!" rejoined the first speaker; "By God, I could not have pulled a trigger at him. No; damn me, I like fair fighting and hot fighting; but I could not single out such a man in cold blood"'[16]. Even an exchange of shot between a garrison and its besiegers could be regarded as unjustified if no obvious attack was imminent; when a British sentry was killed by a French cannon-shot from Bayonne, his comrades showed what they thought of the matter by placing a cannon-ball and an inscription on his grave:

> 'On sentry I fell a sacrifice,
> In cold blood to French cowardice;
> Above my head a cannon-shot you see,
> Resembling that as was the death of me'[17].

Even shooting deliberately at an enemy general, an event which could have had profound effects, was deprecated; George Napier remarked of Busaco that 'I am sorry to say the French general did a most unhandsome thing, and that was to make one of his batteries fire at Lord Wellington as he rode along accompanied by his staff! This was shameful and cowardly, because Marshal Massena knew (the thing was too evident for him not to know) that he was only reviewing and thanking his troops for their bravery, and he should have prevented such an act. Had Marshal Soult or Marshal Marmont been the general in command of the French army they would have scorned such an act'.[18] The same morality was demonstrated at Alba de Tormes in November 1812, when prior to the French attack an officer approached within easy musket-range of the British position when reconnoitering; Lt.Col. John Cameron of Fassiefern of the 92nd Highlanders deliberately prevented his men from firing, and it was said that it was Soult who thus escaped with his life. (Cameron's biographer remarked that 'strange, indeed, are the "chances of war" as they appear to us, though all regulated by a higher Power. The dreadful carnage of the 92d at Maya – the loss of thousands of brave men through the blood-stained passes of the Pyrenees, might have been saved, had not Cameron, at this moment, stayed the deadly weapons of his soldiers'[19]; but even foreknowledge of this might not have led to a violation of this perception of the code of military honour.)

It was not uncommon for the troops of both sides to permit their opponents to forage, and while there was probably an element of expected reciprocation, it demonstrates the absence of animosity. William Surtees recalled how 'three French officers, seemingly anxious to prove how far politeness and good breeding could be carried between the two nations, took a table and some chairs out of a house which was immediately in our front . . . and bringing them down into the middle of the field, which separated the advance of the two armies, sat down within 100 yards of our picquet, and drank wine, holding up their glasses, as much as to say your health, every time they drank. Of course we did not molest them, but allowed them to have their frolic out. During the day also, we saw soldiers of the three nations, viz. English, Portuguese and French, all plundering at the same time . . . they plundered in perfect harmony, no one disturbing the other on account of his nation or colour'[20]. William Lawrence remembered how his regiment 'lay as comfortably as if we had been living in peaceful times; though we were so near the enemy that we very often wandered into the same vineyards, and exchanged compliments by shaking hands'[21]. William Tomkinson of the 16th Light Dragoons described how some French officers 'took off their swords and came down to speak to us, saying their object was only foraging, and that we need not put ouselves to any inconvenience, as they should soon withdraw . . . they invited us to a play at Santarem they had got up, and we them to horse-races, football, and dog-hunts. The communication was put a stop to by general order'. (Despite such friendly relations, shortly after this encounter, Tomkinson chased and captured a French foraging-party of twenty *voltigeurs*, who after running two miles with

120

the cavalry on their heels, 'surrendered without the least resistance . . . they were native French, and the finest men I have seen. They were so blown with running as scarcely able to move'[22].

Such meetings between enemies occurred even in battle. At Busaco George Napier described how he led his men down a hill – regretting his inability to help wounded Frenchmen he passed – and 'When we got to the bottom, where a small stream ran between us and the enemy's position, by general consent we all mingled together searching for the wounded. During this cessation of fighting we spoke to each other as though we were the greatest friends and without the least animosity or angry feeling! One poor German officer in the French army came to make inquiries respecting his brother, who was in our service in the 60th Regiment . . . and upon looking about he found him dead, the poor fellow having been killed. Very soon Lord Wellington, finding we remained as he thought too long below, ordered the bugles to sound the retreat, and the French general having done the same, off scampered the soldiers of each army and returned to their several positions like a parcel of school-boys called in from play by their master'[23]. After the firing ceased at Talavera, Daniel Nicol recalled how the French set up their camp-fires and began to cook their dinner; 'A brook ran through the plain; to it both armies for water as if truce was between us, looking at each other, drinking, and wiping the sweat from their brows, laughing and nodding heads to each other; all thoughts of fighting for the time being forgotten'[24].

Before Pamplona George Wood 'was here highly amused, just before dusk, by observing many of our soldiers run into a field between the hostile picquets, and dig with their bayonets. Soon after I saw many of the enemy do the same thing: they did not molest each other, but appeared even familiar, laughing and joking promiscuously. How strange, thought I, that these men, who to-morrow would be slaying each other, should now be so good-humouredly employed together! They were digging potatoes; and this ground, I believe, is generally, in point of honour, allowed to be neutral'[25]. Criticism was made of those who endeavoured to prevent such civilities; Wellington recalled his anger with Marmont for firing upon British troops drinking from a river: 'I had let his people drink a thousand times, and took care to let him know that I would never do so again'[26].

Charles Parquin recalled his meetings with British officers, the first when he was sent by his commanding officer to invite a party of Englishmen to enjoy a bottle of brandy. A group of his fellow-officers shared the drink with a similar number of British officers of the 10th Light Dragoons, who reciprocated by sharing their rum, and arranged for the transmission of a letter to a British officer held in France. In subsequent encounters, Parquin discovered the British to be very good company if possessed of a somewhat sarcastic sense of humour, and prepared to exchange jovial banter even in combat. Such attitudes were not universal: Marbot described being challenged by a British officer anxious to cross swords with him, resisting the chiding as long as he could, and was then almost captured as he had to fight not only the officer but two cavalrymen who tried to apprehend him.

Most contact between enemies occurred at the 'outposts', the picquets which separated the armies and which in general maintained an attitude of mutual co-existence. One officer recalled that 'the French and English soldier had no feeling of animosity towards each other; they fought bravely in the field, but on picquets they have been known for days to be within musket-shot, the sentinels perhaps separated only by a ditch, yet not a shot was ever fired except at the proper time. They knew how useless it was to harass each other for nothing, and though they both did their duty in the most vigilant manner, confidence was never abused, and we frequently conversed familiarly with the French officers at the advanced posts with as much feeling of security as in our own tents . . . One instance . . . to show the gallant bearing and generous conduct of our foes. An officer commanding a picquet, supped one night with the French officer in charge of the one opposite his post, and, to his own eternal disgrace, actually got drunk, and was brought back about midnight to his own men on the backs of four unarmed French soldiers, laughing and enjoying the joke most heartily'[27].

William Grattan noted that when the armies were encamped on either side of the Douro, 'not one life was lost, nor one shot fired by either army. Indeed so different from hostility was the conduct of both nations, that the French and British lived upon the most amicable terms. If we wanted wood for the construction of huts, our men were allowed to pass without molestation to the French side of the river to cut it. Each day the soldiers of both armies used to bathe together in the same stream, and an exchange of rations, such as biscuit and rum, between the French and our men, was by no means uncommon. A stop was, however, soon to be put to this friendly intercourse; and it having been known in both armies that something was about to be attempted by Marmont, on the evening of the 12th of July [1812], we shook hands . . . and parted the best friends . . . the French officers said to us on parting, "We have met, and have been for some time friends. We are about to separate, and may meet as enemies. As 'friends' we received each other warmly – as 'enemies' we shall do the same"'[28]. Charles Boutflower wrote of the same time that 'a singular mode of warfare is carried on; it is not uncommon to see five hundred of the Enemy, and as many of our men, bathing together in the Douro in the most perfect good humour possible, at the same time that the Cavalry of the two rival Armies come down on their respective sides to water, it being perfectly understood that neither party shall ever approach the River armed'[29].

It was reported in 1810 that 'The 92d Highlanders are about a mile in front of head-quarters, and so close to the enemy that they could (if they understood each other's language) speak to each other. The Highlanders and French are so near and courteous, that they salute each other, when going on or coming off duty; and, a few days ago, a bullock run from the enemy into the 92d's lines, which was immediately shot by one of the Highlanders. Two of the enemy, who were in chase of it, came over, waving white handkerchiefs, who expressed the great want they would be in for food, if the Highlanders kept the bullock from them; on which the Highlanders, with the hospitality which characterises their country, sent half the bullock, with a bottle of whisky over to them'[30].

A British Guards officer recalled that in the later stages of the war, 'I never knew an advanced sentry of either army to be wantonly shot at the out-posts; and I have often myself, when strolling too far in advance of my own picquet, been waved back by the French, but in no one instance was I fired upon'. On one occasion near St Jean de Luz he and another officer, who were in the habit of chatting to their French counterparts, enquired of one whether he could procure some wine for them. The French officer 'expressed every wish to oblige us; but said that he really could not afford to purchase the wine himself, with the chance of losing his money in case any movement should take place in either army; but that, if we chose to take the risk upon ourselves, and would intrust him with the price of it, his regiment would again be at the out-post in three days' time, and that we should then have our wine. He was true to his word: on the third day there was a case of most excellent claret waiting for us, which he had been kind enough to bring upon a mule from St Jean de Luz; and we parted, after exchanging names, and mutually expressing a wish that we might renew our acquaintance at some future period under happier auspices'. Such commercial activities were by no means unusual.

At the same outpost, 'One fine moonlight night our advanced sentry called the attention of Colonel Alexander to the French sentry in his front, who was distinctly seen in the moonlight leaning against a tree, and fast asleep with his musket by his side. Alexander went quietly up to him, and took possession of the musket, and awoke him. The man was at first much frightened upon finding himself disarmed, and in the hands of an English officer. Alexander gave him back his firelock, merely remarking, that it was fortunate for him that he had found him asleep on his post, instead of one of his own officers. The poor fellow expressed the greatest gratitude; and, by way of excuse for such an unsoldierlike act, said, that his regiment having been moved from the extreme left of the French army, he had been marching for many hours through bad cross-roads; and, having been immediately put upon the out-post duty, he was overcome by fatigue'.

Shortly after, Alexander had his kindness repaid, when he, 'in returning from the front on a very dark, stormy night, missed his way, and his horse falling over a bank, both horse and rider came clattering down heels over head into a lane, and close to a French sentry, who instantly challenged. Alexander hearing the *qui vive*, and the click of his musket, thought that he was going to fire, and called out '*C'est l'officier du poste Anglais – ne tirez pas!*'. '*Non, non, mon Colonel*', replied he, '*J'espère que vous n'êtes pas blessé!*' . . . These anecdotes, trifling in themselves, still tend to show that feelings of respect and courtesy may exist between two gallant and chivalrous nations, although opposed to each other in a stern and bloody warfare'[31].

At Bayonne the same officer recalled how he and a comrade 'were amusing ourselves in the garden in front of the picquet-house, by playing at the very intellectual game of "pitch and hustle", when our sentry at the bottom of the walk called us up to him and pointed out a French sentry who had just been posted immediately on the other side of the hedge, and quite within our lines. Col. Alexander, who happened to be at the advance, went up to him and told him that he must go off. The man replied, that he dared not leave his post, and that when the relief came, he would tell "Monsieur le Caporal" what the Colonel said. Alexander desired him to beckon up some one from his picquet, and a non-commissioned officer came directly, who said that he would send the officer. Alexander told the officer that he had no wish to hurt the sentry, but that if he was not withdrawn in a quarter of an hour he would be shot. The French officer was a very reasonable and gentleman-like young man; and after many bows, and the exchange of a pinch of snuff, he went back to his party, taking the sentry with him'[32].

Jonathan Leach remarked upon the difference in relations between the British and French and the inhabitants of the Peninsula; he observed that the Spanish never understood the Anglo-French manner of waging war, 'nor did they ever let slip an opportunity of shooting an unfortunate sentry at his post. Much as such practice is to be deprecated between the armies of civilized nations, it cannot be denied that the Spanish soldiers had a thousand causes of irritation and hatred towards their invaders'[33]. Towards the British, however, he found the conduct of the French 'courteous, and, if I may use the expression, gentlemanly to a degree . . . One morning, in a thick fog, a small patrole of ours

124

suddenly found themselves close to a superior force of French cavalry, and instantly retired; but, in the hurry, one of our dragoons dropped his cloak. Our patrole had ridden but a short distance to the rear, when it was called to by the French, one of whom riding up to within a short distance, dropped the captured cloak on the ground and rode away, making signals to the English dragoon who had lost it, to pick it up. This was carrying on the war as it should be; and it is but justice to add, that we rarely found them deficient on this point'[34].

Such courtesy recalls the incident in 1798 when two Spanish gun-boats captured a boat and crew from the 74-gunner HMS *Edgar*, outside Cadíz, only to return them next day, 'and so particular were the Spaniards, that the Fourth Lieutenant's hat having been left on shore, a flag of truce was afterwards sent off with it on board'[35]. It is noteworthy, however, that British naval officers who visited the army in the Peninsula failed to understand the system then operating; accustomed to attacking the French at sea whenever they were encountered, 'Their first question invariably was, "Who is that fellow there?" (pointing to the enemy's sentry, close to us), and, on being told that he was a Frenchman, "Then why the devil don't you shoot him?"'[36].

Not unexpectedly, there were misunderstandings between sentries and violations of the general system. William Surtees recalled how a sergeant and a few men played a trick on the opposing French picquet, stealing past the French sentry, seizing the arms piled in front of the outpost and smashing them before the French roused themselves, and then running back to the British lines. George Landmann described how he had to intervene in a quarrel between two sentries which had arisen from the differing habits of the two nations. Despite not understanding each other's language, the French and British sentries had become acquainted after the Frenchman had presented the Briton with a piece of bread, and had been invited for a drink in return. After a swig of British rum the Frenchman threw his arms around the Briton, and, with Gallic bonhomie, had kissed him; the startled Briton pulled away, exclaimed 'Do you take me for a girl, or what sort of pranks would you be after?' and followed this with a slap. Landmann jumped between them to prevent further violence[37]. (The British sentry was not alone in his embarrassment with foreign manners; walking around Bordeaux after the end of the war, Lieut. John Ford of the 79th was startled when 'a French soldier ran up to me . . . threw his arms round my neck, kissed my cheek, and hugged me so close as to knock off my highland bonnet with his rough embrace, and this without any previous explanation'[38]; it was a wounded soldier for whom Ford had procured food and medical treatment some months earlier.)

John Kincaid remembered a couple of occasions when normal civilities were violated. One night 'a ball came from the French sentry and struck the burning billet of wood round which we were sitting, and they sent in a flag of truce, next morning, to apologise for the accident, and to say that it had been done by a stupid fellow of a sentry, who imagined that people were advancing upon him. We admitted the apology, though we knew well enough that it had been done by a malicious rather than a stupid fellow, from the situation we occupied'[39]. Another incident occurred at the Nivelle, when Kincaid was sent to order a British picquet commanded by Lieut. John Gardiner to push back the French. 'The enemy's sentries were so near, as to be quite at Mr Gardiner's mercy, who immediately said to me, "Well, I won't kill these unfortunate rascals at all events, but shall tell them to go in and rejoin their picquet". I applauded his motives, and rode off; but I had only gone a short distance when I heard a volley of musketry behind me; and, seeing that it had come from the French picquet, I turned back to see what had happened, and found that the officer commanding it had no sooner got his sentries so generously restored to him, that he instantly formed his picquet and fired a volley at Lieutenant Gardiner, who was walking a little apart from his men, waiting for the expected signal [to advance]. The balls all fell near, without touching him, and, for the honour of the French army, I was glad to hear afterwards that the officer alluded to was a militiaman'[40].

(A similar comment regarding the nature of transgressors was made in relation to the anger displayed by some French officers at the end of the war, who deliberately insulted Allied officers and provoked some duels. One involved Lieut. Ernest von Düring of the 5th Line Battn., King's German Legion, who was challenged by a French officer who 'had invited several ladies "to see him shoot a British officer"; but they only assembled to see the vain braggart fall; for the Frenchman's pistol missed fire, and Düring's ball killed his opponent on the spot. This duel had the good effect of stopping all further insult on the part of the officers of the garrison of Bayonne, who, it is but justice to the French army generally to add, reckoned amongst them many men who had been lately promoted from among the non-commissioned officers and the ranks'[41].)

Communication between armies regarding prisoners and the like was carried on at the highest level, and Wellington once intervened in cutting a possible line of intelligence. He learned that the French general Maximilien Foy was constantly sending envoys to the British to borrow newspapers; 'At that time they were cut off from all intercourse with France, and had no other means of information than those papers afforded. When I heard of Foy's having them, I put a stop to it, and desired Baron Tripp[42] to ask him what he wanted them for. What do you think was the answer? He said that he was speculating in the English funds, and only wanted to know the price of the Three per cents! I desired that he might be informed of the price of the Funds as often as he pleased, but should not see the papers!'[43].

Some attempts were made to interrupt the intercourse between armies, as some realised the hazards of allowing relations to be too friendly. In 1810 Charles Boutflower wrote that it was 'the practice of the men of both Armies to meet in the same Vineyards in the Valleys, and even to talk and shake hands with each other. This has however very properly been put a stop to, it being very justly considered that the Simplicity of our Fellows was no match for the Cunning of a Frenchman'[44]. William Surtees commented on the same subject: 'The French officers were extremely polite, and asked us many questions of the news of the day, &c.; but the commander-in-chief, hearing of the familiarity which subsisted between the two armies, issued an order, prohibiting British officers from holding conversations with the enemy; for as all these conversations were necessarily conducted in French (very few indeed of their officers being able to speak English) he was apprehensive they might gain such information from our people, from their imperfect knowledge of the French language, as might materially injure our future proceedings. Before this order was issued, the most unbounded confidence subsisted between us, and which it was a pity to put a stop to, except for such weighty reasons. They used to get us such things as we wanted from Bayonne, particularly brandy, which was cheap and plentiful, and we in return gave them occasionally a little tea, of which some of them had learnt to be fond. Some of them also, who had been prisoners of war in England, sent letters through our army-post to their sweethearts in England, our people receiving the letters and forwarding them'[45].

George Napier expressed similar fears when recounting how 'some of the French soldiers asked my leave to come across [a river] and get tobacco from our men, as they had none . . . I allowed two of them to come, who immediately stripped off their clothes and swam across (for I would not let them try the ford), got the tobacco, told us all the news from France, and returned quite happy. Now this was all wrong, because, when a man is placed in charge of a post, he should never permit the enemy to come within reach of being able to observe what he is about . . . No harm did happen by these men coming over to my picket, but there might have been danger from it, because the officer might have disguised himself as a private, and come over as such, and, being naked, I could not possibly tell him from a soldier; and when once over, he would have seen the strength of my post and the number of my men, and returned fully aware of all my weak parts of defence'[46].

In general, friendly relations with the enemy did not compromise duty on either side. Henry King recalled how, accompanied by a group of Spanish soldiers, he walked too near to a French picquet; they fired wide to warn him, whereupon he and a companion 'returned the salutation by taking off our hats, and bowing. Clerke heard the enemy say, "Bon soir, messieurs – allez vous en"'[47]. George Napier described how he warned a French general – he discovered later that it was supposedly Marshal Ney – not to approach too near, and fired a warning shot after his instructions were ignored. On another occasion he recalled how his friend Capt. William Mein, commanding an outpost, 'when all was quiet and his sentinels posted and no fear of any surprised, he asked the captain commanding the enemy's pickets to have some supper with him, which the poor fellow, who had been half-starved for some months, was delighted to accept. So he came to Mein's house, and after a good supper – for we had some sutlers come up to the army – and an hour or two of conversation, it was time for him to go back to his own picket; and he had not been gone above a quarter of an hour when he was ordered to retreat from his post. Our men, perceiving that the French sentinels were withdrawn, gave the alarm and off started Mein with his picket after his friend the French captain, firing at him as hard as he could'[48]; which demonstrated that despite their earlier friendship, duty was paramount.

George Gleig recalled that provided he wore his red jacket (to confirm his nationality, the French having no time for civilities with Spaniards), he could approach the French lines so closely and in such safety that they helped him fish for trout, and took advantage of the good relations to barter tea for brandy. He remarked, however, that 'the matter may be pushed too far. Towards the close of the war, indeed, so good an understanding prevailed between the outposts of the two armies that Lord Wellington found it necessary to forbid all communication whatever; nor will the reader wonder at this when I state to him the reason. A field-officer . . . going his rounds one night, found that the whole of a sergeant's picket-guard had disappeared. He was, of course, both alarmed and surprised at the occurrence; but his alarm gave place to absolute astonishment when, on stealing forward to observe whether there was any movement in the enemy's lines, he peeped into a cottage from which a noise of revelry was proceeding, and beheld the party sitting in the most sociable manner with a similar party of Frenchmen, and carousing jovially. As soon as he showed himself his own men rose, and wishing their companions good night, returned with the greatest *sang froid* to their post. It is, however, but justice to add, that the sentinels on both sides faithfully kept their ground, and that no intention of deserting existed on either part. In fact, it was a sort of custom, the French and British guards visiting each other by turns'.

Such civilities doubtless served to alleviate a few of the hardships experienced on campaign, and prevented much unnecessary and aimless bloodshed. Those involved would probably not have disagreed with Gleig: 'There is something extremely agreeable in carrying on hostilities after this fashion'[49].

Notes

1   Anon, *The Military Mentor*, London 1804, II p. 60.
2   *Military Instruction from the Late King of Prussia*, trans. Lt Col T. Foster, London 1818, pp. 120–1.
3   *Morning Chronicle*, 17 December 1804.
4   *The Courier*, 19 April 1811.
5   'A Field Officer', 'Four Years of a Soldier's Life', in *Colburn's United Service Magazine*, 1844, III pp. 46–7. The author has been identified as Frederick Mainwaring of the 51st Light Infantry.
6   Gordon, A., *A Cavalry Officer in the Corunna Campaign 1808–9*, ed. Col H.C. Wylly, London 1913, p. 109.
7   Cooper, J.S. *Rough Notes of Seven Campaigns in Portugal, Spain, France and America*, Carlisle 1869, r/p 1914, p. 22.
8   Jones, Lt Col H., 'Narrative of Seven Weeks' Captivity in St Sebastian', in *United Service Journal* 1841, I p. 193.
9   'A Field Officer', p. 231.
10 Lejeune, L.F., *Memoirs of Baron Lejeune*, trans. Mrs A. Bell, London 1897, II p. 103.
11 Sherer, M., *Recollections of the Peninsula*, London 1825, pp. 353–7.
12 ibid. p. 179.
13 Napier, G.T., *Passages in the Early Military Life of General Sir George T. Napier*, ed. Gen. W.C.E. Napier, London 1884, p. 177.
14 Leach, J., *Rough Sketches in the Life of an Old Soldier*, London 1831, p. 151.
15 Anon., *The Personal Narrative of a Private Soldier who served in the Forty-Second Highlanders for Twelve Years during the Late War*, London 1821, p. 230.
16 Sherer, *Recollection*, p. 349.
17 'Green Feather', 'Reminiscences of Bayonne', in *United Service Magazine* 1842, II p. 84. The author has been identified as Charles Parker Ellis.
18 Napier, *Passages*, pp. 147–8.
19 Clerk, Rev A., *Memoir of Colonel John Cameron, Fassiefern*, Glasgow 1858, p. 56.
20 Surtees, W., *Twenty-Five Years in the Rifle Brigade*, London 1833, p. 263.
21 Lawrence, W., *The Autobiography of Sergeant William Lawrence*, ed. G.N. Bankes, London 1886, pp. 70–1.
22 Tomkinson, Lt. Col. W., *The Diary of a Cavalry Officer in the Peninsular War and Waterloo Campaign 1809–1815*, ed. J. Tomkinson, London 1895, p. 64.
23 Napier, *Passages*, pp. 145–6.
24 Quoted in Low, E.B., *With Napoleon at Waterloo*, ed. McK. MacBride, London 1911, p. 100.
25 Wood, Capt. G., *The Subaltern Officer*, London 1825, p. 206.
26 Ellesmere, Earl of, *Personal Reminiscences of the Duke of Wellington*, ed. Countess of Strafford, London 1904, p. 152.
27 'A Field Officer', pp. 231–2.

28 Grattan, W., 'Badajoz to Salamanca', in *United Service Journal* 1834, I p. 507.
29 Boutflower, C., *The Journal of an Army Surgeon during the Peninsular War*, privately published, n.d., p. 145.
30 *Edinburgh Evening Courant*, 1 December 1810.
31 'Green Feather', 'Out-Post Anecdotes', in *United Service Journal* 1840, I pp. 223–4.
32 'Green Feather', 'Reminiscences of Bayonne', p. 84.
33 Leach *Rough Sketches* p. 97.
34 ibid. p. 189.
35 *Morning Chronicle*, 2 August 1798.
36 Kincaid, Sir John, *Adventures in the Rifle Brigade*, London 1830, r/p with *Random Shots from a Rifleman*, London 1908, p. 18.
37 Landmann, Col. G., *Recollections of My Military Life*, London 1854, II pp. 293–5.
38 Ford, Capt. J., 'The Redoubt "Des Augustins" . . . and some Military Scraps', in *Colburn's United Service Magazine*, 1844, II p. 113.
39 Kincaid, *Adventures*, p. 19.
40 ibid., p. 134.
41 Beamish, N.L., *History of the King's German Legion*, London 1832–7, II p. 305.
42 The name is omitted from this quotation but the officer is identified in Ellesmere, p. 128.
43 Stanhope, Earl, *Notes of Conversations with the Duke of Wellington*, London 1888, p. 54.
44 Boutflower *Journal*, p. 67.
45 Surtees *Twenty-five years* pp. 257–8.
46 Napier, *Passages* pp. 115–6.
47 *United Service Journal*, 1840, II p. 526.
48 Napier, *Passages* pp. 176–7.
49 Gleig, G.R., *The Subaltern*, Edinburgh 1872, p. 235.

CHAPTER VII

Prisoners of War in the Peninsula, 1808–14

Paul Chamberlain

During the long wars with France from 1793 until Napoleon's final defeat in 1815, a total of 200,000 prisoners of war arrived in Britain from all theatres of the conflict. These men (and women) were housed in land prisons and the infamous prison hulks. Captured officers and civilians of rank were offered their parole, giving their word of honour in writing not to violate parole conditions (including not attempting escape), if they were allowed the relative freedom of the towns and villages throughout the country designated as parole depots.

Until 1808, enemy soldiers and seamen had been taken during the numerous campaigns to capture French, Dutch and Spanish territory overseas (especially in the West Indies); the frequent naval actions that produced a large haul of captives, such as the battles of Camperdown and Trafalgar; and the continuous war against enemy commerce. Indeed, this latter aspect of the conflict generated a continuous stream of prisoners into the British war prisons, taken captive on board merchant vessels, privateers, transports and coastal craft. While the Royal Navy was acquiring such prizes on the high seas, the French and Spanish were doing likewise, especially through the many privateers operating out of ports along the Channel coast and in the Mediterranean.[1]

During the Napoleonic Wars prisoners taken by Britain were administered by the Transport Office of the Admiralty, presided over by the Transport Board[2]. Prison ship depots existed at Portsmouth, Plymouth and Chatham, and in 1808 the land prison depots were Forton (Gosport, near Portsmouth), Mill Prison (Plymouth), Stapleton (Bristol), and Norman Cross (near Peterborough). Dartmoor Prison was nearing completion and would receive its first batch of French prisoners in May 1809.

The year 1808 was a significant one for Britain, and was of great importance for the Transport Board and its administration of prisoners of war. With the start of the Peninsular War, Britain could now take the conflict to the enemy by land, in alliance with Portugal and Spain. This latter fact resulted in many thousands of Spanish prisoners being released from British war prisons, thus creating space in the depots that could be filled with Frenchmen, and reducing the financial burden on the Admiralty, albeit only temporarily. British prisoners held in Spain were also immediately released.

The most important effect, however, was evident when a British army under Wellesley arrived in Portugal in August 1808. Wellesley's army was very soon in action against the French, and the first trickle of captives from the Iberian Peninsula began to arrive in England during the autumn. The Commissioners of the Transport Board were well aware that more captives would soon be on their way if a British army remained in that theatre. The opening of the depot at Dartmoor the following year alleviated the space problem for the time being, but with Wellesley's victory at Talavera on 28 July 1809 it was evident that the Peninsular theatre was going to be a major source of captives. Portchester Castle, near the south-coast naval base of Portsmouth, had been a major land prison during the war with Revolutionary France. From 1803 until early 1810 it remained empty of prisoners (although the artillery of the King's German Legion used the barracks as their depot), as many senior military and government officials questioned the wisdom of having a large population of enemy nationals next to a major naval base, especially during the invasion scare of 1803–5[3]. In late 1809 the Transport Board was forced to reconsider Portchester Castle as a depot to accommodate prisoners from the Iberian theatre[4].

The two major conflicts that resulted in an increase in the British war prison establishment were the Peninsular War and the simultaneous Anglo-American War of 1812. Two further barracks were constructed at Dartmoor Prison in 1812, while further depots were built at Esk Mills and Greenlaw/Valleyfield in 1811, and Perth in 1812. The prison ship establishment was increased from twenty-four vessels in 1808 to a total of thirty-six by 1814[5]. The Peninsular War had a notable impact upon the prisoner of war population in Britain (indeed, the depot at Perth was built specifically to house captives from this conflict), and was a theatre that caused many a headache for the Commissioners of the Transport Board.

The battles fought in Spain and Portugal produced many captives. When General Dupont surrendered his army at Baylen in July 1808, a total of 17,635 French troops passed into captivity in Spanish prisons[6]. The Corunna campaign generated a few French prisoners, the pursuing French army taking more captives (2,000) than the retreating British. Many of these were taken as stragglers[7]. Soldiers of both sides were taken prisoner if they were wounded or sick and could not be conveyed from the scene of action. After Talavera 1,500 wounded British soldiers were left in the town, guarded by the Spanish. On the advance of the French the

Spanish troops departed, leaving these wounded soldiers to be captured[8]. The bloody action at Albuera in 1811 resulted in 900 wounded French becoming prisoners after being left in the Allied position[9]. The pursuit of a defeated army generated more captives than were taken in the action itself. The majority of the captive total for the battle of Vittoria was taken during the rout of the French, and included many camp followers. The Spanish took most of the 2,000 prisoners in this action, and many more would have fallen into Allied hands but for the plundering of the French baggage train[10].

Successful sieges gave the victors a large number of captives to be housed, guarded and fed. The Spanish garrison of Zaragosa, totalling 13,000 disease-ridden men, women and children, capitulated to the French in 1809 and were marched off to France[11]. When Ciudad Rodrigo fell nearly 1,400 French soldiers marched into captivity, while nearly 5,000 soldiers joined these captives when Badajoz was successfully stormed by the British army[12].

An army fighting overseas requires constant supplies of munitions, food and reinforcements if it is to continue the conflict. While British and French troops were marching and fighting in Spain, both sides relied on their navies to supply them; the former throughout the war, and the latter in the early stages before the Royal Navy made the supply by sea of French coastal garrisons too hazardous. Throughout the campaign, French privateers made the coastlines of Spain and Portugal dangerous for isolated British merchant vessels, and some of the supplies destined for Wellesley's army fell into the hands of the French in this way, along with the crews of such ships. Only constant patrolling by the Royal Navy kept this menace to a minimum, and a continuous stream of captive privateer crewmen was sent to Britain from this source[13]. After 1812 there were many American privateers captured around the Iberian coastline, having taken advantage of the increase in British commercial traffic. While their countries were not at war with the United States of America, the Spanish and Portuguese authorities detained any American vessels that arrived in their ports, and handed the crews over to the British[14].

The French armies that fought in Spain contained not only French troops, but also Italian, Polish, German (from the many German states allied to France), Irish, Neapolitan, Swiss, Prussian and Dutch soldiers. Many of these men were reluctant allies of Napoleon, and often took the opportunity to desert to the Allied forces, sometimes individually, occasionally en masse. Oman calculates that at Baylen a total of 1,400 Swiss troops deserted to the Spanish forces prior to Dupont's surrender, while during the second siege of Zaragosa in 1809 many Swiss soldiers deserted the Spanish garrison to join the besieging French[15]. Next to the Swiss, the most numerous deserters were from the German units making up a large proportion of the French armies in Spain. From the start of the Peninsular conflict such men deserted at every available opportunity, and the problem (as far as the French command was concerned) was aggravated by the large number of troops that the French army had to employ in procuring food from the countryside. This gave them ample opportunity to desert. Wellington wrote to Lord Liverpool in 1810:

> The difficulties which the enemy experience in procuring subsistence, owing to their having invaded this country without magazines, and having adopted no measures for the security of their rear, or of their communications with Spain, has rendered it necessary for the soldiers to straggle in search of food, and not a day passes that prisoners and deserters are not sent in[16].

Ensign John Aitchison of the 3rd Foot Guards was at the sharp end of the war. Writing from Vizeu on 28 March 1810 he related that:

> Deserters from the enemy arrive here about three times a week and they have almost all been taken into our service . . . three deserters were brought here this morning[17].

Sometimes whole units deserted. In a country where the guerrillas had an ominous reputation there was obviously safety in numbers, even when deserting. Whole units even deserted when they realised the direction the war was going. As Rifleman William Surtees recalled, in December 1813 during the action at the Nive:

> . . . two or three battalions of the Nassau and Frankfurt regiments came over and left the French. They had heard that the Dutch had declared against Bonaparte, and wished to be transported to Holland, with all their arms and appointments, which they brought with them[18].

While many soldiers deserted the French armies, there were also some cases of troops from the British army fleeing to the enemy. The King's German Legion recruited many ex-prisoners of war, both in Spain (from the spring of 1810 onwards) and from within the war prisons of Britain. While this force had a fine fighting reputation under Wellington's command, it experienced constant desertions while in the Peninsula. The records do not state whether these men specifically deserted to the French or away from any form of military service, but the problem was so serious that those Germans enlisting in Spain were sent back to the Legion's depot in England, and more trustworthy troops dispatched in their place[19]. Desertion was also a problem for the other foreign units in Wellington's army, namely the Brunswick Corps and the Chasseurs Britanniques. The latter had an especially bad reputation for desertion and was never employed on outpost duty, although as a fighting force they had a respectable record, due to the professionalism and zeal of their officers[20]. While such men may have deserted to join the other side, initially (and certainly as far as the British army was concerned) they were treated as prisoners of war.

The Peninsular Campaign is notable for the ferocity of the guerrilla war waged against the invading French armies. Popular accounts relate how no quarter was given on either side, and that atrocities were committed by the Spanish upon French soldiers who fell into their hands, which prompted the French to treat the inhabitants with equal brutality. Certainly this situation did occur, but the official records detail numerous French soldiers and civilians who were taken captive by Spanish and Portuguese guerrillas, civilians and the armed forces. Bernard Tolede, for example, was the French manager of an hotel near Madrid. After the French evacuated the area he '. . . was taken by the inhabitants in Spain on 11 November 1812'[21]. Ensign John Aitchison relates how the French garrison of Cuenca quitted the place hoping to reach the main French forces, but found themselves surrounded by Don Pedro Villacampa's guerrillas. These 1,000 French troops were taken prisoner and conveyed to the British for transport to England[22]. Throughout the war both the Spanish and Portuguese armies conveyed their French captives to the British. This act was part of the subsidies paid to both these countries to enable them to continue the war effort. Britain had an efficient war prison system, and so was able to absorb these captives into the depots; neither Spain nor Portugal having the facilities, either moral or physical, to house, feed, clothe and guard large numbers of prisoners of war. Those French troops captured at Baylen, and who survived the Spanish hulks in Cadiz and the island of Cabrera, were eventually transferred to Britain in October 1810, most of them being confined on board the hulks at Plymouth[23].

In Britain the prisoners of war were administered by the Royal Navy, and guarded by regiments of militia in the land depots, and the Royal Marines on board the hulks. In the Peninsula such captives were guarded by soldiers drawn from the British, Portuguese and Spanish armies, while they were transferred to ports such as Lisbon for transport by the Royal Navy to England. During their transfer to the coast they were housed in convenient and temporary prisons such as convents and fortresses. As in

Britain, the officers were offered their parole and if accepted were allowed the relative freedom of Spanish towns, although governed by the same regulations imposed upon them as if they were in Britain. After Vittoria many French officers resided on parole in the town, some even setting up a Masonic Lodge with which to occupy their time![24]

The treatment of prisoners of war in the Peninsular theatre depended very much upon who captured them. British and French soldiers had much in common in that they were both fighting in a strange land far from home, and so there was no personal animosity between the two nationalities. The Spanish and Portuguese, however, had both seen their countries invaded by the French and fought the invaders with a fierce passion, an attitude that was reciprocated. It was to be expected that prisoners taken by these soldiers would not always be treated well. Edward Costello of the 95th Rifles recorded a conversation he had with a particularly savage-looking Spanish guerrilla that summed up the attitude towards the French:

> 'Napoleon loves his soldiers, and so do the ravens,' as he pointed to several of those carrion birds perched on the walls of an old convent . . . 'We find them plenty of food; they shall never want so long as a Frenchman remains in Spain'.[25]

Costello also relates an incident that occurred during the pursuit of the French as they retreated from Portugal. As they advanced into a village, a Portuguese Caçadore whose family lived there rushed to his home and discovered:

> . . . the mangled bodies of his father and mother, the blood still warm and reeking through the bayonet stabs, while an only sister lay breathing her last, and exhibiting dreadful proofs of the brutality with which she had been violated. The unhappy man staggered, frenzied with grief . . . His first act was to dash at some French prisoners that unfortunately were near the spot, guarded by some of our dragoons. These he attacked with the fury of a madman. One he shot and another he wounded, and he would have sacrificed a third, had not the guard made him prisoner.[26]

Undoubtedly the French received the same treatment they themselves meted out to the inhabitants in the Peninsula. This resulted in many of the deserters from the French armies remaining in the mountains until they had a favourable opportunity of surrendering to the British. Sir Robert Porter accompanied Sir John Moore and his army during the Corunna campaign, and witnessed some French soldiers taken captive by British cavalry. He wrote:

> . . . we find the French officers very pleasant men, and far from chagrined by their misfortunes . . . I believe they inwardly rejoice at having fallen into our hands, rather than those of the Spaniards, as they well know the enraged patriots would have given them no quarter . . . mobs of our allies have continually surrounded the house in which our prisoners were confined, awaiting the moment when they hoped we would call the Frenchmen out and have them shot.

These particular Spaniards were to be disappointed as shooting prisoners of war were not in '. . . our laws of war' as Porter put it[27]. Those soldiers were fortunate. In November 1812 Lieutenant Swabey came across some French prisoners huddled together by the side of the road while their Spanish escort was leading them one by one to a tree against which they were being shot. The Spaniards' excuse was that these prisoners were from the hospital in Madrid and were too ill to travel farther. They were simply being put out of their misery! Fortunately some soldiers of the 95th Rifles arrived on the scene and helped Swabey rescue the unfortunate captives[28]. Not all Spaniards treated their captives cruelly however. Swabey relates how he met a Spanish dragoon who was conveying a wounded Frenchman to the rear. The dragoon asked Swabey for assistance, which he could not give as it would mean leaving his post. After refreshing the Frenchman with brandy and water, however, he sent the benevolent Spaniard and his charge on their way. The Frenchman, so it was later discovered, reached the British camp safely[29].

The French made an example of guerrillas (or brigands as they called them) whenever possible, and did not appear to make much of a distinction between these men and Spanish soldiers taken in battle. Captain Charles Boothby, wounded and captured at Talavera, was conveyed by wagon through Spain to imprisonment in France. In his conversations with the people he met en route, both French, Spanish and English, he learnt that the usual treatment for Spanish prisoners, especially if they were sick and could not march, was execution. This was:

> . . . too well corroborated by the carcasses of Spanish soldiers on the road, upon whose bodies the uniform declares their nation, and the wounds the manner of their death.

Boothby regarded this treatment of prisoners to be inhumane and something the British army would never contemplate. The policy reason for these massacres was explained by a French officer who said that '. . . if those wretches were left sick on the road they would only serve to strengthen the brigands'[30].

The British and French treated each other as well as circumstances would allow. Any rough handling experienced by the common soldier when captured was out of a desire for plunder rather than any animosity towards a vanquished foe. Edward Costello was a witness of this attitude after the siege of Badajoz:

> . . . we saw a number of Frenchmen guarded by our soldiers, coming over the bridge. They were the prisoners taken in the Fort San Christobal which but an hour or two previously had surrendered. These were soon surrounded by our men, who began examining their knapsacks, from whence a number of watches, dollars, etc. were quickly extracted[31].

Surgeon James McGrigor was witness to the chivalry displayed by British officers towards their captive counterparts. At Badajoz he recalled:

> In one street, I met General Phillipon, the governor, with his two daughters, holding each by the hand; all three with their hair dishevelled, and with them two British officers, each holding one of the ladies by the arm, and with their drawn swords making thrusts occasionally at soldiers who attempted to drag the ladies away. I am glad to say that these two British officers succeeded in conveying the governor and his two daughters safely . . . to the camp.[32]

Boothby, lying injured in the town of Talavera, heard from his servant that a number of wounded British officers had had their possessions plundered by French soldiers. He was prudent enough to conceal what few belongings he had with him and made his presence known to some French officers, who showed him every courtesy; supplying him with food, clothes and books, and even visiting to keep him company. He had nothing but praise for the French officers he met[33]. This respect was reciprocated by the British.

Costello witnessed the charge of the King's German Legion heavy cavalry under General Bock at Garcia Hernandez in 1812. In this action the cavalry broke the French squares '. . . taking them prisoners, almost to a man'. Costello, suffering the effects of a wound, was sent to the rear as part of the escort for these prisoners many of whom were severely wounded. As Costello noted:

> The escort consisted chiefly of the Germans that had taken them prisoners, and it was pleasing to behold these gallant fellows, in the

true spirit of glory, paying the greatest attention to the wants of the wounded.[34]

All captives taken by the British and their allies were sent to Lisbon where they awaited transport vessels provided by the Royal Navy to convey them to England. These vessels usually discharged their captives at the ports of Plymouth or Portsmouth, which were then in the care of the Transport Office.

When the French acquired prisoners of war, they were marched through Spain under a strong escort of gendarmes. The French treated both British and Spanish officers with the greatest respect, often entertaining them and ensuring their comfort during their journey to France. During the Peninsular conflict only three British generals were captured by French forces, namely Lord John Murray, Sir Edward Paget and Major-General Andrew Lord Blayney, and these gentlemen were treated with the utmost courtesy. Lord Blayney travelled leisurely through Spain (his journey took three months) being passed from one French general to another, dining with each in turn and attending balls, bull-fights and hunting excursions with his hosts[35]. The British had the same attitude to senior French officers taken prisoner. General Ruffin was mortally wounded at the battle of Barrosa in March 1811. He was taken captive and conveyed to England on board HMS *Gorgon*, on board which he died on 15 May, then being conveyed to Portsmouth where he was buried with full military honours[36].

British prisoners were sent to reside in the fortress towns along the east and north-east borders of France. Officers resided on parole in Verdun[37].

Throughout the period the British had a larger population of prisoners of war than the French had British in their hands. This meant that the French could not mistreat their British captives as they did their other foreign prisoners such as the Spanish and Portuguese. The enmity between the nations accounts for much of this, but the French also had considerable supply problems in the Peninsula. They had immense difficulties in feeding their own troops; prisoners of war were an inconvenience and had low priority for food, clothing and shelter. Of the 13,000-strong Spanish garrison of Zaragosa, only 6,000 actually reached France, the remainder dying of disease and neglect en route, typhus accounting for a large proportion of the deaths.

The Spanish and Portuguese were treated as second-class prisoners of war and used as a source of labour on farms and in factories, replacing the French male population who had been conscripted into Napoleon's armies. Many of these captives were used to build roads, embankments and drain swamps, especially at Walcheren in north Holland. Large numbers died whilst working on these projects[38].

While many French prisoners of war taken by the Spanish were eventually transferred to the British authorities, where they received humane treatment, initially those taken experienced just as harsh treatment as did the Spanish in French hands. The Spanish had a number of hulks in Cadiz harbour and a major prison depot on the Balearic island of Cabrera. Conditions in these places of confinement were appalling at the best of times. Many Frenchmen died of hunger, disease and maltreatment. In June 1810, 800 French prisoners arrived at Portchester Castle after having been confined on board one of the Cadiz hulks. They were in poor health, and stated that during their eighteen months in Cadiz they had not once tasted fresh vegetables or meat, and scurvy, typhus and dysentery had reduced their number from an original total of 1,600. This was corroborated by an English officer who related how the dead bodies of prisoners were allowed to float about in the harbour of Cadiz, and on one occasion he had counted thirty bodies washed ashore in one day. In October of the same year, eighty survivors of General Dupont's army were transferred from Cabrera to Plymouth, where it was noted that one of them lay down on the beach and 'died of dirt'.[39]

In the confusion of battle, many soldiers taken prisoner seized the opportunity to escape shortly after capture. Captain Thomas Henry Browne was in the company of a squadron of the 18th Hussars in the pursuit after Vittoria. The force he was with rapidly became depleted as the soldiers '. . . could not resist falling to the work of plunder'. The French rearguard saw this and attacked, taking Browne and some troopers prisoner. He was escorted to the main French force by a party of French dragoons, who, some hours later, were in turn attacked by British cavalry. Browne related:

> . . . the fellow who guarded me swore a tremendous oath, that if he could not keep me he would put an end to me, and lifted up his sword for the purpose of carrying it into execution. I flinched, caught the blow just above the hip, and taking advantage of his stroke having failed started off, ran with full speed towards my countrymen, with several shots fired at me in vain . . .[40]

Some prisoners attempted escape but were unsuccessful in their endeavours. Costello witnessed an attempt at freedom during the Battle of Fuentes de Oñoro:

> During the latter part of the day the enemy had made some prisoners,

which they exhibited to us as they marched them along their lines. One man we saw make a determined attempt to obtain his liberty. He had loitered in the rear as the party were going over a small bridge that crossed the Duas Casas by a mill, when, turning suddenly upon a Frenchman behind him, he threw him into the water, and immediately made a dash for our position, but owing to several of the French being between him and us, we had the mortification of seeing the poor fellow recaptured, without being enabled to render him any assistance; we could see by his kilt that he belonged to the 79th Regiment.[41]

For the majority of prisoners, however, captivity meant remaining in the prison depots until the war ended. During the Revolutionary Wars, a prisoner could expect to remain captive for no more than a year or two, as frequent exchange cartels were arranged between Britain and her enemies. Prisoners were exchanged on the basis of an agreement first arranged between Britain and France in 1780; then they would be exchanged man for man, rank for rank. If no prisoners of a particular rank were held by one side, then the balance could be made up of lesser ranks. This system worked well, with all the belligerents keeping a careful record of prisoners exchanged, so that no side could claim that it was being treated unfairly in the return of its nationals. The system was made easier by Britain treating separately with France, Spain and Holland. During the 1790s the many German states were either allies of Britain or neutral, and so Germans taken prisoner in the French service could be released immediately in the interests of international diplomacy.

This situation changed in 1803. Hanover was overrun by the French, and Napoleon insisted that the 17,000 Hanoverian soldiers who surrendered at the capitulation of General Walmoden be offset against French prisoners in Britain for the purpose of exchange. Britain would not agree to this, insisting that the French make separate arrangements with the Hanoverian authorities over this matter. The problem was that Britain rapidly acquired more French prisoners than France had British captives. Between 1803 and 1814 a total of 122,400 prisoners of war arrived in Britain, mostly French (including Dutch and Germans who were now part of the French empire). During the same period, France acquired approximately 500,000 prisoners of war from throughout Europe, of which only 20,000 were British. In 1811, for example, after captives began arriving in Britain in significant numbers from the Peninsular theatre, the figures reveal that France held approximately 88,000 prisoners, including 40,000 Spanish, 10,526 English and 932 Irish[42]. Britain held a total of 49,130 captives, including 20,000 sent from the Iberian Peninsula in that year alone. The total in Britain reached a maximum of 72,000 in 1814, but this also included a number of Americans. The maximum number of British prisoners in France at any one time was 12,000 in 1812[43].

It was obvious that in any general exchange of prisoners, France would be left with a deficit once all Britons held by her had been sent home. Throughout the Napoleonic period, there were numerous discussions about the possibility of exchange cartels being organised, but very few actually were. The diplomacy involved in these talks was conducted by the French Agent residing in London, Baron Otto, and his British counterpart in Paris, Mr Mackenzie. When such cartels were organised, merchant vessels were hired by the respective governments to convey prisoners across the Channel. It was suspected that both sides used these vessels for intelligence gathering, and occasionally the artillery batteries protecting the Ports would open fire upon these vessels, mistaking them for warships. Such actions would result in a flurry of diplomatic correspondence between London and Paris, during which no further cartel ships would sail[44].

A further problem resulted directly from the Peninsular conflict. France held fewer Britons than Britain held Frenchmen. Therefore, France was willing to exchange British, Spanish and Portuguese prisoners for her own nationals. This Britain would not agree to, stipulating that the Spanish and Portuguese were a matter for their own governments to deal with[45]. This further hindered any exchange cartels being organised, and the Transport Board was well aware that once a prisoner arrived in England, he was incarcerated in the system until either diplomacy prevailed, or the war ended. Likewise, once a British soldier arrived in France, his chance of exchange was minimal. The only prisoners who were sent home without waiting for an exchange cartel were women (who were regarded as non-combatants and therefore not prisoners of war), children under the age of 12, and the chronically sick.

There was a way round this problem however. Some French officers were offered their parole and allowed to return to France, provided they agreed not to engage in any hostile act against Britain or her allies until they had been regularly exchanged. The advantage of this method was that the officer could use his influence with senior civil or military officials to obtain the release of a British officer of equal rank. This means of exchange bypassed the political channels and obtained the release of some officers. British officers were allowed the same arrangement, being granted parole and allowed to return to England.

Wellington and his officers were also aware that once an officer was captured and sent to France the chance of regaining that soldier was slight. The Transport Board was happy to assist in any local exchanges that were arranged in Spain, provided that full details were transmitted to the Admiralty. They would even release French officers on parole in England if a British officer had been released by the French forces in the Peninsula. Captain Joseph Benoit was on parole in Bridgenorth in early 1813, having been captured in Spain during the previous August. He was 'exchanged for Mr Anscott, Paymaster 3rd Dragoon Guards in Spain, at the request of Lord Wellington'[46]. In November 1813 Wellington requested an officer be exchanged for Major O'Hara of the 1st Portuguese Regiment, who had been returned on parole by the French. The Board authorised the release of Major Eman Le Gentil who was residing on parole in England[47].

The British and French in Spain frequently organised their own exchange cartels. Lieutenant Swabey was sent under a flag of truce to arrange the exchange of officers and men taken when General Slade's cavalry lost some troops to the French in the summer of 1812. His mission was a formality according to his account:

When we arrived at the outposts, handkerchiefs were tied over our eyes, a ceremony which, though performed with the greatest civility, was totally unnecessary on this occasion. We were carried to the General Officer's quarters, ascertained that all due care was taken of some wounded men and officers, and set on foot their exchange which was afterwards completed. By the time this was done it was nearly sunset and we were persuaded to remain to dine and sleep. There was nothing very extraordinary in this for there was always great rivalry in generous civility between this part of the French army under Count D'Erlon . . . and Sir Rowland Hill, and the exchange of prisoners was carried on between these officers . . .

In a cavalry action on 13 June 1812 the light cavalry under General Long captured an aide-de-camp, while the French took two British officers. Swabey noted:

The Count D'Erlon treated our people with the greatest kindness and every assistance was given to the wounded; he gave the two officers money, and they are both to be exchanged for the aide-de-camp.[48]

Officers taken captive were allowed to correspond with their commanders to effect an exchange. Captain Boothby, whilst a prisoner, had some letters conveyed across the lines to General Sherbrooke. The latter replied giving details of his efforts to obtain Boothby's release and saying:

. . . if there be any officer of your rank, prisoner with us, about who

. . . the French Generals feel interested, I beg you will send me his name, and that of the place he is supposed to be at, and I will use all the influence I have to effect an exchange between you.[49]

Chivalry and good conduct between the British and French was a characteristic of the conflict in the Peninsula. When Countess Gazan (wife of a French General) was captured after Vittoria along with her children and their nurse, they were treated with the greatest respect and returned to her husband in the French lines[50]. The French had the same approach, returning some children of the British army under a flag of truce in 1812[51]. At the siege of San Sebastian in 1813, some British officers were wounded in an unsuccessful assault on the citadel. As they lay in the breach a French officer appeared from the town holding a white handkerchief. The British ceased firing and this humane officer caused some of his men to help the two Britons into the town, where they were well treated. This chivalrous deed was brought to the attention of the Duke of Wellington who, when the town fell, sent for this officer who dined with him before being restored to liberty and conveyed to Bayonne by sea, with an attestation stating that his '. . . release to be owing to the gallantry of his conduct.'[52]

While the possibility of exchange gave hope to many prisoners in the prison depots, most were wise enough to realise that they were likely to remain there until the war ended, whenever that might be. Many decided that the only way out was by volunteering for service in the forces of their captor. Many of these volunteers did so to escape the war prison and serve in the only profession they knew, whilst undoubtedly many joined the army or navy in the hope that they could desert back to their own side again. This was realised by the authorities who often kept their ex-prisoner of war recruits in the regimental depots, or sent them to stations abroad (such as the West Indies) where the chance of contact with the forces of their own nation was remote. On the British side the units that recruited from amongst prisoners of war were the King's German Legion, the Chasseurs Britanniques, the Duke of Brunswick Oel's Corps and the 5th and 7th Battalions 60th Foot, all of whom recruited not only in the prison depots in England, but also directly in the Peninsula. In 1811 for example, Philippe Fischer, Frederick Schreiber and Johannes Müller, all deserters from the French armies in Spain, enlisted in the 1st Hussars of the King's German Legion. Philippe Fischer at least, was still on the muster records of the regiment in March 1814[53]. The battle of Vittoria convinced many soldiers in the French army that they were on the losing side. The records for Forton Prison detail many Germans who, having been taken during or after this action in June 1813, were transferred to

England to be housed at Forton, and had then enlisted in the British service by the autumn of that year. Theodore Schmitz (ex-4th Dragoons), Heinrich Seymit (ex-2nd Hussars), Adam Plum (ex-17th Regiment of Light Infantry), all enlisted in the 7th Battalion 60th Foot when a recruiting party from that corps visited Forton on 11 September[54].

As the Peninsular War progressed, the British army acquired a plentiful source of recruits. The French acquired a number of deserters from the British army, mainly Irish and never as many as were deserting in the opposite direction, and these were recruited into the Régiment d'Irlandaise. A number of these soldiers deserted from this corps.

The Peninsular War had a significant impact on the prisoner of war population in Europe, but especially so in Britain, as the population of captives swelled and new prison depots were constructed to house them. The belligerent forces (Britain more than France) found new recruits in this theatre, the campaign providing many of the more reluctant troops of Napoleon's armies with the opportunity to avoid fighting for an Emperor and a cause they had no heart for. There is no doubt that this conflict contributed considerably to the expansion of the British war prison system. The Peninsular War had a major impact on the course of the Napoleonic conflict, and especially so over the matter of prisoners of war held by the opposing forces.

Notes

Manuscript sources:

PRO – Public Record Office, Kew, London.

MT – National Maritime Museum, Greenwich, London.

1 For a detailed account of privateering activity during the period, and its effect on the generation of prisoners of war, see Patrick Crowhurst, *The French War on Trade: Privateering 1793–1815* (Gower Publishing, 1989).

2 Until 1795 all prisoners of war were in the care of The Commissioners for taking care of sick and wounded seamen, and for exchanging prisoners of war, popularly known as the 'Sick and Hurt Office.' In that year the administration of prisoners was transferred to the newly formed Transport Board. See Condon, M.E., *The Establishment of the Transport Board – A Subdivision of the Admiralty, 4 July 1794*. The Mariners Mirror 58: 69–84, 1972.

3 Portsmouth was a major centre for the accommodation of prisoners of war. Portchester Castle had a capacity of 7,000; Forton Prison could hold 3,000; and the prison ships in Portsmouth Harbour held 5,000 in 1810.

4 PRO ADM98/252. Admiralty Letters to Agent, Portchester Castle, 1810.

5 For a general account of the war prisons see Francis Abell, *Prisoners of War in Britain 1756–1815* (London, 1914). Details of the prison ships may be found in PRO ADM103 passim.

6 V.J.Esposito and J.R. Elting, *A Military History and Atlas of the Napoleonic Wars* (London, 1980) Map 85: The Campaign in Spain.

7 Charles Oman, *A History of the Peninsular War* (London, 1995) I: p. 648.
8 ibid., II: p. 581.
9 ibid., IV: p. 395.
10 ibid., VI: pp. 435–42.
11 Rudorff, Raymond, *War to the Death: The Sieges of Zaragosa 1808–1809* (London, 1974), p. 262.
12 Oman, *Peninsular War*, pp. 185 and 593.
13 PRO ADM103/145, *General Entry Book of French Prisoners of War at Gibraltar, 1803–1813.* This volume details the prisoners taken in and around the Iberian Peninsula and held temporarily at Gibraltar prior to transportation to England. The General Entry Books are a valuable source of information regarding prisoners of war, detailing their physical features, rank, place of capture, and eventual disposal.
14 PRO ADM103/144, *General Entry Book of American Prisoners of War at Gibraltar 1812–1815.*
15 Oman, *Peninsular War* I p. 191 and II p. 133.
16 Lt.Col.J.Gurwood, *Selections from the Dispatches and General Orders of Field Marshal the Duke of Wellington* (London, 1851), Wellesley to Liverpool, 20 October 1810, p. 393.
17 W.F.K. Thompson (ed.). *An Ensign in the Peninsular War: The Letters of John Aitchison* (London, 1981), p. 88.
18 William Surtees, *Twenty-Five Years in the Rifle Brigade* (London, 1996), p. 262.
19 Daniel Savage Gray, 'Prisoners Wanderers and Deserters: Recruiting for the King's German Legion 1803–15', *Journal of the Society for Army Historical Research*, 53:153.
20 For a detailed discussion of the German troops in Wellington's Army and the problems they posed see Sir Charles Oman, *Wellington's Army 1809–1814* (London, 1986) pp. 220–8.
21 PRO ADM103/368. *General Entry Book of French Prisoners of War at Forton, 1813.* Tolede was sent to England to reside in Forton Prison, along with many other soldiers captured at Salamanca and Badajoz.
22 Thompson, *An Ensign*, p. 198.
23 The Pescott Frost Collection (1888) 1, P. 61 (Portsmouth Central Library).
24 John T. Thorpe, *French Prisoner's Lodges* (Leicester, 1900), p. 116.
25 Edward Costello, *The Adventures of a Soldier or Memoirs of Edward Costello* (London, 1841), p. 207.
26 ibid., p. 103.
27 Sir Robert Ker Porter, *Letters from Portugal and Spain Written During the March of the British Troops under Sir John Moore* (London, 1809, facsimile reprint, 1985) pp. 203–4.
28 Lieutenant William Swabey, *Diary of Campaigns in the Peninsula for the Years 1811, 12 and 13* (Facsimile reprint, London, 1984) p. 153.
29 ibid., p. 111.
30 Captain Charles Boothby, *A Prisoner of France* (London, 1898) pp. 226–7.
31 Costello *Adventures*, pp. 175–6.
32 Sir James McGrigor, *The Autobiography and Services of Sir James McGrigor, Bart – Late Director General of the Army Medical Department* (London, 1861) p. 276.
33 Boothby *Prisoner*, pp. 45–6.
34 Costello, *Adventures* p. 200.
35 Michael Lewis, *Napoleon and His British Captives* (London, 1962), pp. 83–6.

36 The Pescott Frost Collection, p. 121.
37 The prison depots in use in France between 1803 and 1814 were: Arras, Valenciennes, Cambrai, Givet, Sedan, Longwy, Verdun, Sarrelibre, Bitche, Besançon, Auxonne, Briançon, and Montdauphin. Lewis, ibid., p. 84.
38 Edward Fraser, *Napoleon The Gaoler* (London, 1914), pp. 14–16.
39 The Pescott Frost Collection, p. 61.
40 Roger Norman Buckley (ed.), *The Napoleonic War Journal of Captain Thomas Henry Browne 1807–1816* (London, 1987), pp. 214–5.
41 Costello, *Adventures*, p. 124.
42 Francis Abell, *Prisoners of War in Britain 1756–1815* (London, 1914), p. 20.
43 PRO ADM105/44. Commissioners Reports, 14 June 1811.
44 For a detailed account of cartel ships and their regulation, see Abell ibid., pp. 25–6. The Admiralty records in the National Maritime Museum contain much correspondence relating to the problems surrounding cartels during the 1790s – ADM/MT/415 and 416. These problems continued after 1803 – see PRO ADM98/261 passim. *Letters Relating to Prisoners of War at Portsmouth 1810.*
45 *Cobbett's Weekly Political Register* Vol. XVIII. No.40, 26 December 1810, pp. 1307–1312; and No.41, 29 December 1810, pp. 1327–1340.
46 PRO ADM103/611. List of Parole Prisoners A-K.
47 PRO ADM103/614. List of Parole Prisoners L-Z.
48 Swabey, *Diaries*, pp. 105–6.
49 Boothby, *Prisoner*, p. 145.
50 Buckley, *Napoleonic Journal*, p. 218.
51 Costello, *Adventures*, p. 210.
52 Buckley *Napoleonic Journal*, pp. 239–40.
53 PRO WO25/672, *Description and Succession Book 1810–11: Foreign Regiments in British Service* and PRO WO12/11799, *Pay and Muster Records, 1st Hussars King's German Legion.*
54 PRO ADM103/368.

CHAPTER VIII
Wellington: Architect of Victory
Ian Fletcher

The defeat of the French armies in the Peninsula was caused by a combination of several different factors; the undoubted influence of the Spanish guerrillas, the sacrifices and huge contributions made by the long-suffering people of both Portugal and Spain, interference from Paris by Napoleon and his ministers, the squabbling and petty in-fighting of French commanders and, of course, the superiority of the Allied armies in the field over their French adversaries. These are just a few of the causes. But above all, one man stands tall as the real architect of the Allied victory in the Peninsula. That man was, of course, Sir Arthur Wellesley, later to become first Duke of Wellington. To do justice to Wellington's part in the great scheme of things in the Peninsula requires a book in itself. Therefore, this chapter looks briefly at some of his more marked characteristics which proved of greatest significance in his long struggle for supremacy in the Peninsula.

It is a great shame that Wellington never chose to write his memoirs for it would be wonderful to be able to read his own account of the war. Much of what we read was taken down by the gossips of the day, by socialites and by close friends, eager to impart the slightest piece of tittle-tattle or table talk. Fortunately, we have twelve volumes of Wellington's *Dispatches*, which were edited by John Gurwood and published between 1837 and 1839, and the *Supplementary Dispatches*, edited by Wellington's son and published between 1857 and 1872. They may not form an autobiography as we know it, but they are the next best thing and afford us a wonderful insight into the life of Wellington as military commander. One only has to read just a few of the letters to appreciate what an astonishing workload he undertook. Indeed, the level of detail to which he addressed himself is evident to anyone who reads these beautifully written Dispatches. For example, on 4 August 1811, we find him writing letters to Hill, Beresford, Admiral Berkeley (twice), Major General Needham, Torrens, his Military Secretary (twice), to Lord Liverpool and even to Marshal Marmont.[1]

Wellington was thirty-nine years of age when, as Sir Arthur Wellesley, he arrived in Portugal in August 1808 at the head of a small and relatively untried army. Its recent record – the disasters of El Hamet and Buenos Aires – was not particularly good, although many of his future regimental, brigade and divisional commanders were present at Sir John Stuart's fine victory at Maida on 4 July 1806, the manner of which was not lost on them. By the time he approached Toulouse in southern France, almost six years later, he did so at the head of what he considered the finest machine existing in Europe for its numbers.[2] He later called it an army with which he could do anything and go anywhere. Something had happened during the six years of war in the Peninsula to turn the British army from no-hopers to match winners and that 'something' can be laid firmly at Wellington's feet.

Wellington – he was awarded the title in August 1809 a month after his victory at Talavera[3] – has attracted more than his fair share of generalisations over the years, none more so than that of being a cautious, defensive-minded commander. Yes, of course he was, but only to an extent, and one has to understand the reasons for his caution before levelling criticism. For example, when he was faced with great odds with his small Anglo-Portuguese army during the anxious days of 1810, when even some of his own officers advocated an evacuation of the Peninsula in the face of an impending French invasion of Portugal, Wellington knew he had to be careful in order to preserve the only army Britain could put into the field. But not only was he being careful, he was also being wise. Wellington knew exactly what he had to do to defeat the French and was not averse either to retreat or to caution if it suited his objectives. He cared little for personal reputation, and if a retreat was necessary as the means to an end then so be it. One only has to look at the year of 1812 to bear this out, for, after all his great triumphs that year – the stormings of Ciudad Rodrigo and Badajoz, his crushing victory over Marmont at Salamanca, and the occupation of Madrid in August – he still finished the year back where he started, in Portugal, after the infamous retreat from Burgos in October and November. And yet he was left with little choice and so it had to be done.

The retreat to the Lines of Torres Vedras is cited as another example of his defensive-minded nature. But, here again, Wellington had planned his strategy a year in advance, for as early as October 1809, he had issued Colonel Richard Fletcher, his chief engineer, with his *Memorandum for the Construction of the Lines of Torres Vedras*.[4] The troublesome spring and summer of 1810, spent posturing on the Spanish-Portuguese border awaiting the third French invasion of Portugal, was as much about buying time to enable the construction of the Lines as it was about engaging the French under Massena. And when, following the fall of both Ciudad

Rodrigo and Almeida to the French, he was finally forced to retreat to Lisbon, he did so knowing that the Lines were waiting for him. Of course, what he did not know was whether they would actually stop Massena. Indeed, reports by Fletcher's engineer officers indicate that not all of them shared Wellington's belief in them.[5] In the event, however, he was proved correct. The Lines held, Massena's invasion came to nothing, and the French retreated having suffered one of the greatest reverses of the entire war. Even as Wellington was issuing his *Memorandum* in October 1809 he was already planning his strategy for the coming year and, the following year, predicted a retreat to the Lines, anticipated fighting a battle along the way which, of course, turned out to be Busaco, a battle which was never intended to be anything more than a delaying action.[6]

So, cautious and defensive-minded, or just sensible and prudent? Furthermore, the war lasted six years of which only two can really be said to have been spent on the defensive. 1808 saw the initial campaign, of which Roliça was an offensive action, 1809 saw British victories at Oporto – one of the most daring operations of the war – and Talavera, whilst 1810 can be said to have ushered in the period of Wellington's greatest vulnerability and consequent caution. 1811 began with Wellington's offensive operations to expel Massena from Portugal and ended with him consolidating on the Spanish border. 1812 was a momentous year for the Allies with the capture of Ciudad Rodrigo and Badajoz, the defeat of Marmont at Salamanca and the occupation of the Spanish capital, Madrid. The fact that the year ended disastrously with the retreat from Burgos takes nothing away from what was otherwise a great year. From 1813 onwards the Anglo-Portuguese army acted like a juggernaut and rolled back the French over the Pyrenees and into France, the war ending in April 1814. Therefore, can one really call Wellington a defensive-minded general, given the fact that he really only spent about two and a half years on the back foot in the face of French pressure?

The French certainly regarded Wellington as such, but this in fact worked to his advantage. At Fuenteguinaldo, in September 1811, Wellington found himself in a perilous position, outnumbered by Marmont. However, such was the psychological stranglehold which Wellington had over his enemies that Marmont would not attack, fearing the same treatment that Ney and Massena had been dealt at Busaco the previous year. Wellington was reinforced, Marmont never realised just how good a position he was in, and a great opportunity went awry.[7] At Salamanca, in July 1812, Marmont manoeuvred across Wellington's front, believing that he would not attempt an offensive move. Unfortunately for Marmont he was terribly wrong, as the subsequent attack by Wellington's army proved. The hold which Wellington had over the French was still working as late as 1815 when, immediately before the battle of Quatre Bras, Reille, an experienced Peninsula veteran, saw red-jacketed troops along the top of the Allied position. Wellington's troops on this occasion were arriving piecemeal and the crossroads were held, in fact, by a relatively small force. But Reille, after having experienced years of Wellington's reverse slope tactics in Spain, urged caution and Ney's attack was delayed, in part because of Reille's observations. The delay allowed more Allied troops to concentrate and the position at the crossroads, at first seemingly untenable, became rather more stabilised.[8] One final point concerning Wellington's reputation as a defensive general; of the fourteen major battles at which Wellington commanded the Allied army, just five of them (Vimeiro, Talavera, Busaco, Fuentes de Oñoro and 1st Sorauren) involved him in a defensive role.[9] The other nine (Roliça, Oporto, Salamanca, Vittoria, 2nd Sorauren, Nivelle, Nive, Orthes and Toulouse) saw him on the offensive. This does not take into account the four sieges (Ciudad Rodrigo, Badajoz, Burgos and San Sebastian), which were all offensives, the crossing of the Bidassoa and Adour rivers and, of course, his pursuit of Massena in March and April 1811 and the series of battles along the way. This represents a mass of offensive operations, something worth bearing in mind whenever one reads of Wellington as being a defensive general.

There has been, perhaps, another myth which has grown in proportion with Wellington's reputation as a defensive-minded general, and that is his use of the reverse slope as a battle-winning tactic. There is little doubt that the combination of reverse slope and linear tactics proved superior to the columnar tactics employed by the French. But once again, how many times was the tactic actually employed in the major battles? Surprisingly few; at Vimeiro and Busaco, and partially at Talavera, Fuentes de Oñoro and Sorauren. Most of the other named major battles involved Wellington's army in an attacking role – almost exclusively from Vittoria onwards, save for the Pyrenees – and so were devoid of the sort of tactics with which Wellington is most associated. The column against line tactic has long been the source of much discussion and heated argument since the days of the Peninsular War. Much of the cause of the argument, however, was sparked off by events, not in the Peninsula, but in southern Italy, at Maida in July 1806. That Sir John Stuart's victory was won by the firepower of the British line there is little doubt, but it is the formation of Reynier's French troops that caused most controversy. It is clear from evidence that the French came on in columns but deployed into line before engaging the British.[10] However, this was originally missed by the great historian of the Peninsular War, Sir Charles Oman. In a paper given to the Royal Artillery Institution in 1907 and published in their *Journal* the following year, Oman claimed that the triumph of the British line over French column at Maida was a precursor to Wellington's triumph in the Peninsula, but of course this was not true. After discovering that the French did not, after all, attack in column, Oman altered his account of the battle in his *Wellington's Army,* published in 1913, which led other historians such as Sir John Fortescue to alter their accounts of the battle.[11] Unfortunately, the original version of Oman's account of Maida – column versus line and all – reappeared when his *Studies in the Napoleonic Wars* was published in 1929, an error perpetuated further when the book was republished in 1987. The error has since led many an historian a merry dance.[12] For the time being, therefore, we can discount Maida as being the classic origin of the line versus column theory. What is true, however, is that many British officers present at Maida noted what they had seen and the power of the line was not lost on them when they served in the Peninsula.

But it was no magic formula that Wellington employed in the Peninsula. Indeed, the advantage of line over column – a mathematical equation which dictated that every musket in a line could be brought to bear against just the front ranks of a column – was quite clear to the French commanders themselves. What was new was the way in which Wellington used the tactic, for he combined it with judicial use of his skirmishers, his artillery and of his chosen fighting position. For years, French armies had been used to employing heavy columns, born of the need for ease of operation during the years of the mass armies of the revolutionary period, which would more often than not punch their way through whatever enemy troops stood in their way, e.g. Austrian, Russian and Prussian. At Vimeiro on 21 August 1808, however, something very significant happened – the attacking columns failed to break or even shift the British lines which stood stoic, silent, and positively unimpressed by the advance of the noisy French infantry who were driven off in disorder. Wellington's victory at Vimeiro, in a far-off corner of Europe, hardly sent tremors through the halls of the Parisian palaces, but more than one French general was made to sit up and take notice of what they had seen.

So, what had happened? First, the French voltigeurs, whose task it was to drive back the British security line before setting about the main British line, came up against an unusually heavy line of skirmishers. In addition to the light companies of the British line battalions, the French had to endure their first taste of the 95th Rifles, whose Baker rifles took a heavy toll of the enemy as they advanced. In fact, the French voltigeurs had their work cut out in driving back even the British skirmishers, let alone the main British line. Wellington employed the 95th as a whole battalion

– three, in fact, served in the Peninsula – unlike the 5/60th, the other British unit armed with the Baker rifle, which was split into separate companies and allocated to various brigades throughout the army. The British skirmish line, therefore, was a force in itself, as the French were to discover. Wellington also used his artillery wisely, choosing not to engage in counter-battery fire, but instead turned his guns on the attacking enemy columns. By the time the French approached the British units which were in position on or behind the crest of the ridge in front of the village of Vimeiro, their columns had been pretty well shaken up. The final part of the equation consisted of Wellington's positioning of his main infantry line. For reasons of safety and in order to keep the French from discovering his true strength and dispositions, he kept his men out of sight on the reverse slope of whichever ridge he had chosen to fight on, in this case Vimeiro. This meant, of course, that the shaken enemy columns never knew when to deploy into line – if they ever intended to. As a result, the British lay low until the last minute when they were brought forward, made ready and fired. Two or three volleys were usually enough, followed by a loud cheer, before they charged their bayonets and drove the French away. The bayonet was, in fact, rarely used in the Peninsula, but the mere sight of it in the hands of Wellington's men had a tremendous psychological effect on the enemy and was enough to chase them away on battlefield after battlefield.

The end result of this combination of heavy security line, judicial use of both artillery and ground, plus the firepower of the two-deep line, proved decisive in the Peninsula and was still used to dramatic effect at Waterloo in 1815. What is surprising is that the French commanders appear never to have decided to try anything different. Indeed, it is almost tiresome to have to keep relating how the line triumphed over the column. Little wonder, therefore, that at Waterloo Wellington was moved to write to Beresford that Napoleon, 'just moved forward in the old style, in columns, and was driven off in the old style.'[13] There were occasions when the French tried to ape their British adversaries and adopt the two-deep line, but this was only in defensive mode, at Salamanca and in certain places during the battle of the Nivelle, for example. It is strange that, considering the negative results achieved by the French in the Peninsula, they did not get down to analysing the problem and altering their method of attack. Their strategy changed from time to time but their tactics remained predictable and stale from start to finish.

Unlike his French adversaries, Wellington found no problem in employing a variety of formations, both columnar and linear. Much of this was down to brigade and battalion commanders who, under Wellington, grew in confidence as the war progressed. We find British troops attacking in column during the stormings of Ciudad Rodrigo, Badajoz and San Sebastian – although these examples are rather inappropriate – and during the crossing of the Bidassoa and the battles of Orthes and Toulouse, as well as attacking in line at Vittoria, at Salamanca and at the battle of the Nivelle where they also attacked in column. At El Bodon, we even find British infantry attacking cavalry while in line.[14]

There can be little doubt that Wellington's success was based firmly upon the prowess of his infantry. But what of his cavalry? This arm of the service has long since been regarded as the poorer relation, one which presented Wellington with a series of disasters and mishaps that continued throughout the Peninsular War and was perpetuated at Waterloo. The British cavalry in the Peninsula drove Wellington to distraction from the word go, beginning with the charge of the 20th Light Dragoons at Vimeiro, and continuing with the 23rd Light Dragoons at Talavera and Jack Slade's escapade at Maguilla, to name just a few examples. These misadventures were still happening as late as 1815, with the famous charge of the Union Brigade at Waterloo. Indeed, such was Wellington's despair following Slade's infamous gallop at Maguilla, that he was moved to make his famous indictment of the cavalry, saying, 'our officers of cavalry have developed the trick of galloping at everything, and their galloping back as fast as they gallop on the enemy. They never consider their situation, never think of manoeuvring before an enemy – so little that one would think they cannot manoeuvre, excepting on Wimbledon Common.'[15] And yet, there were some very creditable actions performed by the British cavalry, such as Benavente, Sahagun, Usagre, Villa Garcia and Morales, to name the most important. The famous breaking of the French infantry squares at Garcia Hernandez was performed by the cavalry of the King's German Legion, regarded as the best Allied cavalry, and so must fall outside our immediate area of study. The significant aspect of these successful actions was that Wellington himself was never present at any of them, the cavalry being commanded by either Henry, Lord Paget, William Lumley, John Gaspard Le Marchant or Stapleton Cotton. The only occasion on which Wellington was present himself was during the battle of Salamanca, when Le Marchant's heavy cavalry brigade smashed the centre of Marmont's army. So, may we deduce from this that Wellington was unable to command cavalry or was it that he just did not trust them, after his personal experiences with them?

One cannot blame Wellington for being decidedly reluctant to use his cavalry, given their antics, but the reasons for his under-employment of them are far more complex. Space precludes any detailed discussion here, but we can examine some of the causes which lay behind their bad reputation. First of all, the number of cavalry present with Wellington's army was woefully short of the requisite number. At Vimeiro, for example, he had with him just 240 British cavalry[16], a ludicrously low number, and the situation saw little improvement until the Vittoria campaign of 1813. Also, the campaigning country hardly lent itself to decent cavalry operations. Portugal was far too mountainous, whilst the area of the campaigns of 1810 and 1811 on the Spanish-Portuguese border was equally bad for cavalry operations. The Pyrenees were also out of bounds to cavalry. In fact, it was only the rolling plains of Leon, fought over during the 1812 Salamanca campaign, and the land to the south, in Estremadura and Andalucia, which afforded the cavalry any chance to deploy and show what it could do. And as if the combination of insufficient numbers and inadequate campaigning country was not enough, there was the problem of finding a decent cavalry commander. The most able, Henry, Lord Paget, had led the British cavalry throughout the Corunna campaign and had won the battles of Sahagun and Benavente. However, upon his return to England he made the rather unwise decision to elope with Wellington's sister-in-law, and so was *persona non grata* for the rest of the war and only fell back into favour with Wellington during the Waterloo campaign of 1815 in which he again served with distinction, although even here, Wellington probably held his head in his hands when the Union Brigade charged off to glory and destruction when it smashed D'Erlon's corps during the early afternoon. In Lord Paget's absence command of the cavalry was patchy at best, Stapleton Cotton proving the most able commander. Le Marchant was by far the most forward thinking and potentially the natural successor to Paget, but he was killed in action at Salamanca on 22 July 1812. Robert Ballard Long disappointed while 'Mad' Jack Slade caused nothing but vexation at headquarters.

British cavalry could achieve stunning results and, I believe, their bad reputation is based upon the handful of high-profile disasters named above. Yes, picquets were taken on occasion by French cavalry – usually as a result of inexperience on the part of recently-arrived officers who knew little of outpost work[17] – but British cavalry did much fine work in the Peninsula, both on the battlefield and on outpost duty, not to mention the business of gathering intelligence, a role which has long gone without sufficient praise. But the combination of a series of misadventures, poor cavalry commanders, bad campaigning country and low numbers contrived to make Wellington turn to his infantry time and time again as his instruments of victory.

Wellington's siege operations at Ciudad Rodrigo, Badajoz, Burgos and San Sebastian were most unsatisfactory, only those at Ciudad Rodrigo coming off without too many traumas. Few of the causes for the manner in which the operations were conducted could be laid at Wellington's feet, however, and, indeed, he complained bitterly throughout the war about the lack of trained engineers and of a corps of sappers and miners, similar to that employed by the French.[18] The digging of parallels and construction of batteries devolved upon the ordinary line infantry, who positively loathed the work. A lack of decent entrenching tools and, more important, siege guns, hampered matters also, particularly at Burgos where, by his own admission, Wellington overstretched himself and undertook the siege with just three guns. The end result was that he was forced to hurl his men against the walls and rely purely on their own powers to force entry into the fortresses. That they did so at Rodrigo and Badajoz in 1812 and at San Sebastian in 1813 reflected great credit on their remarkable abilities but did little to enhance the army's reputation in siege operations.

The darker nature of Wellington's army was displayed in all its evil following the stormings of the three fortresses above, but it was during the aftermaths, particularly at Badajoz, that Wellington showed two other sides of his often complex character. He was, naturally, very angry at his men following their behaviour at Badajoz, but this was not just because of their treatment of the local population, their allies. He was also worried lest the French garrison form up and counter-attack, in which case the British troops, busy sacking the place, would be in no state to meet them. Wellington has also been called cold-hearted and unfeeling, but on the morning after the storming of Badajoz he broke down and wept at the sight of so many of his men lying dead and dying in the breaches. He wrote to Lord Liverpool, saying, 'The capture of Badajoz affords as strong an instance of the gallantry of our troops as has ever been displayed. But I anxiously hope that I shall never again be the instrument of putting them to such a test as that to which they were put last night.'[19] He also defended his men after the storming of San Sebastian, following which a great fire destroyed most of the town, a fire which the Spaniards accused Wellington of starting deliberately in retaliation for the town's continued trading with the French. Here again, he showed great loyalty to his men.[20]

One of the greatest faults of which Wellington stands accused was his reluctance – and often flat refusal – to delegate. Throughout the campaign in the Peninsula, Wellington rarely entrusted his subordinates with any matters of extreme importance, either on the battlefield, on the march or in matters logistical. When we call it Wellington's army, we do so because that is exactly what it was – it was his army. He had no notion of the idea of a second-in-command and refused to acknowledge even the concept.[21] As such, we have a series of episodes where he himself is responsible for the issuing of orders which he may have considered of such a vital and crucial nature that he could entrust their delivery to no-one but himself. Take Salamanca, for example, where he rode over two miles to deliver his orders to Pakenham, waiting patiently with the 3rd Division at Aldea Tejada. The outcome of the day was probably decided by Pakenham's whirlwind attack on Thomieres' overstretched division at Miranda, and Wellington, appreciating instantly the accuracy of the orders' delivery, galloped over to do the job himself, something which in other armies would surely have been delegated to an aide-de-camp. His officers, from senior officers downwards, were kept on a tight rein and any deviation from his orders usually met with a fearsome backlash as Stewart (reduced to tears), McGrigor (berated in the presence of Goya) and Ramsay (arrested) discovered to their cost. And these were not the only ones. Indeed, any officer unfortunate to incur the Commander-in-Chief's wrath in his Dispatches was very unfortunate, and on at least two occasions the victims (Bevan after Almeida and Sturgeon after Orthes) committed suicide. As John Mills said of him, 'at the table he is as big a boy as the best of them, but when he is angry he is a perfect tiger.'[22] His reluctance to delegate is also reflected in the performances of some of his subordinates, for there were few who could really be regarded as obvious candidates for the post of Commander-in-Chief should something have happened to Wellington. His own choice was Beresford, whilst Graham, Cotton, Brent Spencer and Edward Paget came into the frame also. In fact, Paget, who had lost an arm during the crossing of the Douro in May 1809, returned to the Peninsula in October 1812, apparently in order to act as Wellington's 'second-in-command', but was taken prisoner during the retreat from Burgos.

Of Wellington's lieutenants, only Craufurd, Graham, Beresford and Hill were entrusted with any real degree of independent command, and with varying results. Graham won the battle of Barrosa in March 1811 and was in command during the siege of San Sebastian in July and August 1813, but did little besides as an independent commander. Craufurd was the most controversially brilliant of them all, maintaining the Allied outpost line on the Agueda and Coa rivers in the spring and summer of 1810, and leading his Light Division through a series of memorable battles, sieges and skirmishes. Unfortunately, he suffered from a lapse of judgement and concentration on more than one occasion, although when he was mortally wounded at Ciudad Rodrigo in January 1812, Wellington called his loss a great blow and knew in his heart that he had lost the finest leader of light troops which he possessed.[23] Beresford shone to distinction in reorganising the Portuguese army but failed terribly when in command at Albuera. Indeed, it is somewhat surprising to find him as Wellington's favourite to succeed him in the event of any accident. By far the most successful of Wellington's lieutenants was Rowland Hill, who led his independent command with great success, particularly at Arroyo dos Molinos, Almaraz and St Pierre. But what of men like Cole and the fiery Picton? These men were two of the great fighters in Wellington's army, but at Roncesvalles, for example, when they had to fight the battle on their own, they let their nerves get the better of them and pulled back from one good position to the next in spite of Wellington's explicit orders not to do so. 'They really are heroes when I am on the spot to direct them,' wrote an irritated Wellington, 'but when I am obliged to quit them they are children.'[24] At Vittoria, both Dalhousie and even Graham suffered from the same affliction when in command of their respective independent columns. Indeed, the latter, ordered to tease the French on their right until he considered it prudent to launch a full-scale attack, merely prodded, somewhat hesitantly at times, throughout the day and, although he cut the main road to France, his attack was carried off in a less than satisfactory manner, probably through not having his great chief with him at the time. So, the conclusion to be drawn from this is that although Wellington's senior officers performed heroics when with the main field army, they did not live up to expectation when command was placed upon them, being unfamiliar in the role which Wellington had consistently denied them due to his reluctance to delegate. The subject could be taken a step further – but not here – by examining the subsequent careers of Wellington's lieutenants in India, Africa and, significantly, in the Crimea.[25]

One final point concerns Wellington's own presence on the battlefield. We know that he regarded the sight of Napoleon's hat as being worth 10,000 extra Frenchmen on the field of battle. Similarly, Wellington's own presence had a similar value amongst his own men. Remember, there were other British forces fighting in Europe and, indeed, in the Peninsula, at the same time that Wellington was leading his army to triumph. Those forces, employing similar tactics and, at Walcheren and Bergen-op-Zoom, the very same troops, failed to make an impression on the French. May we draw the conclusion that it was Wellington's own absence from these respective theatres that was significant? Also, his immediate presence at any point of the battle was enough to inspire the men around him to greater efforts, as well as providing a useful barometer as to the crucial phases of any battle. Waterloo is a great example, for wherever Wellington was to be found, we may be sure that it was one of, if not the, most important places on the battlefield at the time. He later explained his philosophy to Larpent, his Judge Advocat General. 'When I come myself the soldiers think that what they have to do is the most important since I am there, and that all depends on their exertions. Of course, these are increased in proportion, and they will do for me what, perhaps, no one else can make them do.'[26] This attitude can possibly be linked to his reluctance to delegate, Wellington choosing to command locally on occasions instead of trusting to his lieutenants. But, if his presence did indeed draw more exertions from his men than other commanders, then perhaps it was not a bad course of action to adopt.

At the beginning of this chapter, I said that it would take an entire volume to study Wellington's character and method of command, something which has yet to be satisfactorily accomplished. His character was explored by Elizabeth Longford in her classic *Years of the Sword*, and in Philip Guedalla's *The Duke*, whilst S.G.P. Ward's *Wellington's Headquarters* remains the definitive work on the workings of Wellington and his army, his staff and the various functions of the army departments. Indeed, although the war in the Peninsula was ultimately won on the field of battle, these actions occupied the army for just a few days of each year between 1808 and 1814, and it would be remiss to forget the contribution Wellington made to the day-to-day running and organisation of his army, for one of his greatest achievements in the Peninsula was, perhaps, the development of the army and its maintenance, something dealt with in great depth by Ward. It is hoped, however, that this brief glimpse into the complex character of this great man, who possessed a unique appreciation of his situation – both political and military – has given a small insight into his character, and will stir the reader into a further exploration of the mind of the architect of the Allied victory in the Peninsula.

Notes

1 John Gurwood (ed.), *The Dispatches of Field Marshal the Duke of Wellington* (London, 1837–9) pp. 166–71.
2 *Dispatches*, Wellington to Lord Bathurst, 21 November 1813, XI, p. 306.
3 Wellesley did not assume the title of 'Wellington' until 16 September 1809. On that day he wrote to the Right Hon. John Villiers regarding certain commissariat matters and signed the despatch, 'Wellington'. In a postcript, he says, 'This is the first time I have used my new name.' *Dispatches*, Wellington to Villiers 16 September 1809, V, pp. 155–6.
4 *Dispatches*, Wellington to Lt Col. Fletcher, 20 October 1809, V, pp. 230–5.
5 See various papers listed under 'Colonel Richard Fletcher' in the Royal Engineers Museum, Brompton, including a letter from Captain Goldfinch to Fletcher in which he suggests that the various redoubts will not hold back the French, and that the Portuguese will run at the first shot fired.
6 Wellington to Admiral Sir Richard Keats, Celorico, 2 August 1810. Unpublished MSS letter, in the collection of Mr Richard Old.
7 See Oman, *History of the Peninsular War* (Oxford, 1902–30), IV, pp. 572–5.
8 See David Hamilton-Williams, *Waterloo; New Perspectives* (London, 1993), p. 198.
9 In fact, although Vimeiro was fought as defensive battles it took place

during an offensive campaign, ie the British march south towards Lisbon in August 1808.

10 See Anderson, J., *Recollections of a Peninsular Veteran* (London, 1913), pp. 12–13. 'They returned our fire without ceasing, then in part commenced to deploy into line.' Dyneley, in his *Letters*, (Cambridge, 1984), p. 9, wrote, 'And sure enough, down they did come, in line, in the finest order it is possible to conceive.'

11 Fortescue's account of Maida had followed Oman's (see *History of the British Army*, 5) but when the second edition was published in 1921 he altered it, taking into consideration Oman's revised account of the battle.

12 See David Chandler's *On the Napoleonic Wars* (London, 1994), p. 143.

13 *Dispatches*, Wellington to Beresford, 2 July 1815, XII, p. 529.

14 See Oman, *History of the Peninsular War*, IV, pp. 565–9.

15 *Dispatches*, Wellington to Hill, 18 June 1812, IX, p. 238.

16 The 240 cavalry were from the 20th Light Dragoons.

17 On 31 March 1812, William Tomkinson, of the 16th Light Dragoons, wrote in his *Diary*, 'In England I never saw nor heard of cavalry taught to charge, disperse, and form, which, if I only taught a regiment one thing, I think it should be that. To attempt giving men or officers any idea in England of outpost duty was considered absurd, and when they came abroad, they all had this to learn.' Tomkinson, *Diary of a Cavalry Officer* (London, 1894), p. 135.

18 Following the carnage at Badajoz, Wellington wrote to Lord Liverpool, 'I assure your lordship that it is quite impossible to carry fortified places by "vive force" without incurring great loss, and being exposed to the chance of failure, unless the army should be provided with a sufficient trained corps of sappers and miners . . . I earnestly recommend to your lordship to have a corps . . . formed without loss of time.' Wellington to Lord Liverpool, quoted in Oman, *Wellington's Army* (London, 1913), pp. 284–5. In another letter Wellington wrote, 'Our loss has been very great . . . The truth is, that, equipped as we are, the British army are not capable of carrying on a regular siege.' *Dispatches*, Wellington to Torrens, 7 April 1812, IX, p. 45.

19 Wellington to Lord Liverpool, quoted in Oman, *Wellington's Army*, p. 284.

20 *Dispatches*, Wellington to Sir Henry Wellesley, 9 October 1813, XI, pp. 171–6.

21 See S.G.P. Ward's *Wellington's Headquarters* (Oxford, 1957), pp. 156–7, for a fine analysis both of the command structure in Wellington's army and the relationships between himself and his senior officers and heads of departments.

22 Ian Fletcher (ed.), *For King and Country* (Staplehurst, 1995), p. 80. Mills goes on to say, 'He makes no-one acquainted with his intentions and laughs at the idea of a Council of War.'

23 On 10 July 1810, Craufurd bungled an attempt to cut off a French foraging party at Villa de Puerco, during which Lt Col. Talbot of the 14th Light Dragoons was killed. Two weeks later, on 24 July, he almost lost the Light Division itself when, after dallying for too long on the right bank of the Coa river in the face of overwhelming French numbers, he was attacked and driven back with a loss of over 300 men. Only the skill and bravery of his regimental officers saved the division from being lost altogether.

24 Quoted in Fortescue's *History of the British Army* (London, 1921), IX, pp. 255–6.

25 See Oman, *History of the Peninsular War*, VII, pp. 524–8, for a review of the subsequent fortunes and careers of some of Wellington's lieutenants.

26 See Larpent, *The Private Journal of F Seymour Larpent* (London, 1853), I, p. 285.

CHAPTER IX

'Keep step and they cannot hurt us¹':
The value of drill in the Peninsular War

Paddy Griffith

There has always been a school of thought which believes that drill is the key to understanding how battles were fought in the Napoleonic era. This idea was rampant in the years before the French Revolution, when Frederick the Great and his Potsdam parades were often seen as the models to be followed. It was also widespread during the Napoleonic Wars themselves, and we find many references to the use of drill in the memoirs of participants. In the years since 1815 there has also always been a steady trickle of books which analyse the way in which drills were supposed to have worked, ranging from late-nineteenth-century authors like Colin or Home,[2] through to modern authors like George Jeffrey and George Nafziger.[3]

One attraction of this view surely lies in the idea that drill is a scientific system, and almost a 'mechanism',[4] which takes the messy human element out of the business of fighting. Regiments which manoeuvre 'like clockwork', 'as if on a parade' or 'like in Hyde Park' will behave in a fashion that their commanders can predict and plan for with 'military precision' (or even 'Prussian efficiency'). The evolution of the battle can be controlled without the bothersome intrusion of chance. Its 'rules' will be more like those of chess than of roulette – and indeed it may be no coincidence that modern hobbyists who wargame the Napoleonic era seem to be particularly fascinated by the idea of drill. From the point of view of the military officers at the time, furthermore, drill always represented a strong reinforcement of their hierarchical authority over their men. It encapsulated the principle of obedience to orders, and as such it has survived as an essential feature of military training right down to the present day, even though its battlefield relevance evaporated at about the time of Omdurman (1898).[5]

The power of drill perhaps comes from the fact that it is by definition 'counter-instinctual', and therefore it seems to give men who possess it an advantage over those who can behave only naturally or instinctively.

Drill forces the soldier to perform strictly defined actions that run against his normal inclinations, and to perform them in concert with a large body of other men who are simultaneously doing the same thing. The whole mass acts together as a single unit, thereby greatly multiplying the power of each man individually. Drill is a concept that is alien to most civilian trades, apart perhaps from the dance troupe or the football squad. Indeed, much of its potency comes precisely from the fact that it overrides civilian expectations and forces its participants to accept that they are soldiers under discipline, no longer masters of their own actions. When the veteran soldier complains into his beer that 'modern youth has no idea how far we had to sacrifice our individuality when we were called up into the army',[6] he is speaking not only a profound truth but also giving a compact definition of the value of drill.

In the Peninsular War, when muskets were primitive and edged weapons had advanced little since Roman times, drill naturally loomed larger in the soldier's armoury than it does today. Drill was a weapon in itself, which allowed a large mass of troops to be gathered together into a formed body to be hurled against the enemy at a chosen time and place, or to be concentrated into a solid knot of resistance against assaults. It was also a 'secret' weapon which insiders belonging to the select guild of European military officers could exploit against either the undrilled rabble in their own countries, or supposedly lesser breeds elsewhere. Napoleon had done this when suppressing riots within France from 1786 onwards; Wellington had done it in his heavily outnumbered battles in India, although he was also consciously following the practice of European mercenary officers who had trained the Mahratta armies in the early 1790s.[7] To paraphrase Napoleon's comments on his cavalry's chances against the Mamelukes in Egypt, an individual French cavalryman might be very inferior in horsemanship and swordsmanship; but a troop of French riders might hope to hold its own against a troop of the enemy, whereas a French squadron would sweep away a Mameluke squadron every time. The secret of the French success lay entirely in their command of drill, which was a skill unknown to Mamelukes – who could be considered as pure children of nature, not least because they happened to live so close to the site of the original Garden of Eden.

There is even a sense in which large battles could not have been fought at all without the power of drill, since it was only by drill that large numbers of men could be gathered in an orderly way on the battlefields. As John Koontz remarked in a 1983 paper, 'I confess that I would be at a loss to understand how a unit in close order could move at all, if not by means of some formal system similar to one of those described in the drill regulations'.[8] Admittedly this comment suggests that its author is

164

blissfully unaware of the apparent ease with which entirely undrilled masses of 40,000 modern football supporters are habitually concentrated into stadia scarcely bigger than 300 yards square, with only about an hour to arrive and another hour to disperse. Such cases demonstrate that quite a high level of celerity and regularity may be achieved by informal, undrilled arrangements. We might even suggest that a Napoleonic army of 40,000 men, exercising under the full rigours of formal drill, could easily waste an entire morning, and not just an hour, aligning itself into an area 300 yards square. The *Grande Armée* of the Boulogne camp, 1804–5, was indeed noted for such parades, while its successor in 1813–15 was known for extending its breakfasts until noon, and getting under way only after that[9] – which was a problem that General Robert E. Lee would also experience at Gettysburg some five decades later. Nevertheless, despite all these caveats, John Koontz's main point remains valid, that most battlefield manoeuvres could normally be achieved rather faster with drill than without it.

Once all the above has been accepted, however, we do soon start to encounter some serious problems with the theory that drill is the key to understanding Napoleonic battles. The first is that the drills themselves were really no more than an ideal to be aimed at – merely a guide to thinking that was intended to be common to the whole army – rather than a description of what would actually happen. It has often been said that 'no plan survives the first contact with the enemy'; but it is surely still more true that 'no drill survives the first contact with uneven or broken terrain'. The more uneven and broken the terrain became, the more it was guaranteed to upset most of the evolutions that were practised mainly on flat, open fields. The drill manuals were admittedly fully aware of this basic fact; but they were still forced to become successively more desperate and unrealistic as the difficulty of the postulated terrain increased. The advance of a line, for example, soon began to look more like the advance of a column, once it encountered obstacles which restricted the frontage and forced some platoons to be doubled upon others.[10]

Even on flat fields marching units tend to concertina out, and increase their size or miss their alignments. Forces of more than a couple of battalions were also notoriously difficult to keep in order, even when they did not make such elementary mistakes as taking their direction from the position of cows, rather than of trees (because, of course, cows tend to move around whereas trees do not). There was really no hope at all for drill on some of the truly hostile terrain upon which some of the real battles would be fought – such as the dramatically steep slopes of the 800-foot-high Busaco ridge up which the French had to attack;

the kilometre-wide Bidassoa estuary through which the British infantry had to wade; or the densely wooded two-mile area between the mayor's house at Barrouillhet and Biarritz, through which the same infantry would advance in line. On many Napoleonic battlefields, in fact, there was really no alternative to some form of skirmish order, which was notoriously the formation that was least well covered by drill manuals.

Even the most modern expert, George Nafziger, is very tellingly forced to compare the speeds of formation changing, as between the various drill books, only after he has systematically cut out out all 'real' factors such as rough terrain, incoming fire, the morale of the troops, etc., etc.[11] He is left with a set of notional ideals, showing how the Westphalians' times for forming square on a flat parade ground might be compared with the French; or the British times for deploying into line might stack up against the Prussians. In theory this procedure is impeccable, because it is itself a highly theoretical exercise – but in practice his results actually look very odd indeed. He finds, for example, that the victorious British of 1813–15 were slower in their drill changes than the French they defeated, just as the tactically *very* superior Prussians of 1792–4 were *very* much slower than the French they defeated. So glaring is this last anomaly, in fact, that George himself can only explain it by the plainly ridiculous suggestion that the Prussians maybe left the War of the First Coalition in order to win time to smarten up their conversions from line to column.[12]

Terrain was not, of course, by any means the only factor which might upset the regularity of drill. The action of the enemy was perhaps even more worrying, since men would not behave normally when they feared for their very lives. The proximity of the enemy might easily make drill quite impossible, and it was axiomatic that all formation changes should be completed, calmly and carefully, while he was still at a great distance. Guibert himself, whose 'revolution' is so much praised in George Nafziger's book, went so far as to say that 'One must not try to manoeuvre [ie change formation] close to the enemy.'[13] The implication of this is that drill was actually irrelevant to fighting a battle, since it could not be used at close quarters. If one started an advance in massed columns – a handy formation for manoeuvres – one would not feel confident about deploying into a firing line once one came close to the enemy. It would be safer to carry on with the assault in column, rather than risking everything by stopping to do drill. Thus the French army regularly made column attacks that they had not really intended, simply because 'one must not try to manoeuvre close to the enemy'. This had been true during the campaigns of the *Armée du Nord* in 1792–4,[14] and it would continue to be true of many French attacks in the Peninsula and at Waterloo. Whatever else one may say of Oman's interpretation of British infantry tactics, he is surely to be trusted in the case of his repeated listing of occasions when the French were thought by observers to be attacking in columns. Sometimes they might attempt to deploy when close to the British; but usually this endeavour failed, and they continued in column up to the last.[15] They knew as well as the British did that the column was a weak formation for combat; but they felt they had to continue with it once they found themselves at close range.

Perhaps it was enemy cavalry which provided the harshest reality that might upset the ideal world of infantry drill, and the French army of the early Revolution certainly suffered innumerable panic routs at the hands of Austrian, Prussian, British and even Spanish horsemen. The use of drillbook square formations did not seem to offer any protection, and so some pretty irresolvable debates ensued. On the one hand there was a common-sense view that troops threatened by cavalry should form themselves into the deepest possible mass, who would use their fire, and especially their bayonets, to warn off the attacking horses and keep them at a respectful distance. Normally this implied that the infantry would be in a square or some other type of flankless line, and that the line itself would be three rather than two ranks deep. Against this, however, there was a widespread awareness that any deep formation was intrinsically inflexible and wasteful of manpower, as well as very vulnerable to enemy artillery and liable to irrational panics. The more ranks were massed together, in fact, the less they could be subjected to precision drill and the more they resembled a formless football crowd. Indeed, even when it did perform its drill religiously, even a three-deep line could easily turn into a self-inflicting death trap. Gouvion St Cyr complained that as many as a quarter of the wounds among French infantry were caused by the men of the third rank firing into the men of their own first rank.[16] Because they were being asked to shoot 'through' two ranks of their comrades, they found it almost impossible to get a clean shot at the enemy, and many accidents resulted. Many different drills were proposed to avoid this embarrassment, such as making the first rank kneel or having the third rank act only as reloaders for the first two: but in the event these expedients all proved to be rather futile or impracticable, and the third rank was sometimes expected to shoot into the air rather than to commit any mischief. The third rank eventually came to be recognised as a potential source of weakness, apart from the special case of providing depth against cavalry, or reinforcements to the front two ranks if the unit had suffered particularly heavy casualties.

By about 1800 the British had adopted the two-deep line, which had also been widely discussed by the French – and even adopted by them on some occasions. George Nafziger suggests that the British formation two-deep was an unavoidable result of the habitual undermanning of their battalions,[17] although there were doubtless other influences at work, such as the light infantry traditions derived from the American War of Independence. From wherever it came, the two-deep line seemed to represent a certain degradation of the formal complexity of drill, in favour of a lighter and more 'common-sense' approach. Two lines were safer and more effective than three for firing, whereas for squares against cavalry it was thought better to double two lines to four, rather than just to stand unquestioning in the regulation three lines.[18]

Almost all the drill manuals, however, were frustratingly reticent about the actual business of fighting. They might explain how a line should be formed, or how it could be transformed into a column. They might even explain how firelocks should be discharged in the general direction of the enemy; but they would not normally say much about what could happen after that, or what effects the enemy's retaliation might produce. If the square was broken and the colonel was killed, for example, there was no 'first aid' advice in the manuals apart from some rather technical explanations about re-taking dressing and closing up intervals – and of course the second-in-command was so obviously the person to take charge, if the colonel should be unavoidably detained for whatever reason, that no further comment was thought to be required. Conversely, if the enemy had received our volley and might be wavering in his resolution, there was no advice about what tell-tale signs one should look for or try to exploit. In practice experienced commanders often came to know instinctively when the enemy was 'ripe' for a charge – i.e. when he was visibly wavering, and losing even a vestigial grasp on drill formations. In those cases it was cheaper and safer to chase his entire force away with the bayonet rather than to try to shoot a proportion of his men with musketry[19] – but there was not a word in the drill books to suggest that the skill of spotting the right moment might have any actual importance in battles.

During the Napoleonic era the drill manuals were not at all the same as tactical manuals. They did not tell a commander which formation was the best for defence against cavalry, the best for storming a battery or the best for sustaining a firefight. Indeed, they did not even say whether a firefight was something to be desired or shunned, or whether it should include skirmishers, artillery and cavalry as well as formed infantry. Such omissions should warn us that the inner agenda of the drill books was rather different from the actual business of combat, and that they were really about self-discipline, military neatness and an unattainable ideal of how things ought to have been arranged if only the enemy wasn't shooting back.

For the French, particularly, the wars of the Revolution and early Empire seem to have shone a spotlight upon the serious limitations of the 1791 drillbook. Much of the fighting was conducted in skirmish order (which was not even mentioned in the drillbook), while assaults were habitually conducted in columns (which were generally discouraged for close combat by the drillbook, even if some ambiguities still remained). On a real battlefield the neat lines recommended in the drillbook would almost always degenerate into formless mobs or 'blobs'. Many post-1791 authorities, from Marmont to Morand and from Meunier to Gouvion and Ney,[20] therefore called for a 'tactics of common sense' in which men were no longer expected to follow a detailed and complex choreography. They were to be shunted around in small groups, as informally and quickly as possible, without too much pedantry, fuss or 'bull'. That normally meant that they would give fire in some approximation of a skirmish line, and make movements – including most assaults – in battalion masses rather than any more complex arrangement of lines.

This conception had been stated most specifically in the fighting instructions for the Army of Italy issued by General Schérer just before he was replaced in that command by Bonaparte in 1796;[21] but it is worth remembering that Guibert had been saying almost the same thing as early as 1772. There was apparently nothing that had changed in the interim apart from a general decline in the quality of the available recruits, and hence a decline in their ability to perform detailed drills. Even though the *Grande Armée* of the Boulogne camp had managed a great deal of drilling in 1804–5, and had even maintained its drill skills in Germany during the wars of 1805–6, it was apparently already starting to lose those skills in and after the cruel Polish winter of 1806–7. Then it would deploy only its 'second best' units for most of the Peninsular War, so that only a relatively poor attainment in drill could ever be expected in that particular theatre.

By the time of the Peninsular War it seems reasonable to suppose that all the engaged armies had essentially come to terms with the practical limitations on drill that real battlefields imposed. They had adopted a shorthand form of drill, or a 'tactics of common sense', in which groups of men moved around by the easiest and shortest routes, rather than by the stuffy technicalities of pedantic drills. Despite a great deal of propaganda in its favour, therefore, drill could not by any means provide the full answer to the soldier's problems in a battle. It could never be more than one weapon among many, and was often even a somewhat marginal one. In this context it is fascinating to reflect that of all the nationalities engaged in the Peninsular War it was possibly the Spanish who were most aware of the need for drill. This was doubtless because, like the French in 1793, they believed they could not match their opponents in this activity, and so suffered from a disproportionate inferiority complex. They often sought to fight in difficult mountainous terrain, where drill was of little importance, because they knew they would normally be defeated in open terrain where drill was inescapable. They also concentrated rather more of their efforts on drill training than was normal in other armies, just as the French of 1793 had done before them (and, ironically, not least when facing the Spanish themselves).[22] In a letter of 14 May 1812 Wellington says that the Spanish system was to give intensive drill training to their recruits before they were sent to their units, although he also complains that it was a poor system because, once arrived, the recruits found their units lacked military cohesion and 'habits of obedience' based on effective officers.[23] For Wellington, at least, it seemed to be far more important to get high quality officers who could form confident and properly subordinate teams of soldiers, than it was to get soldiers who could perform accurate parade ground manoeuvres.

Here, perhaps, lies the true Achilles' heel of the 'drill' school of thought. What Wellington was saying was basically that you could drill a recruit until he was a perfectly choreographed individual performer (like Colonel Elmer Ellsworth's prancing circus Zouaves in 1860)[24]; but it would all be tactically meaningless unless he went on to join an effective battalion team or 'military family' in which there was full trust between man and man and, more importantly, between man and officer. The driving force behind that battalion family would not be the drill or the bull or the gymnastic contortions, but the mutual trust and understanding between its members of all ranks. Despite scrappy drill, in fact, such a battalion could still confidently hope to defeat all comers, regardless of whether it met them in open ground or in extreme terrain like the Busaco ridge, the Bidassoa estuary or the Barrouilhet woods. If its square was broken by cavalry – which must surely have been the ultimate imaginable breakdown of drill – such a battalion would still keep on fighting doggedly until all the enemy who had got into the square had been defeated. In 1793 many French squares had simply run away when – or even before – they had been broken by enemy cavalry: but from Alexandria in 1801 to Quatre Bras and Waterloo in 1815, the British infantry seemed to shrug off such catastrophes as if they were of only minor importance. They were able to keep up their mutual trust, even after they had lost all semblance of drill.

Notes

The author is grateful to everyone who helped him form his views on these issues, especially Professor Norman Gibbs in Oxford, John Lynn in Chicago, and Jean Lochet's team at 'Empires, Eagles and Lions'.

1 The title of this chapter is taken from a quote in 'The Letters of Private Wheeler', (edited by B.H. Widdell-Host) London 1951 p. 56.

2 J. Colin, La Tactique et la Discipline dans les Armées de la Révolution (Paris, 1902) is the most important book on Napoleonic minor tactics ever written: widely quoted although rarely read. He makes the case, albeit perhaps excessively, that the French used linear drills in battle more often than had normally been assumed. R Home, A Précis of Modern Tactics (Clowes, London, 1882) is one among many minor competitors appearing at around the same time.

3 George Jeffrey, Tactics and Grand Tactics of the Napoleonic Wars (edited by Ned Zuparko, The Courier Publishing Co., Brocton, MA, 1982); George Nafziger, Imperial Bayonets, Tactics of the Napoleonic battery, battalion and brigade as found in contemporary regulations (Greenhill, London, and Stackpole, Mechanicsburg, Pa, 1996).

4 A book was published in 1808 by 'A French Officer' which actually had the title 'Essay on the mechanism of war, or the application of the first principle of mechanics to the movement and action of army corps' (my translation).

5 This of course refers to close order drill on the parade ground, as opposed to 'battle drills' or 'drills for weapon handling' etc., which continue to be of direct importance in combat, even for helicopter pilots.

6 Bill Jackson of the Mercia Military Society, 25 November 1996, in conversation with the author.

7 Napoleon helped suppress riots in Lyon, August 1786; Seurre, April 1789; Auxonne, July 1789; Ajaccio, June 1793; and Paris, October 1795 – see G Six, Dictionnaire Biographique des Généraux et Amiraux Français de la Révolution et de l'Empire (2 vols. Paris, Saffroy 1934, reprinted 1989). For Wellington's 'Indian' tactics, see Griffith Forward Into Battle (A Bird, Chichester, 1981), chapter 3; and for the work of Western mercenaries in India, see H Compton, A Particular Account of the European Military Adventurers of Hindustan, from 1784 to 1803 (T Fisher Unwin, London, 1892).

8 John E.Koontz, 'Reasons for studying Napoleonic drill regulations' in Empires, Eagles and Lions, #74, 1 September 1983.

9 Jac Weller, Wellington at Waterloo (Longman, London 1967) pp. 73–4, ff.

10 The convoluted methods by which a line was supposed to cross broken ground may be followed in e.g. David Dundas, Principles of Military Movements, chiefly applied to Infantry (London, 1788), upon which the official 1792 'Rules and Regulations' would be based, and the Règlement concernant l'exercise et manoeuvres de l'infanterie (Paris, 1 August 1791; 1812 edition).

11 Nafziger, Imperial Bayonets, p. 54.

12 Ibid., p. 85.

13 Ménard, ed., Guibert, écrits militaires, 1772–1790 (Copernic, Paris, 1976), p. 128. It is very unfortunate that Nafziger actually makes no bibliographical references to Guibert.

14 John Lynn, *The Bayonets of the Republic, motivation and tactics in the army of revolutionary France, 1791–94* (University of Illinois Press, Chicago, 1984), pp. 243–59, 287–91.

15 C.W. Oman, *A History of the Peninsular War* (7 vols, Oxford, 1902–30): the classic work on the subject, containing innumerable accounts of French assaults.

16 Quoted and discussed in Nafziger, *Imperial Bayonets* p. 44.

17 *Ibid.*, pp. 45, 66.

18 This 'doubling' was done at Waterloo: Weller, *Wellington at Waterloo*, pp. 205–12.

19 E.g. Wellington's 'Go on Colborne! Go on! They won't stand. Don't give them a chance to rally', quoted in *Weller, Wellington at Waterloo* p. 150, citing Clinton.

20 All cited in Colin, *La Tactique*, especially in section VII of his Preface.

21 *Ibid.*, Preface, section VIII, p. lxxxv. Cf Schérer is quoted at length, but alas mistaken for Gouvion St Cyr, in Nafziger, *Imperial Bayonets*, p. 172.

22 For the 'first' Peninsular War, 1793–5, see especially J-N Fervel, *Campagnes de la Révolution Française dans les Pyrénées Orientales* (2 vols., Pillet, Paris, 1851).

23 Wellington, *Selections from the Dispatches and General Orders of Field Marshal the Duke of Wellington* (J Gurwood, ed., London, 1841), p. 591.

24 See Griffith, *Rally Once Again* (A Bird & Crowood Press, Swindon, 1987), pp. 101–2.

CHAPTER X

Wellington's Fighting Cocks:
The Portuguese army in the Peninsula

John Grehan

In 1807 the Portuguese army was incapable of defending the frontiers of its own country. The small French force under General Junot which invaded Portugal in the autumn of 1807 met with no resistance and the country succumbed without a shot being fired in its defence. Yet the Portuguese army underwent a remarkable transformation and forged a partnership in arms with Britain which was to defeat the French on a dozen battlefields and eventually drive the invaders from the lands of Iberia.

Though the Portuguese army had not dared to oppose the French invasion Junot ordered its disbandment which was effected by the Marquis d'Alorna, the Inspector General of the Army, on 5 March 1808. The Marquis was invited to raise a corps of Portuguese troops for service with the French army to which many of the more able officers and the best of the other ranks enlisted. Portugal therefore lost its finest soldiers to the enemy before the fighting had even begun.[1]

So it was that when Sir Arthur Wellesley landed in Portugal with an Expeditionary Force to help liberate the Peninsula he found the Portuguese without an army. Wellesley defeated Junot's corps at Roliça and Vimeiro and the French were forced to evacuate the country. However, it was inevitable that the French would attack Portugal again and the Portuguese government immediately ordered the complete restoration of its armed forces.

All the former officers and men were recalled to the colours but this measure failed to produce the required numbers to fill the ranks. A severe lack of money and equipment also hindered the development of the new army, and when the French attempted a second invasion of northern Portugal in 1809, the Regency Council asked Britain to take over the task of rebuilding the army.

The man that the Portuguese wanted for this job was Wellesley, but Sir Arthur, who knew that the Portuguese command would be subordinate to the British field commander in the Peninsula, declined the position. Instead the offer was passed on to Major-General William Carr Beresford who, on 15 February 1809, was made Commander-in-Chief of the Portuguese Army. 'The choice was not left to me,' Beresford was to write shortly after his appointment, 'and the first thing that I was told was that it was not optional.' Beresford had previously served as Governor of Madeira and had some knowledge of the Portuguese language.[2]

Beresford found the army in a truly wretched condition. 'I am sure that the state of the Portuguese army is quite misunderstood in England,' wrote Sir John Craddock who commanded the British troops in Lisbon in 1809. 'Their army have not in their possession ten thousand firelocks fit for service . . . their battalions of infantry are one half without arms or clothing . . . Many of their cavalry regiments are without arms . . . This cavalry is unformed, and totally unfit for any sort of service.' Beresford's first task was to weed out all the old and inefficient Portuguese officers. To help him Beresford was allocated twenty-four British captains and majors who transferred from their regiments to the Portuguese service. These officers were given one step in rank in the British service and another in the Portuguese. Therefore a lieutenant, for example, became a British captain and a Portuguese major, and he was permitted to receive the pay from both commissions.[3]

The poor standard of Portuguese officers was due in part to low pay and very few and arbitrary opportunities for promotion. Commissions were sold or given away 'by intrigue and corruption' often to men with no military training. Advancement for those officers without money or influence was almost impossible. In the 14th Line 'the most senior captain has served 37 years, the 1st Lieutenant 25, the 1st ensign 16: that's encouragement for aspiring minds!' commented Haviland Le Mesurier who had been promoted from a captain in the 21st Foot to lieutenant-colonel in the 14th Portuguese Line regiment. In the 19th Line regiment seven officers were over sixty, and in one cavalry regiment 'the three eldest cornets make up near 180 years.' Many of the more senior General officers had left the country with the Royal Family when it fled to the Portuguese colony of Brazil in 1807, and those that were left behind had almost no experience of warfare. 'The officers of the Portuguese army have for many years done little or no duty,' Wellington explained to Lord Liverpool, 'Their country having, with trifling and short exceptions, been at peace since the year 1763, they were generally throughout their service employed in the same garrison, if they remained with their regiments; or they lived with their families at home.'[4]

As a consequence, between 15 March and 4 July 1809 Beresford relieved 108 officers of their commissions and a month later he ordered a further 107 to be retired. To fill the gaps that these retirements created Beresford was allowed to enlist more British officers and they came forward in considerable numbers. Beresford, though, had to be careful not to injure Portuguese pride and patriotism, for simply to remove all the senior officers would have appeared a gross insult. His way of solving the problem was to ensure that whenever a Portuguese officer was in command of a regiment or a battalion he had a British officer as his second-in-command and, similarly, if a British officer commanded the unit then his immediate subordinate was Portuguese. At brigade level, if the brigadier was Portuguese, then the colonels of the two regiments that formed the brigade were both British and vice versa. Altogether some 350 British officers served with the Portuguese army throughout the war, including twenty-three sergeants who received Portuguese commissions.[5]

Beresford's next task to bring the army up to full establishment. The old army had been organised into three regional Grand Divisions, with each regiment permanently based in its own recruiting area, this district or town usually being named in the regimental title. This helped give the regiment a strong local identity and it meant that in times of war all available men from the district with previous service in the ranks could be quickly summoned back to the colours. In theory the twenty-four line infantry regiments, the twelve cavalry regiments, the four artillery regiments, and the six battalions of Caçadores should have totalled 51,653 men but the army had been under strength for many years, and by November 1808 only 22,361 infantry, 3,422 cavalry and 4,031 artillery had been mustered. It was the responsibility of the Capitaos Mor of each district to select and collect the required number of recruits from all the able-bodied young men who could be removed from their lands with the least inconvenience to local agriculture. There were few exemptions and no rights of appeal against the decision of the Capitaos Mor, but the local authorities failed adequately to enforce the recruiting laws. Military service was so unpopular that many of the conscripted peasants deserted before they reached the training depots. Possibly as many as half of all those selected never arrived at their regiments. Even at its highest point, in September 1809, the Portuguese regular army numbered only 44,000 officers and men.[6]

The return of the old troops to their regiments and the trickle of new recruits to the depots created further problems. Junot had confiscated and destroyed most of the store of weapons of the old army and in September 1808 the authorities were able to arm and equip only 13,000 men. Vast quantities of muskets were imported from Britain between August and December and by the end of December there were 31,833 troops fully equipped for service in the field, including 2,052 cavalry.

Items of uniform – shakos, trousers, knapsacks and greatcoats – were also supplied from Britain as well as field guns and ammunition. There was one problem, though, that could not be resolved. The cavalry force should have amounted to over 7,000 sabres, but Portugal was not a horse-breeding country and with the British cavalry and artillery also desperate to procure remounts it was not possible to obtain sufficient horses for all the regiments. As a result four of the twelve regiments were sent to perform garrison duty in the country's fortresses and their mounts were distributed amongst the remaining eight.[7]

Having mustered and equipped the various regiments as far as was possible, they now had to be turned into a cohesive fighting force. Depots were established in every province to accommodate and train the new recruits. They were situated at Lisbon, Peniche, Elvas, Evora, Chaves, Viseu, Vianna and Oporto, and each regiment was assigned to a particular depot. Every line infantry regiment and artillery regiment was required to maintain a minimum of 155 men in its depot. As it was impracticable to attempt to retain the brigade structure of the old divisional system, on 29 September 1809 Beresford issued a General Order revising the pairing of the line regiments.[8]

The Portuguese were found to be 'well enough, very obedient, willing and patient', but the Portuguese army still used the old Prussian system of formations and manoeuvres introduced into the army in the middle of the previous century. For the Portuguese regiments to be able to integrate with the British on the battlefield their entire drill had to be changed to the British pattern. This job was undertaken by Major-General John Hamilton who was appointed Inspector-General of Infantry. Hamilton had the British drill books translated into Portuguese as the 'Instruccoes para a formatura, exercicio e movimentos dos Regimentos de Infanteria' and issued to each battalion. The Caçadores were likewise trained on the 'Rifle Regulations' of Coote Manningham and the cavalry also received their 'Instruccoes para a Cavallaria' based on the British regulations.

The troops, nevertheless, continued to desert even when they had reached the depots. General Blunt, who commanded the largest of the training depots at Peniche, reported 'with regret the dangerous extent to which desertion is appearing in this encampment – fifty men from two regiments in two nights.' That they deserted is hardly surprising as the troops endured almost continuous privations. Britain had agreed to pay for 20,000 and later 30,000 Portuguese troops to serve with the British army, but the responsibility for feeding them still lay with the Portuguese authorities. The Portuguese Commissariat was divided into two departments, one being responsible for the supply of provisions, the other for transportation. The former, the *junta da direccao geral dos provimentos das municoes de boca para o exertio*, had Intendants in every province and storekeepers, or Feitors in every town. The method of supply was that the Portuguese government contracted with the junta for the different kinds of provisions and forage at a fixed price and the Feitors were then directed to purchase on the spot what was required at the cheapest possible price. The impecunious farmers could not afford to sell their products at such low prices and consequently 'every art is used by the farmer to bury and conceal his grain,' noted a British surgeon with the Portuguese army, 'and it has not unfrequently happened that the army has been starving for the want of provisions, when the country, nay the very village where they were quartered, was full of it.' What food the army did manage to acquire, whether by purchase or simply by seizing what it could find, was paid for in government bills which were generally regarded as worthless. As a result the troops were half-starved. 'The Portuguese army could not be in the distress under which it suffers, from the want of provisions,' wrote Wellington in 1810, 'if only a part of the food it receives from the country were paid for.' Although Wellington ordered changes in the commissariat structure this problem was never satisfactorily addressed and the Portuguese troops were always inadequately supplied.[9]

In the depots and the fortresses the training of the troops continued throughout the winter of 1809–10, and it was during this period that the real improvement in the effectiveness of the army took place. Each infantry battalion consisted of five companies, and as both battalions of a Portuguese infantry regiment fought together in the field, this produced a ten-company organisation allowing exact replication of the manoeuvres of the standard ten-company British battalion. By the end of the winter the British and Portuguese regiments could be moved in the same formations and by the same words of command. The Portuguese army was now ready to go to war.

In the spring of 1810 Beresford moved five brigades of infantry from their quarters around Thomar and Abrantes to join the British army on the frontier near Ciudad Rodrigo. Wellington added a Portuguese brigade to each of the 3rd and 4th Divisions and two to the recently formed 5th Division. The 1st and 3rd Caçadores were with the Light Division and the two brigades of Hamilton's Portuguese Division were attached to Hill's 2nd Division. In addition there were four independent Portuguese brigades, each composed of two line infantry regiments and one battalion of Caçadores. There were also four regiments of cavalry with the army brigaded together under General Fane, and seven brigades of artillery totalling forty-two guns drawn from all four artillery regiments. Out of Wellington's 52,274 men, 24,429 were Portuguese. The new Allied army's first battle was at Busaco. This was the battle that by Wellington's own admission was 'to save the country'. There was no more important event in the entire war. If the Portuguese troops failed to stand before the French onslaught, then Wellington's small British force would not be able to maintain its foothold in Portugal. As a French staff officer was to observe, it was at Busaco 'that the fate of the Peninsula was to be decided'. Despite Wellington's fears that 'much still remains to be done, with very insufficient means . . . towards the enrolment, organisation and equipment of this force', at Busaco the Portuguese proved to be 'as steady under arms as any in the world'. The French were decisively beaten with the Portuguese infantry and artillery facing as much of the fighting as their British counterparts. In fact the Allied casualties at Busaco numbered 1,252 of which exactly half (626) were Portuguese.[10]

The battle of Busaco gave the Portuguese troops 'a taste for an amusement to which they were not before accustomed' and they became a fully integrated and essential part of Wellington's army. Yet the Portuguese proved to be 'a most daily and uncertain sort of fighting people' and just how effective a fighting force the Portuguese army really was has never been fully established.[11]

Their exploits at Busaco stand comparison with any troops of the period. In one well documented incident an isolated French battalion came face to face with a single Portuguese battalion. In the attack upon the Busaco heights the 2nd Battalion of the 32nd Leger had become separated from its parent brigade. Although unsupported, the 32nd (413-strong) continued up the hillside to where the two battalions of the 19th Portuguese Line Regiment were posted. As the 32nd approached, the 19th fired a single volley and one of the battalions (approximately 560 men) charged down the slope. The 32nd stood their ground and a desperate hand-to-hand struggle took place 'some of the Portuguese . . . got so wedged in amongst the French that they had not room to use their bayonets. They turned up the butt ends of their muskets and plied them with such vigour that they promptly cleared the way.' The Portuguese pursued the 32nd 'headlong down the steep', wrote Beresford, until 'a heavy [French] battery opened upon them [the Portuguese] from the opposite side of the ravine; the regiment immediately, under the fire, reformed, faced to the right about, as if manoeuvring on a parade, and regained its original position, amid the acclamations of all the left of the British Army who were spectators of their conduct.' This incident became 'a matter of notoriety' throughout the whole army and caused Wellington to write that 'they have proved that the trouble taken with them had not been thrown away; and that they are worthy of contending in the same ranks with the British troops.'[12]

Despite all the public praise that Wellington lavished upon the Portuguese after Busaco, privately he continued to doubt their ability. In a letter to his brother just four months after Busaco he wrote that he had 'seen too much of the troops of the Peninsula, even the Portuguese when not united with our own, to form any calculation of the effect of any operation of theirs. Even when the troops are encouraged and inclined to behave well, the impatience, inexperience and unconquerable vanity of the Officers lead them into errors.'[13]

The cavalry was unquestionably the weakest and least reliable arm of the service. The Portuguese army was primarily a defence force designed to maintain the country's independence from its larger neighbour, Spain. The mountainous regions near the frontier where the army was expected to operate were not suitable for large-scale cavalry manoeuvres and the establishment strength of each cavalry regiment was far lower than in most armies of the period. Beresford attempted to increase the size of the cavalry regiments but the dearth of horses prevented this and usually each regiment was able to field only 300 to 400 men.

The unpredictable nature of the Portuguese cavalry was fully revealed in the summer of 1812. With Wellington's army was a brigade of the 1st, 11th and 12th regiments under the command of Sir Benjamin D'Urban. At the battle of Salamanca in July of that year the 1st and 11th regiments, numbering just 482 men, charged and routed a French battalion which it caught before it could form square. Encouraged by this exemplary conduct Wellington allowed D'Urban's brigade to form part of the advance guard of the Anglo-Portuguese army as it marched towards Madrid. As the allies approached the Spanish capital D'Urban encountered the French outpost line composed of two regiments of dragoons. D'Urban pushed back the dragoons, reaching the town of Majalahonda on the morning of 11 August. D'Urban ordered his men to cook their midday meal and to wait until later in the day before continuing their advance. However, just before 1600 hours six regiments of French cavalry – over 2,000 strong – appeared in front of Majalahonda. Outnumbered almost three to one D'Urban should have fallen back upon the rest of the Allied vanguard. But the performance of his brigade at Salamanca encouraged him to attempt to fight the French dragoons and lancers. Whilst messengers were sent to bring up the Allied cavalry D'Urban deployed the 1st and 12th regiments into line, threw one squadron of the 11th out in skirmish order in front, and placed the other squadron of the 11th in reserve. The opposing lines of cavalry drew sabres and charged 'but just at the moment when contact was to be expected', the Portuguese stopped, turned and galloped away leaving D'Urban and the two colonels of the 1st and 12th regiments in the very midst of the enemy. The two colonels were severely wounded and captured, D'Urban managing to cut his way free and escape.

A troop of K.G.L. Dragoons and a detachment of horse artillery which had come up in support were left stranded by the flight of the Portuguese and were completely overrun. The Germans were cut to pieces and three guns were taken. 'The same men who at Salamanca followed me into the French ranks like British dragoons,' wrote an astonished D'Urban, 'left me alone, and vanished from before the helmets [of the French] like leaves before the autumn wind.' Wellington responded to this 'devil of an affair' with a stinging rebuke, 'the occurrences of the 22nd of July [Salamanca] had induced me to hope that the Portuguese dragoons would have conducted themselves better, or I should not have placed them at the outposts of the army. I shall not place them again in situations in which, by their misconduct they can influence the safety of other troops.'[14]

Despite some notable achievements, such as the charge by Madden's brigade (3rd, 5th and 8th regiments) at Fuente Cantos which saved the whole of La Romana's Spanish army, Wellington continued to regard the Portuguese cavalry as 'worse than useless'. A more balanced view is given by D'Urban. 'They require a little incentive of shouts, and the inspiring cheers of a British line advancing near them. I am afraid they will never be quite safe by themselves.'[15]

The infantry, in contrast to the cavalry, 'was always well and gallantly led, fought well, and', according to an officer of the 34th Foot, 'ranked next to the English troops in all ways.' This same officer also observed in 1813 that the Portuguese were 'well disciplined and well clothed, with an esprit de corps not so well understood by the Espanoles'. Another British officer, Leith Hay, whilst condemning the 'very unsoldierlike conduct' of the Portuguese cavalry, wrote that 'I do so without the slightest intention of casting any reflection that can generally be attributed to the troops of that service. I have previously stated my humble tribute of respect for their undeviating good conduct on every occasion, wherein I had opportunities of witnessing their demeanour in contact with the enemy.' George Simmons of the 95th Rifles wrote that 'the Portuguese, led on by English officers, fight like Tigers. They have behaved astonishingly well. I have witnessed several regiments of them come on with the greatest enthusiasm.' Major-General Robert Long, who arrived in the Peninsula in 1811, was 'really astonished' with the appearance of the Portuguese troops. 'It is in every respect equal to our own, and in some instances finer, and their conduct hitherto before the Enemy had commanded the most decided approbation.'[16]

The four regiments of artillery occupied the principal fortresses along the border with Spain and around the sea coasts. Although Beresford found the artillery in a much better state than the other arms, the fortresses mounted a confusing assortment of different calibres and there were very few field pieces available. At first the field brigades had only 3- and 6-pounders, twelve of which formed a battery. Later, as more British equipment became available, the brigades were reduced to six guns each of either 6- or 9-pounders, and as the war progressed British 5 inch howitzers came into service. There were also a number of Independent, or Invalid, companies of gunners (some 1,300 men in total) called *peses de castello* who garrisoned some of the less important fortresses and who were never expected to serve in the field.

In May 1809 there were only two field brigades, one of which was a 'mountain' brigade of 3-pounders. A year later there were five brigades with Wellington's army organised into two unequal 'Divisions' with another brigade attached to the Lusitanian Legion. The personnel for each of these brigades were taken somewhat haphazardly from any of the four regiments, although some effort was made in the later years of the war to ensure that troops serving together on campaign were taken from the same regiment. The artillery always performed well and as early as December 1809 D'Urban saw 'The Artillery in a most excellent state, working rapidly and correctly', and at the siege of Badajoz one British officer was moved to write that 'the Portuguese artillery under British officers, was uncommonly good.'[17]

Officers of the Corps of Engineers held positions in all the major fortresses, and three Portuguese engineers assisted in the building of the Lines of Torres Vedras. There was also a small body of sappers which was raised and trained by the Engineers in 1809. The corps generally appears to have suffered from many of the excesses and abuses of the old army, and Wellington did not employ them in the field until 1813 when the entire body of sappers was moved to the front under the command of a major of the Engineers. A number of Portuguese naval officers and sailors were also used with the army's pontoon train in the later years of the war.

Because so many of the Portuguese brigades were integrated into the British divisions it is difficult to analyse their effectiveness. George Bell noted that 'the red-coats were always expected to do the real fighting business', and Colonel Colborne of the Light Division recalled that, if the Portuguese were beaten back in an attack, the British troops would continue the assault, but if the British attacked first and failed the Portuguese would abandon the attempt. Possibly the most accurate assessment of the Portuguese must come from the soldiers who fought against them. At Busaco, Chef de Bataillon Pelet reported that 'the Portuguese were interspersed among the British; they acted perfectly', and some of the French firmly believed that they had been engaged by British troops dressed in Portuguese uniforms. This impression was no doubt heightened by the fact that the Portuguese fought and manoeuvred in two-deep lines and were moved by British words of command. Lemonnier-Delafosse wrote of the Portuguese infantry's steady discipline under fire, and the Baron de Marbot was not alone in regarding the Portuguese as 'the equal of British troops'.[18]

In numerical terms the Portuguese became less important as the war progressed. At Busaco they formed almost half of the entire Allied force, yet just two years later at the Battle of Vittoria in 1813 the Portuguese constituted less than a third of Wellington's army. Yet by the end of the war the Portuguese were regarded as veterans. 'We do what we please now with the Portuguese troops,' wrote Wellington, 'we manoeuvre them under fire equally with our own,' and after the siege of Badajoz William Warre remarked that 'it is difficult to say which troops, the British or the Portuguese are most indifferent to danger. In both it is quite remarkable.' Certainly Wellington was quite correct in stating that 'Portugal has done as much, and will do more, in the contest than any province in Spain of the same extent and population', and he would not have been able to achieve his remarkable victory in the Peninsula without the Portuguese who became, in Wellington's own words, the 'fighting cocks of the Army'.[19]

Notes

1 A. Halliday, *Observations on the Present State of the Portuguese Army* (London, 1811) p. 3. These troops formed the Légion Portugaise comprising three infantry regiments and one regiment of light cavalry.

2 M. Glover, 'History Today', April 1976, p. 263.

3 Extracts from various dispatches from Sir John Craddock 1808–9, cited by W. Napier in *History of the War in the Peninsula and in the South of France*, (London, 1828–45) II, Appendix Section III; C. Oman, *Wellington's Army* (London, 1913), p. 232.

4 W. Warre, *Letters from the Peninsula* (London, 1909) p. 81; J. Gurwood (ed.), *The Dispatches of Field Marshal The Duke of Wellington*, (London, 1837–9) V, p. 275.

5 Oman, *A History of the Peninsular War* (Oxford, 1908) III, p. 174. Only the initial batch of twenty-four British officers that transferred to the Portuguese service were granted the double step in rank, all the subsequent transferees received a single step in the Portuguese army with no advancement in their British rank. This led to much acrimony. *Dispatches*, IV (1838) pp. 368–81, V pp. 151–3 and p. 284; B. D'Urban, *The Peninsular Journal of Major-General Sir Benjamin D'Urban*, (London, 1930) p. 59.

6 R. Howard, *The Portuguese Regular Army 1806–1814* (1979) p. 1; Oman, *History*, II p. 214; Halliday, *Observations*, pp. 57–8.

7 The 2nd (Moura) and 3rd (Estremoz) cavalry regiments never took the field. The 9th (Chaves) was dismounted and sent to the fortress of Almeida, and the 12th (Miranda) was dismounted at Lisbon in March 1810. Halliday, *Observations*, pp. 34–40.

8 For details of the new brigade structure see S. Ward, 'Journal of the Society for Army Historical Research', LIII pp. 103–12.

9   G. Nafziger, *The Armies of Spain and Portugal 1808–14* (Privately Printed, 1992)
    pp. 78–80; Foy, *History of the War in the Peninsula* (1827) I, p. 273; Halliday,
    Observations, p. 80; *Dispatches*, V, pp. 452–7; D'Urban, *Journal*, p. 104.

10 J.Fortescue, *A History of the British Army* (London, 1935) VII, pp. 469–70;
    Dispatches, VI, p. 6; J. Pelet, *The French Campaign in Portugal 1810–11* (ed.
    D.Horward 1973) p. 157; W. Tomkinson, *The Diary of a Cavalry Officer*
    (London, 1894) p. 42.

11 Wellington (ed.), *Supplementary Despatches and Memoranda* (London 1857–72)
    VI, pp. 606–7.

12 G. Chambers, *Wellington's Battlefields Illustrated* (London 1910), p. 126; W.
    Beresford to Dom Miguel Forjaz, 30 September 1810, quoted in Chambers,
    pp. 122 and 127.

13 Oman, *History*, V, p. 194; *Dispatches*, VIII, p. 194.

14 Oman, *History* V, pp. 509–14; *Dispatches*, IX, p. 354.

15 Oman, *History*, III, p. 333; *Dispatches*, VIII p. 230; D'Urban, op.cit. pp. 282–3.
    Beresford went even further, stating that 'they must not be employed again,
    alone, or with our own cavalry, who gallop too fast for them.'

16 G. Bell, *Soldiers Glory* (London, 1956), p. 101; A. Leith Hay, *A Narrative of
    the Peninsular War* (London, 1850) II, p. 189; G. Simmons, *A British Rifleman*
    (London, 1899) p. 126. R. Long, *Peninsular Cavalry General* (London, 1951)
    pp. 68–9.

17 Howard, 'Portuguese Army'. pp. 6–7; D'Urban, *Journal*, p. 78; J. Kincaid,
    Adventures in the Rifle Brigade (London, 1907), p. 84.

18 Bell, *Soldier Glory*, p. 71; G. Moore Smith, *Life of Sir John Colborne* (London,
    1903) p. 192; Horward, *French Campaign p. 181*; Tomkinson, *Diary*, p. 44; J.
    Lemonnier-Delafosse, *Campagnes de 1810 a 1815* (Le Havre, 1850), pp. 161–2;
    Memoirs du Baron de Marbot Paris, (1891), I, p. 485.

19 *Dispatches*, VI, p. 68, Warre, letters, p. 239, Larpent, *The Private Journal of
    Judge-Advocate Larpent* (London, 1854) p. 139; *Dispatches*, X, p. 569.

CHAPTER XI

Wellington's Army: a bibliographical essay

Ian Fletcher

They say the pen is mightier than the sword and, indeed, one is tempted to suggest that more paper has been consumed on the Peninsular War itself than ammunition was fired during it, for there exists today an absolute wealth of literature on the war, at the forefront of which are accounts by Wellington's men who were only too eager to recount their part in the victory. This is understandable, however, as the Peninsular War was the British army's main contribution to the Napoleonic Wars, and with such a successful outcome it is not surprising that so many memoirs, diaries, biographies and autobiographies have been published over the years. Spanish accounts of the war are plentiful enough too, as one would expect from a country wishing to record its liberation from the French invaders. Portugal has also contributed to the study of the war in a likewise fashion, whilst French Napoleonic memoirs, understandably, are more concerned with events in central Europe where Napoleon commanded. This is not to say that good French accounts of the war in Spain do not exist. Far from in, in fact, for there are many fine histories and some good personal accounts of the war which have helped us put together a picture of the French experience, as Philip Haythornthwaite has demonstrated in this book. This particular bibliographical essay, however, is mainly concerned with British accounts of the war

The British army had been in the Peninsula barely a year before its officers and men began to put pen to paper, and by the end of the war some extremely graphic accounts of the conflict had been published. There had been some very ordinary ones too. Amongst the former were Ker Porter's *Letters from Portugal and Spain*, and, by coincidence, Adam Neale's work of the same title, which were mainly concerned with the retreat to Corunna. Hawker's *Journal of a Regimental Officer*, published in 1810, and dealing with the Oporto and Talavera campaigns, is another of the early memoirs. Among the more mundane accounts, which today might be termed travelogues, were Mackinnon's *Journal of the Campaign* and Stothert's *Narrative of the Principal Events*, both published in 1812. While the war was in progress scores of officers and men were writing

185

home to their families, providing invaluable barometers as to the war's progress. The majority of these letters were not published until long after the war had ended and, indeed, still continue to be published today. In recent years we have seen published the letters of George Hennell, John Aitchison, John Mills, John Douglas and William Thornton Keep, and there are still letters and diaries which have yet to be published. In a way, these are among the most valuable of our sources as they were written as events unfolded. As Sir Charles Oman wrote in his *Wellington's Army*, a soldier writing about the retreat to Corunna after the war had ended did so with the knowledge that battles such as Salamanca, Vittoria and Waterloo were to follow, and therefore could do so with a great air of optimism, whereas the soldier writing of Corunna in the winter of 1808–9 had no such luxury, and as far as he was concerned had no cause for optimism at all. Hindsight is a wonderful thing and is something from which the post-Peninsular period writers greatly benefited, unlike those writing at the time. For, even as late as November 1812, Wellington's men were writing home full of bad tidings and doubts. 'The Marquis [Wellington] has ruined his reputation . . . and Spain I fear is lost,' wrote John Mills in November 1812 following the debacle at Burgos. And all of this in the year of Ciudad Rodrigo, Badajoz and Salamanca.

The immediate post-Peninsular and Waterloo period gave rise to even more memoirs, including Gleig's *The Subaltern*, Green's *The Vicissitudes of a Soldier's Life*, Sherer's *Recollections*, Buckham's *Personal Narrative* and Wood's *The Subaltern Officer*. The period also saw two of the first histories of the war, Londonderry's *Narrative of the Peninsular War* and Southey's *History of the Peninsular War*. But things were to begin to change drastically in 1828 with the publication of the first volume of William Napier's *History of the War in the Peninsula* which, despite its faults, remains not only the indispensable work on the war but also one of the finest works in English literature. Napier served with the 43rd Light Infantry, one of the great regiments in Wellington's army, which saw more than its fair share of action as part of the famous Light Division. Napier was, therefore, an eye-witness to many of the events described in his book. He was also able to glean much information from those around him who had been present at those actions where he was absent. Unfortunately, his own prejudices often get in the way of historical accuracy and, indeed, his work prompted a vitriolic correspondence between himself and William Carr Beresford, Napier's 'devil', following his account of Beresford's handling of the battle of Albuera, a battle which Napier never witnessed. But in spite of its flaws – and there really are not many – its six volumes remain a work of supreme importance to all students of the Peninsular War.

But Napier's work was more important than simply a historical account of the war. It was an inspiration to scores of veterans who, upon reading his work, were anxious to record their part in the war and so came a deluge of writings, either in book form or in journals such as Colburn's United Service Magazine. Wellington's men were relatively young at the time of the war, and by the 1830s and 1840s were still capable of recalling the events of 1808–14. However, by the 1850s, the memories of more than a few veterans had begun to fade and Napier was the obvious stimulus for them. Consequently, some veterans described events which they could not possibly have witnessed, and their accounts are based either on the recollections of comrades, perhaps told in camp afterwards, or, more likely, on the pages of Napier's *History*. This does not devalue them in any way whatsoever, for they were still participants in the war and many of them saw its great battles and sieges. It is just that we should be wary of what might be called 'the Napier factor' when using post-1840 memoirs. A prime example is Charles O'Neil's *Military Adventures*, published in 1851. O'Neil served with the 28th Regiment at Barrosa, Badajoz and Waterloo and wrote some graphic descriptions of army life. However, whenever the major actions occur he simply draws upon the writings of William Napier which is very frustrating, leaving the reader wondering why O'Neil chose not to write about his own experiences.

During the years of the publication of Napier's work, 1828–45, some truly fine memoirs also appeared, amongst which were Blakiston's *Twelve Years' Military Adventure*, Cadell's *Narrative of the Campaigns of the Twenty-Eighth Regiment*, Donaldson's *Recollections*, Cooke's wonderful *Memoirs of the Late War*, Surtees' *Twenty-Five Years in the Rifle Brigade*, Leach's *Rough Sketches* and perhaps the most famous memoir of all, Kincaid's *Adventures in the Rifle Brigade*. The post-Napier years likewise delivered up some gems such as Cooper's *Rough Notes of Seven Campaigns*, Frazer's *Letters* and Henegan's *Seven Years' Campaigning*.

As the 19th century wore on the veterans began to fade away of course. But their reminiscences lived on. Some veterans dictated their memoirs to be published later, like Harris's famous *Recollections*, whilst the letters and diaries of many veterans remained in family hands or with friends or regiments until they too were published either by relatives or by historians. In this way some very famous and valuable memoirs were published. Amongst these are Lawrence's *Autobiography*, Tomkinson's *Diary of a Cavalry Officer*, Smith's *Autobiography*, Larpent's *Private Journal* and Grattan's *Adventures with the Connaught Rangers*. Other shorter reminiscences appeared in magazines and journals such as Colborn's and Blackwood's and in regimental journals.

By the end of the 19th century so many good memoirs had been published that the historian Sir Charles Oman decided it was time for a new history of the war. After all, it had been sixty years since Napier's work, and with so many memoirs published subsequently he felt justified in producing another history. The result was his momentous seven-volume work, *The History of the Peninsular War*, published between 1902 and 1930. Oman travelled extensively throughout the Peninsula and studied the terrain and the battlefields for himself, an important aspect of his research. He also benefited from having the papers of some prominent soldiers such as Craufurd, D'Urban and Scovell, loaned to him by their descendants. His research took him deep into the politics of the war and into the affairs of all of the combatant nations, and the result was a work which is unlikely ever to be surpassed. In such a massive work it seems churlish to criticise errors, which do indeed exist, and it rightly stands alone as the definitive history of the war.

While Oman was writing his *History*, another great historian was likewise writing about the Peninsular War. Sir John Fortescue's 13-volume *History of the British Army* appeared at much the same time as Oman's work, and at the core of his work was the Peninsular War on which no fewer than seven volumes concentrate. The two great men corresponded with each other and freely acknowledged their mutual assistance. They likewise acknowledged their disagreements which were more than a few. Fortescue's work has the additional benefit of having some superb atlas volumes containing maps of all the major Peninsular battles as well as detailed campaign maps. Like Oman, Fortescue is of immense value to students of the war.

Memoirs continued and still continue to appear long after their authors had died. So far this century we have seen published such books as Anderson's *Recollections*, Boutflower's *Journal*, Warre's *Letters*, Hay's *Reminiscences*, Schaumann's *On the Road With Wellington*, Wheeler's *Letters* and Wheatley's *Diary*. As late as the 1990s Mills' *For King and Country*, Rous's *A Guards Officer in the Peninsula*, Douglas's *Tale of the Peninsula and Waterloo* and Thornton Keep's *In the Service of the King*, have appeared and one suspects there are still more to follow. Biographies and memoirs of most of the senior officers in Wellington's army have been published too, including Picton, Leith, Colborne, Cole, Pakenham, Craufurd and Hill. The one exception remains Beresford who, somewhat surprisingly, has yet to be the subject of a major biography.

We have already mentioned the diaries and memoirs of Wellington's men, but of course the great man himself chose never to put pen to paper in recording his experiences in the Peninsula, nor did he ever do so about Waterloo. We do, however, have his *Dispatches* which were edited by John Gurwood and published in 1837. These provide a unique insight into Wellington's character and demonstrate the minute detail with which he busied himself during the war. Amongst these beautifully written *Dispatches* we find him addressing an astonishing array of aspects concerning the war, the army and the Allied governments and regencies. We know much about Wellington's own routine during the war which saw him rise at around 6am and go to work almost immediately. This is not surprising when one reads the *Dispatches*. On a typical day, 8 August 1811, we find him writing to Major General Peacocke, the governor of Lisbon, twice to the Earl of Liverpool, Secretary of State, and to Rowland Hill, concerning such topics as the movement of troops, their payments, appointments, diseases and the overall situation in the Peninsula. The following day we even find him writing to Marshal Marmont. Gurwood's edition of the *Dispatches* is marred by his habit of deleting names from many of them, probably from a desire not to offend any persons still living at the time. It is not particularly difficult to discover who these officers were, however, but it is time consuming. Five years after Wellington's death the 2nd Duke published the equally important *Supplementary Dispatches*, which contained Wellington's incoming correspondence. In addition to the *Dispatches* are the volumes of *General Orders*, published between 1809 and 1814 which contain Wellington's orders issued in the Peninsula. Together with the *Dispatches* they provide an absolutely indispensable source for any study of the war.

Wellington himself has been the subject of scores of biographies of which perhaps Guedalla's *The Duke* and Longford's *Years of the Sword* are amongst the best. Otherwise, there are numerous books one can turn to in search of Wellington's opinion on any given subject. And, indeed, it would appear that at almost every dinner party at which the Duke was present there seems to have been at least one guest hanging on every word the great man said. It is as though he had only to sneeze and it would be recorded for posterity. Croker, Creevey and Stanhope are to be found amongst these.

Sir John Moore has naturally been the subject of many biographies, the best of which is Carola Oman's, *Sir John Moore*, published in 1953. His Corunna campaign of 1808–9 attracted its fare share of criticism in England which even his gallant death at the moment of victory could not deflect. One of the motivations behind James Moore's *A Narrative of the British Army in Spain*, was a defence of his brother. The book was published in 1809, only a few months after the campaign had actually come to an end. *The Life of Lieutenant General Sir John Moore*, written by James Moore and published in two volumes in 1834, was another defence of his brother, but we have to wait another seventy years, until 1904, before one of the most valuable works on Moore was published. This was *The Diary of Sir John Moore*, edited by Major General J F Maurice, in two volumes.

Other popular biographies include Parkinson's *Moore of Corunna*, whilst Fuller's *Sir John Moore's System of Training* deals with the tactical legacy left to us by its subject.

With such a wealth of memoirs at our disposal it is possible to break them down into their respective areas, i.e. infantry, cavalry, artillery, etc. The majority of memoirs listed so far are from the infantry, but if one wishes to make a study of cavalry it is to the volumes of Bragge, Le Marchant, Gordon, Hay, Hawker, Long, Combermere, Thackwell and Tomkinson one must turn. This is by no means an exhaustive list, but within the pages of these volumes can be found excellent accounts of that much-maligned arm of Wellington's army. For the artillery, one simply must use *The Dickson Manuscripts*. Alexander Dickson commanded the artillery in the Peninsula and within his manuscripts, published in 1913, can be found a vast store of information relating to ammunition, guns, personnel, the operations themselves, transport and a host of charts, sketches and tables. Frazer's *Letters* are invaluable for the artillery as are Swabey's *Diary* and Dyneley's *Letters*. The siege operations in the Peninsula are regarded as being an aspect of the war which Wellington never quite mastered. Good accounts of the siege operations can be found in Jones's classic *Journal of the Sieges*, of which the 3rd edition, published in 1846, is the best. Burgoyne's *Life and Correspondence* is essential whilst Landmann's *Recollections* is of use also. It is somewhat unfortunate that Sir Richard Fletcher, Wellington's chief engineer, left no account of his part in the war, due of course to his untimely death at San Sebastian, although some of his observations regarding the Lines of Torres Vedras can be found in the library of the Royal Engineers, Chatham.

The journals of some of Wellington's surgeons have been published, such as McGrigor's *Autobiography*, Boutflower's *Journal* and Henry's *Events of a Military Life*. None of these actually go into the business of surgery itself, however, and apart from McGrigor, whose major contribution to the war effort was as Inspector of Hospitals, there is little to be found in these three listed works other than the usual journal of events, marches, etc. Indeed, if one seeks to discover more about military surgery one must use Guthrie's *Commentaries* and Hennen's *Principles of Military Surgery*. This latter work is filled with scores of case histories from both the Peninsular War and Waterloo campaign and makes fascinating, if a little gory, reading.

The Commissariat Department played a vital role in the Peninsula, and works by officers in its service include Henegan's *Seven Years' Campaigning*, Daniel's *Journal of an Officer*, Dallas' *Autobiography* and Bisset's *Memoranda and Observations*. This latter work was written by Sir John Bisset, head of the Commissariat Department in Kennedy's absence, and includes much information about the department and its work. It is interesting to note the conflict between the views expressed in Hennen's *Military Surgery* and Bisset's *Memoranda*. Hennen was a great admirer of Larrey's 'flying ambulance' which saw widespread use in the French army. Hennen would have liked to see a similar vehicle in the British army but Wellington was apparently against this as he wished to see as much wheeled transport as possible used by the Commissariat Department for transporting supplies. The spiritual side of the army was not neglected and works by chaplains include Ormsby's *Operations of the British Army* and Stevenson's *A Soldier in Time of War*. The letters of Wellington's own chaplain, the Reverend Briscall, exist although they have never been published.

So far we have dealt mainly with personal reminiscences but there is an equally large number of histories and specialist studies which are far too numerous to mention, save for a few. Amongst the better studies of Wellington's army are Glover's *Wellington's Army in the Peninsula*, Haythornthwaite's *Wellington's Military Machine* and *The Armies of Wellington*, Brett-James's *Life in Wellington's Army*, Oman's *Wellington's Army* and Ward's superb *Wellington's Headquarters*. This latter work is the definitive study of the relationship at headquarters between the various departments of the army, their functions and the men who ran them. What emerges is the fact that it was indeed 'Wellington's army' as Ward demonstrates that Wellington clearly had no notion of the idea of a second-in-command and would not even admit its existence. It is also clear that only George Murray, the Quartermaster General, had any real independence within Wellington's 'inner circle' of departmental heads and it is a shame that his own memoirs have never been published. If one wishes to consult the numerous volumes of his own papers it is to Edinburgh and the National Library of Scotland that one must travel, for it is there that the majority of the Murray Papers are to be found.

There are scores of first-rate regimental histories which contain eye-witness accounts, whilst others concentrate heavily on the Peninsular War. Verner's *History and Campaigns of the Rifle Brigade* is the obvious example of the latter, covering the Peninsular campaign up until Vittoria. Other excellent histories include Moorsom's *History of the 52nd Light Infantry* and Levinge's *43rd Light Infantry*. My own *Gentlemen's Sons* covers the history of the Foot Guards between 1808 and 1815, whilst my *Wellington's Regiments* gives histories of every single regiment which served in the Peninsula. Strangely enough, there are very few histories of single campaigns. Lawford and Young's *Wellington's Masterpiece* covers the Salamanca Campaign whilst Chambers' *Busaco* is an excellent account of that particular battle. The battle of Vimeiro and the Convention of

Cintra is the subject of Glover's *Britannia Sickens*, the siege of Badajoz in 1812 is covered by my *In Hell Before Daylight*, whilst Beatson's trilogy, *With Wellington in the Pyrenees*, *The Bidassoa and the Nivelle*, and *The Crossing of the Gaves*, covers most of the Peninsular campaign between June 1813 and February 1814. Other than these, individual campaign histories are pretty scarce in English. The study of military dress has been widely covered. As early as 1812, Hamilton Smith's *Dress of the British Army*, a series of uniform plates, began to appear and remains one of the finest sources for study of British military uniforms. Windrow and Embleton's *Military Dress of the Peninsular War* is one of the standard modern works on the subject as is Haythornthwaite's *Uniforms of the Peninsular War*. The same author has written several fine works on the subject which are too numerous to list here. The final word on British works on the Peninsular War goes to Bernard Cornwell's *Sharpe* novels. Love them or hate them, there is no denying their appeal and, certainly, the television series which they spawned has helped immensely in bringing before the general public a war about which many people knew very little or nothing at all. One should never forget they are simply novels but, like the *Death to the French* novel of C.S. Forester, they contain a wealth of detail based upon true events whilst the characters themselves are drawn heavily from the memoirs listed above.

Bibliography

Aitchison, John. *An Ensign in the Peninsular War; The Letters of John Aitchison*. Ed. W.F.K. Thompson. (London, 1981.)

Alexander, D.W. *Rod of Iron: French Occupation Policy in Aragón during the Peninsular War*. (Wilmington, Delaware, 1985.)

Alvarez, F. Carantona. *La guerra de la independencia en Asturias*. (Oviedo, 1983.)

Anderson, J. *Recollections of a Peninsular Veteran*. (London, 1913.)

Anon. *Medios de salvar el reino*. (Cadiz, 1810.)

Anon. *The Military Mentor*. (London, 1804.)

Anon. *The Personal Narrative of a Private Soldier who served in the Forty-Second Highlanders for Twelve Years during the Late War*. (London, 1821.)

Ardenne, Armand von. *Bergische Lanziers, Westfälische Husaren Nr. 11*. (Berlin, 1877.)

Balagny, Dominique. *Campagne de l'Empereur Napoléon en Espagne 1808–1809*. (Paris, 1902–06.)

Barkhausen, Georg H. *Tagebuch eines Rheinbund-Offiziers*. (Wiesbaden, 1900.)

Barrès, J.B. *Memoirs of a Napoleonic Officer*. Ed. M. Barrès. Trans. B. Miall. (London, 1925.)

Beamish, N.L. *History of the King's German Legion*. (London, 1832–7.)

Beatson, Maj.Gen. F. *With Wellington in the Pyrenees*. (London, 1914.)

Beatson, Maj.Gen. F. *Wellington; The Crossing of the Gaves and the Battle of Orthes*. (London, 1925.)

Beatson, Maj.Gen. F. *Wellington; The Bidassoa and the Nivelle*. (London, 1935.)

Beck, Fritz, Karl von Hahn and Heinrich von Hahn. *Geschichte des Grossherzoglich Artilleriekorps*. (Berlin, 1912.)

Belmas, J. *Journaux des Sièges faits ou soutenus par les français dans la Péninsule, de 1807 à 1814*. (Paris, 1836.)

Berdrow, Hermann, Ed. *Vor 1813*. (Leipzig, 1933.)

Blakiston, J. *Twelve Years' Military Adventure in three quarters of the globe*. (London, 1829.)

Blaze, E. *Lights and Shades of Military Life*. Ed. Sir Charles Napier. (London, 1850.)

Boutflower, C. *The Journal of an Army Surgeon during the Peninsular War*. (Manchester, 1912.)

Bragge, W. *Peninsular Portrait, 1811–1814; the letters of Captain William Bragge, Third (King's Own) Dragoons*. Ed. S.A.C. Cassells. (London, 1963.)

Brandt, H. von. *The Two Minas and the Spanish Guerrillas*. (London, 1825.)

Brett-James, A. *Life in Wellington's Army*. (London, 1972.)

Brokenburg, August von. 'Erinnerungen aus den Jahren 1808 bis 1811.' *Beilage z. Schwarzb-Rudolstädtischen Landeszeitung*. (September, 1906.)

Buckham, E.W. *Personal Narrative of Adventures in the Peninsula during the war in 1812–1813*. (London, 1827.)

Burgoyne, Sir John. *Life and Correspondence*. Ed. G. Wrottesley. (London, 1873.)

Cabanes, F.X. de. *Historia de las operaciones del Ejército de Cataluña en la primera campaña de la guerra de la usurpación, o sea de la independencia de España*. (Tarragona, 1809.)

Cadell, Charles. *Narrative of the Campaigns of the Twenty-Eighth Regiment since their return from Egypt in 1802*. (London, 1835.)

Chambers, Lt.Col. G. *Wellington's Battlefields Illustrated; Busaco*. (London, 1910.)

Chandler, David. *On the Napoleonic Wars*. (London, 1994.)

Clerk, Rev. A. *Memoir of Colonel John Cameron, Fassiefern*. (Glasgow, 1858.)

Cole, M.L. and Gwynn, S. *Memoirs of Sir Lowry Cole*. (London, 1934.)

Combermere. *Memoirs and Correspondence of Field Marshal Viscount Combermere, GCB*. (London, 1866.)

Comellas, J.L. (Ed). *Historia general de Espana y America, XII: del antiguo al nuevo régimen*. (Madrid, 1981.)

Cooke, J. *Memoirs of the Late War*. (London, 1831.)

Cooper, J.S. *Rough Notes of Seven Campaigns in Portugal, Spain, France and America*. (Carlisle, 1869.)

Craufurd, A. *General Craufurd and his Light Division*. (London, 1891.)

Daniel, J.E. *Journal of an Officer in the Commissariat Department of the Army*. (London, 1820.)

Dallas, A. *Autobiography of the Rev. Alexander Dallas, including his service in the Peninsula in the Commissariat Department*. (London, 1870.)

Delavoye, A.M. *Life of Thomas Graham, Lord Lynedoch*. (London, 1880.)

Dickson, A. *The Dickson Manuscripts, 1809–1818*. Ed. J.H. Leslie. (Woolwich, 1905.)

Donaldson, J. *Recollections of the Eventful Life of a Soldier*. (Edinburgh, 1845.)

Douglas, John. *Douglas's Tale of the Peninsula and Waterloo*. Ed. Stanley Monick. (London, 1997.)

D'Urban, Sir Benjamin. *The Peninsular Journal of Major-General Sir Benjamin D'Urban, 1808–1817*. Ed. I.J. Rousseau. (London, 1930.)

Dyneley, T. *Letters Written by Lieutenant General Thomas Dyneley, while on active service between the years 1806 and 1815*. (Cambridge, 1984.)

Elias, J. Torras. *La guerra de los agraviados*. (Barcelona, 1967.)

Ellesmere, Earl of. *Personal Reminiscences of the Duke of Wellington*. Ed. Countess of Longford. (London, 1904.)

Ellis, C.P. 'Reminiscences of Bayonne', in *United Services Magazine*, 1842.

Elting, John. *Swords Around a Throne*. (New York, 1988.)

—*Napoleonic Uniforms*, (New York, 1993.)

Esdaile, C.J. 'The Spanish guerrillas: heroes or villains?' *History Today*, XXXVIII, No.4 (April, 1988.)

Esdaile, C.J. *The Spanish Army in the Peninsular War*. (Manchester, 1988.)

Esdaile, C.J. *The Duke of Wellington and the Command of the Spanish Army, 1812–14*. (London, 1990.)

Fernández, X. Barreiro. *Historia de Galicia*. (Vigo, 1981.)

Fiebig. 'Das Bataillon des Princes', *Zeitschift für Heeres- und Uniformkunde*. Heft 61/63, 1934.

Fletcher, Ian. *In Hell Before Daylight; The Siege and Storming of the Castle of Badajoz, March-April 1812*. (Tunbridge Wells, 1984.)

Fletcher, Ian. *Craufurd's Light Division; The Life of Robert Craufurd and his command of the Light Division*. (Tunbridge Wells, 1992.)

Fletcher, Ian. *Wellington's Regiments; The Men and their Battles, from Roliça to Waterloo, 1808–1815*. (Staplehurst, 1995.)

Fletcher, Ian. *Wellington's Army*. (London, 1997.)

Fletcher, Ian & Poulter, R. *Gentlemen's Sons; The Foot Guards in the Peninsula and at Waterloo, 1808–1815*. (Tunbridge Wells, 1992.)

Ford, Capt. J. 'The Redoubt "Des Augustins" . . . and some Military Scraps', in *Colburn's United Service Magazine*, 1844.

Fortescue, J.W. *A History of the British Army*. (London, 1899–1930.)

Foy, Maximilien. *History of the War in the Peninsula*. (Felling, 1989.)

Frazer, A. *Letters of Colonel Sir Augustus Frazer, KCB, commanding the Royal Horse Artillery in the army under the Duke of Wellington*. Ed. E. Sabine. (London, 1859.)

Fuller, J.F.C. *Sir John Moore's System of Training*. (London, 1924.)

Garzon, J. Pérez. *Milicia nacional y revolución burgesa: el protitipo madriléno*. (Madrid, 1978.)

Gates, David. *The Spanish Ulcer: a History of the Peninsular War*. (London, 1986.)

Gleig, G.R. *The Subaltern*. (London, 1825.)

Glover, M. *Britannia Sickens; Sir Arthur Wellesley and the Convention of Cintra*. (London, 1970.)

Glover, M. *The Peninsular War, 1807–1814*. (Newton Abbott, 1974.)

Glover, M. *Wellington's Army in the Peninsula, 1808–1814*. (Newton Abbott, 1977.)

Gonneville, A.O. Le H. de. *Recollections of Colonel De Gonneville*. Trans. C.M. Yonge. (London, 1873).

Gordon, Alexander. *A Cavalry Officer in the Corunna Campaign 1808–1809*. Ed. Col. H.C. Wylly. (London, 1913.)

Gouvion Saint-Cyr, Laurent. *Journal des Opérations de l'Armée de Catalogne*. (Paris, 1821.)

Grasset, Alphonse. *La Guerre d'Espagne*. (Paris, 1914–32.)

Grattan, W. 'Badajoz to Salamanca', in *United Services Journal*, 1834.

Grattan, W. *Adventures with the Connaught Rangers, 1809–1814*. Ed. Sir Charles Oman. (London, 1902.)

Green, John. *The Vicissitudes of a Soldier's Life, or a series of occurrences from 1806 to 1815*. (Louth, 1827.)

Grehan, John. *The Forlorn Hope; The Spanish Frontier, 1811–1812*. (London, 1898.)

Griffith, Paddy. *Forward Into Battle*. (Chichester, 1981.)

Griffith, Paddy. *Wellington Commander; The Iron Duke's Generalship*. (Chichester, 1985.)

Grolman, Ludwig von. 'Aus dem Tagebuche eines deutschen Offiziers über seinen Feldzug in Spanien 1808', in Friedrich M. Kircheisen, Ed. *Memoiren aus dem spanischen Freiheitskampfe 1808–1811*. (Hamburg, 1908.)

Guedalla, P. *The Duke*. (London, 1831.)

Guthrie, J. *Commentaries on the Surgery of War*. (London, 1853.)

Hagen, Benno von. *Das Reussische Militär in den Kriegsjahren 1806–15*. (Gera, 1904.)

Hamnett, B. *La politica española en una edad revolucionaria, 1790–1820*. (Mexico City, 1985.)

Harris, B. *Recollections of Rifleman Harris*. Ed. H. Curling. (London, 1928.)

Hawker, Colonel Peter. *Journal of a Regimental Officer during the recent campaign in Portugal and Spain under Lord Wellington*. (London, 1810.)

Hay, Capt. W. *Reminiscences, 1809–1815, under Wellington*. Ed. S. Wood. (London, 1901.)

Haythornthwaite, P.J. *Wellington's Military Machine*. (Tunbridge Wells, 1989.)

Haythornthwaite, P.J. *Uniforms of the Peninsular War, 1807–1814*. (Poole, 1978.)

Haythornthwaite, P.J. *British Infantry of the Napoleonic Wars*. (London, 1987.)

Haythornthwaite, P.J. *The Armies of Wellington*. (London, 1994.)

Hellrung. 'Die Organisation der Westphälischen Armee'. *Minerva*, December 1840.

Helmes, Hermann. 'Die Würzburger Truppen vor Hundert Jahren'.

Archiv des historischen Vereins für Unterfranken und Aschaffenburg, 55. 1913.

Henegan, Sir Richard. *Seven Years' Campaigning in the Peninsula and the Netherlands from 1808 to 1815.* (London, 1846.)

Henen, J. *The Principles of Military Surgery.* (London, 1818.)

Hennell, George. *A Gentleman Volunteer; The Letters of George Hennell from the Peninsular War, 1812–1813.* Ed. Michael Glover. (London, 1979.)

Henry, W. *Events of a Military Life.* (London, 1843.)

Hermes, Sabina and Joachim Niemeyer. *Unter dem Greifen.* (Rastatt, 1984.)

Herrmann, Friedrich. 'Bergische Reiter', *Zeitschrift für Heereskunde*, 287, 1980.

Hohenhausen, Leopold von. *Biographie des Generals von Ochs.* (Cassel, 1827.)

Horward, Donald. *Napoleon and Iberia.* (Tallahassee, 1984.)

Iribarren, J.M. *Espoz y Mina, el guerrillero.* (Madrid, 1965.)

Isenbart, Wilhelm. *Geschichte des 2. Nassauischen Infanterie-Regiments Nr. 88.* (Berlin, 1903.)

Jones, Lt Col. H. 'Narrative of Seven Weeks' Captivity in St Sebastian,' in *United Services Journal*, 1841.

Jones, Sir J.T. *Journal of the Sieges carried on by the army under the Duke of Wellington in Spain, between the years 1811 and 1814.* (London, 1846.)

Kallenberg, Fritz. 'Die fürstentümer Hohenzollern im Zeitalter der Französischen Revolution und Napoleons'. *Zeitschrift für die Geschichte des Oberrheins*, vol. 111, 1963.

Keep, William Thornton. *In the Service of the King; The Letters of William Thornton Keep, at Home, Walcheren and in the Peninsula, 1808–1814.* Ed. Ian Fletcher. (Staplehurst, 1997.)

Keim, August. *Geschichte des 4. Grossherzoglich Hessischen Infanterie-Regiments (Prinz Karl) Nr. 118 und seiner Stämme.* (Berlin, 1879.)

Kincaid, Capt. J. *Adventures in the Rifle Brigade.* (London, 1830.)

Kincaid, Capt. J. *Random Shots from a Rifleman.* (London, 1835.)

Klessmann, E. Ed. *Unter Napoleons Fahnen.* (Bielefeld, 1991.)

Koch, J.B. Ed. *Mémoires de Massena.* (Paris, 1850.)

Landmann, Col. G. *Recollections of My Military Life.* (London, 1854.)

Larpent, Francis S. *The Private Journal of F.S. Larpent.* (London, 1853.)

Las Cases, E.A.D.M.J. *Memoirs of the Life, Exile and Conversations of the Emperor Napoleon.* (London, 1836.)

Lawrence, W. *The Autobiography of Sergeant William Lawrence.* Ed. G.N. Bankes. (London, 1886.)

Lazaro, J. Fontana. *La quiebra de la monarqia absoluta, 1814–1820: la crisis del antiguo régimen en Espana.* (Barcelona, 1971.)

Leach, J. *Rough Sketches in the Life of an Old Soldier*. (London, 1831.)

Leith, J. *Memoirs of the late Lieutenant General Sir James Leith, GCB*. (London, 1818.)

Lejeune, L.F. *Memoirs of Baron Lejeune*. Trans. Mrs A. Bell. (London, 1897.)

Le Marchant, Denis. *Memoirs of the late Major General Le Marchant, 1766–1812*. (Staplehurst, 1997.)

Levinge, Sir R. *Historical Records of the Forty-Third Monmouthshire Light Infantry*. (London, 1868.)

Londonderry, the Marquess of. *Narrative of the Peninsular War from 1808 to 1813*. (London, 1829.)

Long, R. *Peninsular Cavalry General (1811–1813); the correspondence of Lieutenant General Robert Ballard Long*. Ed. T.H. McGuffie. (London, 1951.)

Longford, E. *Wellington; The Years of the Sword*. (London, 1969.)

Low, E.B. *With Napoleon at Waterloo*. Ed. McK. Macbride

Lucas, M. Ardit. *Revolución liberal y revuelta campesina: un ensayo sobre la desintegración del regimen feudal en el pais valenciano, 1793–1840*. (Barcelona, 1977.)

Lünsmann, Fritz. *Die Armee des Känigreichs Westfalen*. (Berlin, 1935.)

Macdonald, J.E. *Recollections of Marshal Macdonald*. Ed. C. Rousset. Trans. S.L. Simeon. (London, 1892.)

Mackinnon, Major General Henry. *A Journal of the Campaign in Portugal and Spain*. (Bath, 1812.)

Mainwaring, F. 'Four Years of a Soldier's Life'. in *Colborn's United Service Magazine*. 1844.

Marbot, Jean Baptiste, Baron de. *The Memoirs of Baron de Marbot*. (London, 1905.)

Martinien, A. *Tableaux par Corps et par batailles des Officers Tués et Blessés*. (Paris, 1984.)

Maurice, Sir J.F. *The Diary of Sir John Moore*. (London, 1904.)

McGrigor, J. *The Autobiography and Services of Sir James McGrigor, late Director-General of the Army Medical Department*. (London, 1861.)

Military Instruction from the Late King of Prussia. Trans. Lt. Col. T. Foster. (London, 1818.)

Mills, John. *For King and Country; The Letters and Diaries of John Mills, Coldstream Guards, 1811–1814*. Ed. Ian Fletcher. (Staplehurst, 1995.)

Moore, James. *A Narrative of the British Army in Spain*. (London, 1809.)

Moore, James Carrick. *The Life of Lieutenant General Sir John Moore, by his brother*. (London, 1834.)

Moorsom, W.S. *Historical Record of the Fifty-Second Regiment (Oxfordshire Light Infantry) from the year 1755 to the year 1858*. (London, 1860.)

Morgenstern, Franz. *Kriegserinnerungen*. Ed. H. Meier. (Wolfenbuettel, 1912.)

Napier, G.T. *Passages in the Early Military Life of General Sir George T. Napier*. Gen. W.C.E. Napier. (London, 1884.)

Napier, W.F.P. *History of the War in the Peninsula and in the South of France, from the year 1807 to the year 1814*. (London, 1828–45.)

Napoleon I. *Correspondence de Napoléon Ier*. (Paris, 1858–70.)

—*New Letters of Napoleon I*, Trans. Lady Mary Loyd. (New York, 1897.)

—*Lettres Inédites*. Ed. Léonce de Brotonne. (Paris, 1898.)

—*Orders et Apostilles de Napoléon*. Ed. Arthur Chuquet. (Paris, 1911–12.)

—*Unpublished Correspondence of Napoleon I Preserved in the War Archives*. Eds. Ernest Picard and Louis Tuetey. (New York, 1913.)

Neale, Adam. *Letters from Portugal and Spain*. (London, 1809.)

Neff, W. *Geschichte des Infanterie-Regiments von Goeben*. (Berlin, 1890.)

Oesterhaus, Wilhelm. *Geschichte der Fürstlich Lippischen Truppen in den Jahren 1807–1815*. (Detmold, 1907.)

Oman, Carola. *Sir John Moore*. (London, 1953.)

Oman, Charles. *A History of the Peninsular War*. (Oxford, 1902–30.)

Oman, Sir Charles. *Wellington's Army, 1809–1814*. (London, 1913.)

O'Neil, Charles. *The Military Adventures of Charles O'Neil*. (Staplehurst, 1997.)

Ormsby, J.W. *Operations of the British Army in Portugal and Spain, 1808–9*. (London, 1809.)

Parkinson, R. *Moore of Corunna*. (London, 1976.)

Parquin, C. *Charles Parquin: Napoleon's Army*. Trans. & Ed. B.T. Jones. (London, 1969.)

Patterson, J. *The Adventures of Captain John Patterson*. (London, 1837.)

Pelet, Jean-Jacques. *The French Campaign in Portugal*. Ed. Donald Horward. (Minneapolis, 1973.)

Pérez, M. López, & Martin-Portugués, Lara. *Entre la guerra y la paz: Jaen, 1808–1814*. (Granada, 1993.)

Picard, E. *Préceptes et Jugements de Napoléon*. (Paris, 1913.)

Pigeard, Alain. *L'Armée Napoléonienne*. (Paris, 1993.)

Porter, Robert Ker. *Letters from Portugal and Spain*. (London, 1809.)

Rigel, Franz Xavier. *Der siebenjährige Kampf auf der Pyrenäischen Halbinsel*. (Rastatt, 1819.)

Rocca, Albert de. *Memoirs of the War of the French in Spain*. (London, 1815.)

Rocca, Albert de. *In the Peninsula with a French Hussar*. (London, 1990.)

Rässler, Philip von. *Die Geschichte der Herzoglich Nassauischen Truppe*. (Wiesbaden, 1863.)

Robinson, Maj. Gen. C.W. *Wellington's Campaigns, Peninsula to Waterloo, 1808–1815*. (London, 1907.)

Robinson, H. *Memoirs of Lieutenant General Sir Thomas Picton*. (London, 1836.)

Rous, J.E.C. *A Guards Officer in the Peninsula*. Ed. Ian Fletcher. (Tunbridge Wells, 1992.)

Runkel. 'Zur Geschichte der Besatzung der Burg Hohenzollern', in *Mittheilungen des Vereins für Geschichte und Altertumskunde in Hohenzollern, 1899/1900.*

Sauer, Paul. *Napoleons Alder über Württemberg, Baden und Hohenzollern*. (Stuttgart, 1987.)

Sauzey, Camille. *Les Allemands sous les Aigles Françaises*. (Paris, 1987–8.)

Schaumann, August. *On the Road with Wellington*. (New York, 1925.)

Schräder, Karl. *Zwischen Französischer Revolution und Preussens Gloria*. (Eitorf, 1989.)

Schuster, Joseph. *Das Grossherzoglich Würzburgische Infanterie-Regiment in Spanien 1808–1813*. (Munich, 1909.)

Seebach, L. von. *Geschichte der Feldzüge*. (Weimar, 1838.)

Sherer, M. *Recollections of the Peninsula*. (London, 1825.)

Sidney, Rev. E. *Life of Lord Hill, late Commander of the Forces*. (London, 1845.)

Six, Georges. *Dictionnaire Biographique des Généraux & Amiraux de la Révolution et de l'Empire*. (Paris, 1974.)

Smith, G.C. Moore. *The Life of John Colborne, Field Marshal Lord Seaton*. (London, 1903.)

Smith, Harry. *The Autobiography of Lieutenant General Sir Harry Smith*. Ed. G.C. Moore Smith. (London, 1901.)

Southey, Robert. *History of the Peninsular War*. (London, 1823.)

Stanhope, Earl. *Notes of Conversations with the Duke of Wellington*. (London, 1888.)

Stevenson, J. *Twenty-One Years in the British Foot Guards*. (London, 1830.)

Stothert, Captain William. *A Narrative of the Principle Events of the Campaigns of 1809, 1810 and 1811 in Spain and Portugal*. (London, 1812.)

Suchet, Gabriel. *Memoirs of the War in Spain*. (Felling, 1986.)

Surtees, W. *Twenty-Five Years in the Rifle Brigade*. (London, 1833.)

Swabey, W. *Diaries of Campaigns in the Peninsula for the Years 1811, 1812 and 1813*. Ed. F.A. Whinyates. (Woolwich, 1895.)

Thackwell, J. *Military Memoirs of Lieutenant General Joseph Thackwell*. Ed. H.C. Wylly. (London, 1908.)

Thiébault, Paul. *Memoirs*. (Felling, 1994.)

Tomkinson, Lt Col W. *The Diary of a Cavalry Officer in the Peninsular War and Waterloo Campaign, 1809–1815*. Ed. J. Tomkinson. (London, 1895.)

Tone, J.L. *The Fatal Knot: the Guerrilla War in Navarre and the Defeat of Napoleon in Spain*. (Chapel Hill, 1994.)

Umhey, Alfred. 'Das Infanterie-Bataillon des Grossherzogtums Frankfurt' in *Der Bote aus dem Wehrgeschichtlichen Museum*, 1985.

Ussher, Capt Thomas. 'Narrative of the Embarkation and Conveyance of Napoleon from Frejus to Elba, in the Undaunted Frigate, with Personal Anecdotes and Opinions of the Ex-Emperor on the Voyage and after his Occupation of that Island.' in *United Services Journal*, 1840.

Valdés, R. Alvarez. *Memorias del levantamiento de Asturias en 1808.* Ed. M. Fuentes Acevedo. (Oviedo, 1889.)

Verner, W. *History and Campaigns of the Rifle Brigade, 1800–1813.* (London, 1919.)

Ward, S.G.P. *Wellington's Headquarters; a Study of the Administrative Problems in the Peninsula, 1809–1814.* (Oxford, 1957.)

Warre, William. *Letters from the Peninsula, 1808–1812.* Ed. Rev. E. Warre. (London, 1909.)

Weech, Friedrich von. *Badische Truppen in Spanien 1810–1813.* (Karlsruhe, 1892.)

Weller, Jac. *Wellington in the Peninsula.* (London, 1962.)

Wellington, Arthur Wellesley, first Duke of. *Dispatches of Field Marshal the Duke of Wellington.* Ed. J. Gurwood. (London, 1834–8.)

Wellington, Arthur Wellesley, first Duke of. *General Orders in Portugal, Spain and France from 1809 to 1814, and the Low Countries and France, 1815.* Compiled by J. Gurwood. (London, 1839.)

Wellington, Arthur Wellesley, first Duke of. *Supplementary Dispatches and Memoranda. Ed. 2nd Duke of Wellington.* (London, 1852–72.)

Wheatley, W. *The Wheatley Diary; A journal and sketch book kept during the Peninsular War and the Waterloo Campaign.* Ed. C. Hibbert. (London, 1964.)

Wheeler, W. *Letters of Private Wheeler, 1809–1828.* Ed. B.H. Liddell Hart. (London, 1951.)

Windrow, M. & Embleton, G. *Military Dress of the Peninsular War.* (New York, 1974.)

Wood, Capt. G. *The Subaltern Officer.* (London, 1825.)

Xylander, R. von. *Geschichte des 1. Feldartillerie-Regiments.* (Berlin, 1909.)

Young, P. and Lawford, J.P. *Wellington's Masterpiece; The Battle and Campaign of Salamanca.* (London, 1972.)

Zimmermann, P. *Erinnerungen aus den Feldzügen der bergischen Truppen in Spanien und Russland.* (Düsseldorf, 1840 and 1842.)

Notes on the Contributors

IAN FLETCHER was born in London in 1957. His first book, *In Hell Before Daylight*, was published in 1984, since when he has written eight others, *The Waters of Oblivion, Crauford's Light Division, Gentlemen's Sons, Wellington's Foot Guards, Fields of Fire, Wellington's Regiments, Wellington's Army*, and *Salamanca*. He has also edited *Letters from the Front*, a collection of First World War letters, *A Guards Officer in the Peninsula, For King and Country*, and *In the Service of the King*. He has written numerous articles and papers, and has written Introductions for *Rough Notes of Seven Campaigns*, and *Twenty Five Years in the Rifle Brigade*. He has made frequent radio broadcasts, and lectured in Britain, Europe and the USA. Ian travels regularly to the battlefields of the Iberian Peninsula, and escorts guests of his own company, Ian Fletcher Battlefield Tours. He is a member of the British Commission for Military History, and is a Fellow of the International Napoleonic Society. He lives in Rochester, Kent with his partner, Debbie, and has two children, Jack and Harriet.

PHILIP HAYTHORNTHWAITE is a native of Lancashire, where he still lives. He combined a business career with many years of historical research. He is the author of many books, mainly covering 18th- and 19th-century military history, and including *The Armies of Wellington* (1994), *The Napoleonic Source Book* (1990), *Napoleon's Military Machine* and *Wellington's Military Machine* (both Spellmount Publishers). He is the author of numerous papers and articles, as well as *The World War One Source Book* (1992) and *The Colonial Wars Source Book* (1995). He has acted as historical consultant to a number of commercial companies.

DAVID CHANDLER is well known for his writings on the Napoleonic and Marlburian periods. A former Head of the Department of War Studies at the Royal Military Academy, Sandhurst, he retired in 1994 after thirty-three years at the Academy. He has published twenty-seven books, including *Campaigns of Napoleon, Napoleon's Marshals, Waterloo – the Hundred Days*, and *On the Napoleonic Wars*. His various appointments bear witness to the high regard in which he is held in the military field: Honorary President of the British Military History Commission; Honorary Founding President of the European Union Re-enactment Societies, and, for six years, a Trustee of the Royal Armouries at HM Tower of London and at Leeds. For many years he was a Council Member of the Society for Army Historical Research, and is a Fellow of the Royal Historical Society.

Married with three sons and a granddaughter, David counts war games and model ship building among his hobbies.

JOHN (JACK) H. GILL is the author of *With Eagles to Glory: Napoleon and his German Allies in the 1809 Campaign* (Greenhill, 1992). His other works include papers, *Proceedings of the Consortium on Revolutionary Europe*, and articles in *The Age of Napoleon* and *First Empire*. He contributed a chapter on the Nazi nuclear programme to *The Hitler Options* (ed. Kenneth Macksey, Greenhill, 1995). He received his BA from Middlebury College in 1977 (double major: History and German), and his MA from The George Washington University in 1987 (International Relations). A lieutenant-colonel in the US army, he is assigned to the Strategic Plans and Policy Directorate (J-5) of the United States Pacific Command as Political-Military Desk Officer for south Asia. Jack lives with his wife, LTC Anne Rieman, and their two sons, Grant (6) and Hunter (3).

CHARLES ESDAILE was born in Epsom, Surrey in 1959. He graduated with a 1st Class Honours degree in History from the University of Lancaster, where he subsequently was awarded his PhD for his thesis on the Spanish army in the period 1788–1814. He has held a number of academic posts, and is currently a lecturer at the University of Liverpool. Dr Esdaile has written extensively on the Napoleonic period and is the author of *The Spanish Army in the Peninsular War* (Manchester University Press, 1988), *The Duke of Wellington and the Command of the Spanish Army, 1812–1814* (Macmillan, 1990), and *The Wars of Napoleon* (Longman, 1995). He was for many years a keen wargamer, was a founder member of the Napoleonic Association, and is a long-standing member of the Sealed Knot. Currently working on a history of modern Spain, Charles Esdaile recently spent a year's research leave in Madrid. He is married, with three small children, and lives near Formby.

PAUL CHAMBERLAIN is a government scientist. His interests in the Napoleonic period embrace naval and military campaigns and he has a particular interest in the study of prisoners of war held in Britain at that time. He lectures in the UK and overseas, and presents tours of Napoleonic sites in Britain for Midas Battlefield Tours and English Heritage. He regularly contributes articles to publications such as *First Empire*, *Age of Napoleon*, and the *Bulletin of the Napoleonic Alliance*. He has written papers for the journals of the Napoleonic Association, the 1805 Club, and the *Bulletin of the Napoleonic Society of America*. Paul is a Trustee of the Norman Cross Eagle Appeal (a project to restore a prisoner of war memorial near Peterborough), Research Officer of the Napoleonic

Association, for which he organises regular conferences in London, and a Fellow of the International Napoleonic Society.

PADDY GRIFFITH was born in Liverpool in 1947. Educated at Liverpool College and Corpus Christi, Oxford, he was awarded an unviva'd 1st Class Honours BA in Modern History in 1968 (converted to MA in 1972), and went on to pursue doctoral studies in Paris, London and Aughton, Lancaster from 1970 to 1973. His DPhil was awarded in 1976 for his thesis, *On Military Thought in the French Army, 1815–51* (published in a revised edition by Manchester University Press in 1989). Paddy was Senior Lecturer in War Studies at the Royal Military Academy, Sandhurst, and became involved in a number of radio and television projects. He is the author of *Forward Into Battle* (Bird, 1981), *Battle Tactics of the American Civil War* (Yale University Press, 1989), and *Battle Tactics on the Western Front* (Yale, 1994). He has also written extensively on the Zulu War, the Vikings, the French Revolution, the English Civil War, and World War II. His 'Military Lessons for the UK of the Second Gulf War, 16 January to 28 February 1991' was cited in a House of Commons debate. Now a freelance writer and publisher, and currently researching World War I, Paddy and his wife, Genevieve, have a son, Robert.

JOHN GREHAN is a regular contributor to military history magazines and journals. His first book, *The Forlorn Hope – the Battle for the Spanish Frontier 1810–11*, was published in 1990. In 1995, he co-authored an illustrated guide to Napoleon's Imperial Guard; a similar guide to the Portuguese army is shortly to follow. He has travelled extensively throughout Spain and Portugal in the course of his researches, and is currently working on a major study of Wellington's strategy in the Peninsula. He is a member of the Napoleonic Association, and the Friends of the Waterloo Committee.